Chinese Adolescents in Britain and Hong Kong

Identity and aspirations

GAJENDRA VERMA
University of Manchester

YIU MAN CHAN
University of Manchester

CHRISTOPHER BAGLEY
University of Southampton

SYLVIA SHAM
Manchester Metropolitan University

DOUGLAS DARBY
University of Manchester

DEREK WOODROW
Manchester Metropolitan Universtiy

GEORGE SKINNER
University of Manchester

Routledge
Taylor & Francis Group
LONDON AND NEW YORK

First published 1999 by Ashgate Publishing

Reissued 2018 by Routledge
2 Park Square, Milton Park, Abingdon, Oxon, OX14 4RN
711 Third Avenue, New York, NY 10017

Routledge is an imprint of the Taylor & Francis Group, an informa business

A Library of Congress record exists under LC control number: 99072979

ISBN 13: 978-1-138-61822-0 (hbk)
ISBN 13: 978-1-138-61827-5 (pbk)
ISBN 13: 978-0-429-46128-6 (ebk)

Contents

List of Tables vi
Acknowledgements viii
The Authors ix

1 The Context and Background of the Study 1

2 The Chinese Community in Britain 8

3 Self Esteem and Cultural Identity 23

4 The Design of the Study and Sample Characteristics 42

5 Identity and Migration Experience in Chinese Adolescents 61

6 Language and Identity 75

7 Demographic Factors in Cultural Identity 83

8 Cultural Identity in Cross-Cultural Perspective 90

9 The Experience of School and Educational Aspirations 111

10 Qualitative Study of Chinese Families in Britain 124

11 Conclusions and Policy Recommendations 167

References 190

List of Tables

Table 2.1	Chinese-born residents in Britain, 1851–1931	9
Table 2.2	Chinese residents in Great Britain 1951–81: by country of origin	10
Table 2.3	The Chinese population of Great Britain: by region	11
Table 2.4	The Chinese in Great Britain: economic activity	13
Table 4.1	Age by country of residence	51
Table 4.2	Gender by country of residence	51
Table 4.3	Place of birth	51
Table 4.4	Length of stay	52
Table 4.5	Parents' place of birth	52
Table 4.6	Parents' education	53
Table 4.7	British-Chinese: fathers' occupations	55
Table 4.8	British-Chinese: mothers' occupations	56
Table 4.9	European British: fathers' occupations	57
Table 4.10	European British: mothers' occupations	58
Table 4.11	Hong Kong Chinese: fathers' occupations	59
Table 4.12	Hong Kong Chinese: mothers' occupation	60
Table 5.1	Adolescents' self description of ethnic status	61
Table 5.2	Self described ethnic status and place of birth	66
Table 5.3	Self described ethnic status and age on arrival in Britain	66
Table 5.4	Self described ethnic status and length of stay	66
Table 5.5	Self described ethnic status and language normally used with parents	67
Table 5.6	Self described ethnic status and language normally used with siblings	67
Table 5.7	Self described ethnic status and language normally used with friends	68
Table 5.8	Self described ethnic status and best spoken language	68
Table 5.9	Self described ethnic status and those important to please	69
Table 5.10	Self assigned category and cultural attitudes	70
Table 5.11	Desire not to be Chinese	71

Table 5.12	Self ascribed ethnicity and the sense of not wanting to be Chinese	71
Table 5.13	Experiences of racism	73
Table 5.14	Friends' experience of racism	73
Table 6.1	Language spoken the best	75
Table 6.2	Language spoken the best and place of birth	76
Table 6.3	Language spoken best and age on arrival	76
Table 6.4	Language spoken best and length of stay	77
Table 6.5	Language mostly used with parents, siblings and friends	78
Table 6.6	Reasons for attending Chinese community school or equivalent	79
Table 6.7	Ability to read the Chinese language	80
Table 6.8	Frequency of attendance or involvement in Chinese cultural activities	81
Table 7.1	Length of stay and educational attitudes	84
Table 7.2	Length of stay and self identity	86
Table 7.3	Length of stay and cultural identity	87
Table 7.4	Gender and cultural identity	88
Table 8.1	Culture and ethnicity	103
Table 8.2	Spare time spent with friends	110
Table 9.1	Attitudes towards schooling	118
Table 9.2	Attitudes towards academic achievement	118
Table 9.3	Attitudes towards activity participation	119
Table 9.4	Relationships with teachers	120
Table 9.5	Experiences of praise and blame	121
Table 9.6	Preferred working methods	122
Table 9.7	Post-school aspirations: intentions to enter higher education	122

Acknowledgements

Pride of place in these acknowledgements must go to the Trustees of the Leverhulme Trust who showed their faith in us in the most practical possible way: by generously providing the grant which made this research possible. Not for the first time, we express our gratitude to them.

Secondly, we would like to be able to thank all those young people who completed our questionnaires and agreed to be interviewed, here in Britain and in Hong Kong. As we thank them, we would also wish to express our appreciation to the schools and other institutions who kindly assisted us in gaining access to them.

We are also grateful for the help received from many people who contributed in a variety of ways to the success of the research project. Among these it is a pleasure to include Mr Peter Ma (Hong Kong Government Office), Rev. Dr J. Tsang for their helpful suggestions, Mr George Skinner who was involved in planning the original research, and Dr A.R. Neesham who did the final proofreading of the manuscript.

The research was conceived and directed by Gajendra Verma. Data on Chinese pupils were collected by Yiu Man Chan and Sylvia Sham, and parts of their doctoral theses are incorporated in this volume. Data collection and interviewing of European British students was undertaken by Douglas Darby, who was also responsible for writing parts of the text. Further data analysis and most of the writing were undertaken by Douglas Darby and Chris Bagley, who were also responsible for the final text editing.

The Authors

Professor Gajendra K. Verma is Sarah Fielden Professor of Education at the University of Manchester.

Dr Yiu Man Chan was formerly Research Associate, School of Education, University of Manchester, and is now doing research in Hong Kong.

Professor Christopher Bagley, formerly of the City University of Hong Kong, is Professor of Social Work Studies, University of Southampton.

Dr Sylvia Sham is Research Associate, School of Education, Manchester Metropolitan University.

Mr Douglas Darby is Research Associate, School of Education, University of Manchester.

Professor Derek Woodrow is Professor of Education at Manchester Metropolitan University.

Mr George Skinner is a Lecturer in Education at the University of Manchester.

1 The Context and Background of the Study

Introduction

The subject of a study has no objective existence. Its formulation grows from the interplay of the curiosity of the researcher, or researchers, and some aspect of the observed world about them. In this chapter we briefly outline the concerns which led us to attempt this study, describe how it was that its foci were established and how its general shape emerged.

In 1985 the Home Affairs Committee observed that:

> ... remarkably little research has been carried out into the Chinese community, and the lack of reliable information extends even to its size and distribution (HAC, 1985).

Since that time there have been some educational studies of Chinese children and adolescents in Britain, but much more needs to be learned about how these children are experiencing life in Britain.

The 1991 Census, and the 1994 census of ethnic minorities have at least provided some background information. It is now known that there are about 200,000 people of Chinese ethnic origin living in Britain. Compared with other, more visible minority groups it is a not inconsiderable number. To put the number of Chinese people in Britain in perspective, it is almost identical to the Bangladeshi population and approximately one third the size of the Pakistani or Afro-Caribbean communities. In the next chapter, we give an account of the way the Chinese community in Britain grew between 1851 and 1991. At this stage we point to the two crucial differences between the Chinese community and those formed by settlers from the New Commonwealth and Pakistan (NCWP). These can be summarised in a few words: time and patterns of settlement.

Those arriving from NCWP countries, for reasons both complex and varied from one group to another, tended to form relatively compact settlements in well defined areas of Britain's cities. This allied to their visibility, made them a focus of interest from neighbouring indigenous populations, Local Authorities, and researchers, not least because of the racism which these visible minorities were subject to. The Chinese community was by contrast, diffused throughout Britain so that, with the exception of London, Manchester and Liverpool no immediately recognisable 'Chinese districts' existed. Even in those cities, the Chinese districts were concerned largely with businesses and social activities: few Chinese people actually lived in these 'China Towns'.

Chinese men first started to settle, though not necessarily permanently, in the very early years of the nineteenth century and their numbers grew undramatically but steadily until, within the last 30 years and ending with the Commonwealth Immigration Act 1971 there was a marked acceleration in their arrival. This contrasts with the main process of settlement by NCWP migrants who arrived in larger numbers and in definable waves, over relatively short periods of time between 1950 and the 1970s. There was of course a significant African population in Britain during late Tudor times and again in the eighteenth and early nineteenth centuries. However, this nineteenth century African population was wholly absorbed into the general British European[1] working class population through intermarriage.

Little academic work has been carried out on the needs of Chinese children. The Swann Report (DES, 1985) observed that:

> The educational needs of children from this group have not tended to be the focus of as much attention as the needs of other Asian or West Indian children .... We were met by two very different interpretations of their situation – firstly, that they were 'ideal' pupils who had no problems and represented a 'success story' amongst ethnic minority groups, or, alternatively, that they were a 'forgotten minority': invisible pupils whose needs remained unrecognised and thus unmet by schools.

That Swann had said this more than a decade ago, allied to the fact that little substantial research had been undertaken since, encouraged us to believe that research was now long overdue though other factors contributed to this belief. First among these was our perception of the socio-psychological situation of Chinese children in Britain. The 1991 Census made it clear that the majority of youngsters in schools were the children of first generation Chinese settlers. From this it followed that they were growing up in homes which were likely to be traditional in character whilst attending schools operating according to very different principles.

In the final chapter, we reflect on the results of this study, and discuss the nature of the Chinese family. Here we simply record that Chinese parents often adopt child-rearing practices based on Confucian precepts of filial piety and obedience. These emphasise the duty owed by children to their parents and justify what to Western eyes appears to be autocratic powers within the family exercised by the father.

We were tempted to assume that the daily transition between homes operating on these principles and schools whose ethos was informed by western European beliefs and practices, might result in cultural conflicts for these young people with all that this implied for their psychological growth and development. It also seemed possible that these conflicts might be exacerbated by the fact that these Chinese youngsters would be in a position to observe the differences between their own homes and those of their European British peers. Again, the differences were profound. Where the traditional Chinese child owed unquestioning obedience to his or her father, he or she would be able to see the way that most British families operated on a system of continuous negotiation between the generations, and perhaps make unfavourable comparisons.

However tempting it was to make these assumptions, there was little evidence to support them. The differences between the two communities, the British-Chinese and the European British, were not self-evident: but their reality could readily be tested. What was unproven also was whether assumptions that existed would give rise to 'conflict' in the minds of British-Chinese adolescents, with perhaps a harmful effect on identity and self esteem. Alternatively, the family system itself might buffer the self esteem of Chinese children and adolescence in making difficult social and psychological transitions in British society.

Allied to this concern was the question of whether there is evidence to show that British-Chinese adolescents were losing their cultural heritage as a result of growing up in a society whose cultural roots were firmly embedded in the western European tradition.

In seeking to discover an answer to these questions we were not adopting a judgmental stance. Many British Europeans believe, naively, that the way forward to social equality and stability depends on the willingness of ethnic minority groups to discard their cultural heritages and accept those of the majority community as their own. This view is implicitly racist in assuming that 'strange' religious and cultural practices should be discarded, and explicitly racist when groups who have done so continue to be discriminated against. Ideologically, we argue that tolerance of different religious and cultural practices is easily practised in a liberal, plural society and indeed will enrich the society which is able to practise such tolerance. One aim in this study was to discover if young British-Chinese are in fact losing their distinct cultural identity.

It seemed likely that some evidence on this question could be obtained from assessing their general self-esteem. If the British-Chinese adolescents were engaged in a struggle over their cultural identity in which they were faced with the prospect of discarding the beliefs and practices which had shaped their parents' lives, this might affect their views about themselves. Additionally, such an assessment might also indicate the degree of robustness with which they were dealing with their experience of racism.

It is unfortunate that, in the public's perception, the Chinese community in Britain is relatively free from racist persecution. Ample evidence exists to the contrary (Phillpotts, 1990; Seabrook, 1987; CRE, 1988): the Chinese community shares with other ethnic minority groups the widespread experience of racism. What is of interest is the effect of racism on their psychological well-being and their assessment of their worth as people. Racial assault, whether it be as trivial as name-calling by one small child to another or physical assault carried out on adults by adults, is characterised by a sense of superiority on the part of the racist. It is an attack on the ethnic and cultural identities of the victim. If racism were part of the lives of young British-Chinese, how was it affecting their psychological growth?

Finally, we were well aware of the pattern of settlement adopted by the Chinese community in Britain. Given the economic niche (take-away restaurants) which they have come to occupy, they had little choice but to spread themselves thinly through the British European majority. The nature of their work and other factors such as their limited ability in English inevitably resulted in social isolation for them and their children. This was particularly true for the children in their primary schools when they were likely to find themselves the only Chinese child in the school, perhaps unable to socialise with their classmates because they spoke little or no English. Although matters might improve when they arrived in their secondary schools – there were more likely to be fellow students from other Chinese families and they were, by that time, more fluent in English – their opportunities for forming friendships with other British-Chinese youngsters were still circumscribed.

It was these considerations which led us to propose a study, the main focus of which was the cultural identity of British-Chinese adolescents. By adopting this as the primary focus it would enable us to test the validity of the assumptions discussed above, all of which were closely related.

Thus, growing out of these interests and assumptions, the outlines of the study began to take shape. There would be three groups of respondents drawn from the British-Chinese, European British and Hong Kong Chinese populations respectively. Two of the groups would consist of youngsters drawn from members of dominant cultures and the third would come from a minority group growing up in a culture very different from that of their parents and them. At that stage, our expectations were that the British-Chinese group would provide us with findings that differed significantly from those of the other two, reflecting their position as a transitional ethnic minority. We anticipated that there would be evidence of what might be called 'cultural stress' with the young British-Chinese being perhaps ambiguous about the attractions of British cultural norms and those of their parents.

Associated with this there might be indications of reduced self-worth and some loss of personal and cultural identity. There was also the possibility that their educational aspirations would be depressed. Finally, as a group subjected to racism, they were under additional stress. By comparing the findings from this group with those from their White British and Hong Kong peers, some estimate could thus be made of the nature and severity of their problems. Proposals could then be made as to how they might be helped, and what social and educational policies to advocate.

In a later chapter devoted to the design of the study we show how these broad outlines were translated into the more detailed research strategies. Since self-esteem and cultural identity are concepts at the heart of this study, a subsequent chapter is devoted to a discussion of them.

Chinese Educational Styles

In order to understand the educational attitudes and aspirations of Chinese parents of Chinese youth in Britain, as well as the early educational experiences of some of the youth who came to Britain quite recently, we must understand the traditional educational system of Chinese culture in general, and of Hong Kong in particular. These educational attitudes and aspirations are crucial aspects of the identity of many Chinese children.

According to Murphy (1987):

> Hong Kong students display almost unquestioning acceptance of the knowledge of the teacher or lecturer. This may be explained in terms of an extension or transfer of the Confucian ethic of filial piety. Coupled with this is an emphasis on strictness of discipline and proper behaviour, rather than an expression of opinion, independence, self-mastery, creativity and all-round personal development (p. 43).

In contrast, the Chinese school student in England will experience an emphasis on the need for investigation, creative thinking, debate, discussion, group and project work, in other words, self-responsibility for his or her own learning and the formulation of ideas and knowledge. In extreme contrast, the Confucian influence on the development of a Chinese cultural identity, and thus on learning styles passed down through the family, goes back many centuries. The well known Confucian phrase that:

> ... those who labour with their brain should govern those who labour with their brawn ...

gave the development of learning the highest priority.

In Chinese culture the individual practising the values of filial piety and industrious scholarship is central to the dynamic process of a continuing family lineage and the specific ancestry of one's family; each individual is part of ethnic continuity and is defined within relationships (Tu Wei-Ming, 1985). As a result everyone is expected to behave in an exemplary fashion and in accordance with an ascribed role (e.g. father, mother, teacher, student, worker, Party member, etc.). Traditional culture and its system of ordered roles are extremely important. Standards of behaviour and self-development are determined by clearly defined societal roles and shared, subject to sometimes rigidly enforced cultural values.

Cultural pressures to conform have affected learning style: filial duty, the actions one performs, are inextricably linked with filial loyalty or commitment. It is essential within Chinese society to know what to do in all circumstances. This is understood and accepted. There is a strong sense of duty and of obligation which has been ingrained since childhood. Doing one's best is paramount. Perseverance, obedience, duty and loyalty are the essential qualities of a good son or daughter.

Confucian influence is also evident in the suppression of creativity. The age-old 'golden mean' doctrine, advises people to take a middle or neutral stance and this is still observable today:

> The bird that stands out will be shot first.
> The taller tree will catch the wind first.

Chinese children are warned not to take risks but to 'play it safe' while still 'doing their best'. Traditional Chinese education was considered an essential method of moulding the character of its citizens as it complemented the family influence. Chinese teachers were listed among the five categories of being who should be most admired by society: the God of Heaven, the God of the Earth, the emperor, parents and teachers (Zhou, 1988). Education is absolutely important.

For many centuries the process of learning and education resulted in the mechanical memorisation of the ideals of antiquity, of which principally the Four Books and Five Great Classics constituted the major content to be mastered in schooling for civil service examinations. Classical instruction suppressed the spirit of free inquiry and any initiative on the part of the learner. Learners were to be submissive to the dominant teaching style which was the transmission of factual classical knowledge. In reality, education was primarily for a scholarly elite and not for the common citizen or worker (Zhou, 1988).

As education spread to the masses the educational values persisted, and schooling in Hong Kong, as experienced by the several of the researchers and many of those currently being researched, had changed little. One of the aims of this research was to explore the degree to which this traditional learning style, reinforced by the values of filial piety which parents from Hong Kong bring to Britain, causes problems of learning and adaptation for their children experiencing the life of British schools, and of British peer culture.

Note

1. We prefer the term 'British European' rather than the crude term 'white', with its connotations of racial classification. 'British Europeans' are the long-settled group in the British Isles who are descended in the main from the ancient British settlers, who absorbed successive waves of immigrants, namely Celts, Romans, Vikings, Anglo-Saxons, Normans and other Europeans. Rather than focusing on 'race' we focus on 'ethnicity', a compound of cultural characteristics which makes a group more or less unique. Cultural ethnicity is also a relatively fluid concept, open to many social influences.

2 The Chinese Community in Britain

Introduction

In this chapter we trace the growth and development of the Chinese community in Britain. The time-span and pattern of their settlement differs markedly from that of other substantial ethnic minority groups now living in Britain, notably those from the West Indies and the Indian subcontinent.

Although not all of the Chinese people now living in Britain can trace their descent from ancestors who lived in Hong Kong, it would be true to say that most of them could (Home Affairs Committee, 1985). Taylor (1987) suggests that approximately 70 per cent of the Chinese in Britain are Cantonese from Hong Kong and the New Territories and a further 20 per cent are Hakka, with the remainder mostly from Taiwan, Singapore and Malaysia.

The earliest record of Chinese people living in Britain may be found in an 1814 medical report indicating that two had settled in London having served as seamen in the British East India Company (Jones, 1979). An indication of how these numbers grew is provided in Table 2.1 which covers the years 1851–1931. It will be seen that the increase in population was slow until the beginning of the present century. The table also shows how their primary occupation changed over the years from seamen to laundrymen, though there is also an intimation of the future in the data for 1921 with some of them featuring as restaurateurs.

Numbers built up more rapidly after World War II when most of the immigrants were men from Hong Kong. Immigration was stimulated by the recession in Hong Kong and the boom which Britain was enjoying. Thus there was the classic push-pull situation. Men already in Britain were able to write to their relatives and friends about the opportunities here at a time when those at home were under pressure to move anyway, whilst the British Nationality Act of 1948 meant that they had right of abode. Ng (1968) found that many intended, ultimately, to return. They were hard-working, remitted money on a regular basis to their families with whom they kept in close touch,

Table 2.1 Chinese-born residents in Britain, 1851–1931

Year	Number	Characteristics
1851	78	All living in London
1861	147	Now spreading outside London
1871	202	Chinese cheap labour
1881	–	–
1891	582	–
1901	387	80% single males, mainly seamen between 20–35
1911	1,319	Plus 4,595 seamen of Chinese origin serving in the British Merchant Navy
1921	2,419	Included 547 laundrymen, 455 seamen and 26 restaurant workers
1931	1,934	Over 500 laundries in Britain and two or three Chinese restaurants in Soho

Source: Chan (1994) using material adapted from Ng (1968) and Clegg (1988).

and planned to retire to their original villages. In these respects they were comparable with other early postwar settlers, notably those from the West Indies and the Indian subcontinent.

The 1962 Commonwealth Immigration Act, which abolished Hong Kong citizen's automatic right of entry to Britain, stimulated the decision-making process of many and resulted in a rapid inflow between its inception and the date of its coming into force. However, even after the Act, many Chinese emigrated to Britain through close family relationships or by acquiring a valid work permit. It was the Immigration Act 1972, which came into force in 1973, which crucially affected the lives of many Hong Kong people. Under this Act the wives and children of members of the Commonwealth lost their rights to join husbands and fathers living in Britain with the result that many who might otherwise have postponed the decision, arrived during the early 1970s. Table 2.2 shows how these factors affected the population growth between 1951–81.

It should be noted that the figures provided by the censuses on which the table relies have to be treated with some caution. It was not until the 1991 census that a direct question on ethnicity was included. Information on ethnicity in previous surveys depended on a question which asked for the country of origin of the Head of Household. Thus, ethnic Chinese born in Britain would be recorded as British. Conversely, respondents of British origin born in China would be included as Chinese. Finally, large numbers of students, nurses and

Table 2.2 Chinese residents in Great Britain 1951–81: by country of origin

Year	China	Hong Kong	Malaysia	Singapore	Total
1951	1,736	3,459	4,046	3,255	12,496
1961	9,192	10,222	9,516	9,820	38,750
1971	13,495	29,520	5,680	27,335	76,030
1981	17,569	58,917	45,430	32,447	154,363

Source: Censuses, 1951–81.

visitors from China would be included in the 1981 census. Simsova and Chin (1982) estimated that 2,000 Malaysian students and 5,000 nurses had been included.

The 1991 Census provided more reliable data by asking respondents to define their ethnic origin and Table 2.3 gives the total Chinese population of Great Britain at just under 157,000. The table shows major concentrations in the South East and North West with the remainder dispersed among the other regions.

The circumstances leading to this pattern of settlement were well-established in the early part of the century. Ng (1968) showed how with the rise in the numbers of Chinese seeking employment other than as seamen, many became involved in the laundry business which he described as useful but dirty work, not wanted by the British and requiring little capital. Their perception of this niche within the British economy was significant and characteristic. It enabled them to operate independently and provide a useful service without competing for either jobs or capital with the indigenous population. It was as Ng described it, the beginning of a 'symbiotic customer-waiter relationship' which was reproduced when, with the introduction of the launderette (and subsequently the home washing machine) in the 1950s, the laundry business collapsed and they moved into the restaurant trade.

With the end of rationing the British public was looking for a diet that was more varied and interesting than the one that most people had endured since 1939. Chinese food, which was perceived as being both exotic and delicious, was seized on with delight and the number of restaurants grew rapidly between 1956–65. This growth created a demand for workers which was met, in the main, by Chinese from the New Territories of Hong Kong who were relatives, or friends of relatives, of those already in the business. It was, as Verma and Darby (1994) observed, a prime example of chain migration.

Table 2.3 The Chinese population of Great Britain: by region

Region	1000s
North	*5.0*
Tyne and Wear Metropolitan County	2.8
Remainder of North	2.2
Yorkshire and Humberside	*8.3*
South Yorkshire Metropolitan County	2.2
West Yorkshire Metropolitan County	3.9
Remainder of Yorkshire and Humberside	2.2
East Midlands	*7.6*
East Anglia	*3.7*
South East	*137.5*
Greater London	56.6
Inner London	28.4
Outer London	28.2
Remainder of South East	24.3
South West	*6.7*
West Midlands	*9.6*
West Midlands Metropolitan County	
Remainder of West Midlands	
North West	*17.3*
Greater Manchester Metropolitan County	8.3
Merseyside Metropolitan County	5.6
Remainder of North West	3.4
England	*141.7*
Wales	*4.8*
Scotland	*10.5*
Great Britain	*156.9*

Source: 1991 Census.

Men settled and started businesses and were then able to recruit willing employees from within their own families. In this way, the business was able to grow without help being required from outside their own community. In the early days, many restaurants were cooperatives with the starting capital contributed by the founders who then worked in them. Watson (1977) points to the 1970s as the time when the restaurant business effectively reached saturation point – certainly in the major towns and cities.

The second stage of the process was the development of the 'take-away' business. During the 1970s, many fish and chip shops were taken over by Chinese families and converted to take-aways in response to public demand for increased choice and service at times when most traditional fish and chip shops were closed. This development had crucial consequences for the distribution of the Chinese community. From the commercial point of view, it made no sense for a prospective take-away proprietor to set up a business close to an existing business so the families dispersed through towns and cities and out into the villages – wherever sites became available with no pre-existing competition.

Their general economic strategy has been successful as Table 2.4 shows. It presents a picture of a community which is predominantly youthful, entrepreneurially active, with a relatively low unemployment rate. It also shows a high proportion who are students.

This geographical dispersal through the indigenous community goes some way towards explaining the 'invisibility' of the Chinese presence in Britain. Other recent settlers from the West Indies and South Asia for economic and social reasons have generated compact communities which, taken with their colour, made them far more visible from the time of their arrival. To be sure, the Chinese generally are fewer in number but their diffusion through the indigenous population is at least as significant a factor in accounting for their low profile in British life as their numbers.

Bearing in mind the relatively small numbers and their geographical dispersion, it is perhaps not altogether surprising that the response to their particular needs by the host country at government and institutional levels has been small. They were, of course, affected by the general responses to immigration in force at the time of their arrival and subsequently. It may be convenient to summarise them here.

It is difficult to avoid the view that successive British governments since the 1950s have regarded all immigrants, except those from the Old Commonwealth, as 'problems'. Over the years, it became almost an article of faith that continued good race relations required that no more additions to

Table 2.4 The Chinese in Great Britain: economic activity

Economic positions		Male	Female	Total
16 and over		58,777	61,522	120,299
Economically active		41,191	32,665	73,856
of whom, aged under 25		5,287	4,995	10,282
Employees –	full-time	22,736	16,775	39,511
	part-time	1,658	6,636	8,296
Self-employed –	with employees	7,340	3,048	10,388
	no employees	4,555	2,926	7,481
On a government scheme		580	574	1,154
Unemployed		4,322	2,704	7,026
of whom aged under 25		814	707	1,521
Economically active students		534	542	1,076
Economically inactive		17,586	28,857	46,443
Students		13,048	9,970	23,018
Permanently sick 1,044		768	1,812	
Retired		2,604	2,985	5,589
Other inactive		890	15,134	16,024

Source: OPCS (1991) Census.

existing ethnic minority communities be allowed. The increasingly draconian legislation to control immigration speaks for itself whilst the parliamentary debates which preceded the enactment of each statute provided many well-taken opportunities for Members of Parliament to reinforce the message by stressing the importance for the social stability of the state in ensuring that the numbers of 'immigrants' were kept at the irreducible minimum.

Legislation designed to govern the inflow of immigrants has affected the Chinese as well as those from other countries wishing to settle in Britain. One result of this has been to distort the age profile so that the population in the young adult and early middle age groups (20–35 year-olds) is larger than would be expected in a mature, long-settled community (OPCS, 1991). This has obvious consequences for the likely growth rate of families in this age range. The assumption must be that the Chinese population will increase rapidly in the next few years as families reach their desired sizes. It is worth noting here that unlike some ethnic minority communities in the UK., the average size of a Chinese family – 1.9 children (OPCS, 1990) – is, for all practical purposes, the same as that of the European community (i.e. those with British, Celtic, Anglo-Saxon and other European descent) – 1.8 children. Thus, their anticipated growth in numbers is related to the age profile of their community and not to high fertility rates.

It remains in this brief account of the growth of the Chinese community in Britain, to draw attention to the guarantee given in 1990 by the British government that 50,000 Hong Kong households would be given British passports and be permitted to enter Britain – an offer designed to defuse anxiety about the hand-over of Hong Kong to China in 1997.

To be eligible for a British passport, applicants had to be able to demonstrate by virtue of their education and economic status that they would be of positive benefit to this country. In spite of the intense anxiety about the future of Hong Kong felt by many of its citizens, only some 6,000 had availed themselves of this opportunity up to 1998, the majority preferring to seek residence in the Commonwealth countries of Australia, Canada and New Zealand. There may also be a significant remigration to Hong Kong once the immigrant has secured residence in the Commonwealth country.

It seems possible therefore, that the Chinese community in Britain will not substantially increase in the near future. The supposition must be that it will remain at about its present size since the normal family size, unlike that of many ethnic minorities which tend to be larger, is about the same as that of the Anglo or European community resident in Britain. Immigration Acts now in force (which it must be supposed will not be relaxed in the foreseeable future) will prevent people of modest means from increasing their numbers in Britain by immigration from China, whilst those for whom the British Nationality Act (Hong Kong) 1990 was intended as an attraction show little sign of wishing to avail themselves of its provisions.

Chinese People and The 1994 Sample Census of Ethnic Minorities

The Policy Studies Institute has since 1966 published regular surveys of ethnic minority groups in Britain, based on a stratified random sample. The 1994 survey (Modood et al., 1997) contains much interesting information on Chinese people and their families in Britain.

Using the 1991 Census to identity areas with high proportions of the seven ethnic groups studied (European British, Afro-Caribbean Britons and other Britons – the Indian, African Asian, Pakistani, Bangladeshi and Chinese ethnic groups), intensive sampling within these areas identified a sampling frame of the relevant ethnic group, with one adult (16 or over) in a sample of the households being interviewed. The proportion interviewed was sufficiently large for generalisations to made to the total population, with a known sampling error. In this way 214 Chinese people were interviewed. While the sample reflects those who migrated to Britain before the larger migration in the two years prior to 1998 and the absorption of Hong Kong as a special administrative region within the People's Republic of China (PRC), there are no grounds for supposing that these latter migrants differ greatly from those interviewed for the PSI survey.

Religion The Chinese community in the PSI survey had the highest proportion (compared with all other ethnic groups) who were classified as having 'no religion', at 58 per cent. In practice, we know from Hong Kong research that this label of 'no religion' often includes a group holding reverence for ancestors and a degree of filial piety that is often metaphysical in nature, but as a concept this cannot be grasped by Western frameworks of religion (Bagley et al., 1997). In addition, many Chinese people often have statues and altars to minor gods (hence the name of the famous novel *The Kitchen God's Wife*). Twenty-three per cent of the Chinese sample were Christian, reminding us that many Chinese school pupils have a strong (often fundamentalist) set of Christian beliefs. Ten per cent were listed as having adherence to 'other religious beliefs', not specified but almost certainly Buddhism.

People, family and household Along with people of Indian ethnic ancestry, the Chinese group had the smallest proportion (at 28 per cent) with children aged 0 to 15, with five percent being aged 60 plus, compared with 19 per cent of the British European ethnic group. Eighty-eight per cent of Chinese children (0 to 15) were born in Britain, and of the six ethnic minority groups studied, the Chinese community respondents had been resident in Britain for the longest period. Along with Bangladeshis, Chinese adults had a very low rate (below one per cent) of couples 'living as married' as opposed to being legally married, the figure for the British European group being nine per cent. No less than 15 per cent of the Chinese adults surveyed had a British European ('white') marital partner, an indicator presumably of assimilation and absorption into local communities. Bagley, De Clerk and Young (1997) in a comparative study of mixed marriages in Britain and The Netherlands found that Chinese-European marriages (often based on shared membership in Christian churches) were quite frequent.

Seventy-one per cent of the British-Chinese couples aged 20 to 59 had children (compared with 49 per cent of the British European sample) a figure exceeded only by the Bangladeshi and Pakistani ethnic group samples: 24 per cent of the Chinese couples had three or more children. Seventy two per cent of the Chinese families had an adult aged 60 plus living with them, the highest proportion for any ethnic minority, and much in excess of the 13 per cent of British European families in which parents and adult children lived in the same household. The Chinese community had the highest proportion of all the ethnic minority groups who kept in touch with an overseas parent by telephone – 59 per cent of Chinese adults had called in the previous four weeks, and 15 per cent had actually visited an elderly parent overseas in the last four weeks, compared with five per cent of the South Asian respondents. These findings are compatible with the popular view of Chinese people as being particularly concerned about the welfare of their elderly parents.

Qualifications and English language Despite their length of residence in England, the Chinese males tended to speak English 'fluently or fairly well' (in 76 per cent) somewhat less often than several ethnic groups who had, on average, been resident for a shorter time. Chinese women tended to be better at English than their counterparts in other minority communities, partly because they were more likely to work outside the home. However, full verbal fluency in English was achieved only by Chinese people born in UK: Chinese men who had migrated more than 25 years before were fluent or fairly good at English in only 55 per cent of cases. This is presumably a reflection of the fact that in Hong Kong (as opposed to Singapore, where English is the *lingua franca*) English is not spoken as a common language, and was introduced (up to 1998) as a second language quite late in the secondary school curriculum. Even then, verbal fluency rarely resulted.

That the Chinese community in Britain is generally well-qualified there is no doubt, from the results of this sample survey. Males had the highest proportion of all the ethnic minorities with a university degree (26 per cent, compared with 11 per cent of the British European group), and the lowest proportion (31 per cent) with no GCE/GCSE qualifications. Chinese British women too were more than twice as likely (17 per cent versus 8 per cent) as British European women to have a university degree. Seven per cent of Chinese women were qualified nurses, more than in any other minority group, and twice the proportion in white European women. Two thirds of the Chinese degree holders had obtained their degree in Hong Kong, Malaysia or Singapore. Of Chinese people who had all or most of their secondary education in the UK, 27 per cent were degree holders, more than any other ethnic minority and much higher than the 12 per cent in the British European sample.

Chinese people in this survey emerge as a very well qualified group, although their English fluency does not always match their high level of qualifications. The generation of Chinese young adults born and educated in Britain are however doing exceptionally well in terms of educational achievements.

Employment and income profiles Compatible with their high level of educational qualifications, Chinese women in the survey of ethnic minorities in Britain were the most likely to work full or part-time outside the home (in 71 per cent of cases), compared with 64 per cent in the European ethnic group (i.e. the mainstream 'white' group of Briton, Celtic, Anglo-Saxon, Norman and Other European origin). Chinese men, both in manual and non-manual occupations had the lowest recorded rates of unemployment of any group, probably because many are self-employed small entrepreneurs: 46 per cent of Chinese men were professionals, managers or directors of enterprises, a far high proportion than in any other ethnic minority, and higher than the 30 per cent in the mainstream British European ethnic group.

Many Chinese people were employed in Chinese-run small businesses, particularly in catering. Chinese people were much less likely than other ethnic minorities to work in industrial enterprises, but were over-represented in hospital and educational work (20 per cent in this sector, more than twice as many as any other ethnic group, including mainstream 'British Europeans'). The mean weekly earnings of the Chinese men sampled were markedly higher than those of any other ethnic group, and on a par with those of mainstream 'British Europeans'. Earnings of Chinese women were significantly higher than even those of the mainstream group. No Chinese women were, reportedly, single parents or received the bulk of their income from state benefits.

Earnings of self-employment and in small businesses were relatively high for the Chinese group, suggesting that the many restaurants run by this ethnic group are financially quite successful. Linking the location of these Chinese enterprises to census data confirmed that these restaurants served a very mixed ethnic population, and clearly were not restaurants for the Chinese ethnic group as such. Chinese people were relatively unlikely to report racial discrimination or its likelihood, compared with all other ethnic minorities, seven per cent reporting such experience, compared with 28 per cent of people of Caribbean origin. It appears, from comparing data from surveys of ethnic minorities in Britain over several years, that the Chinese minority group are probably the most upwardly mobile. Average total household income reported by the Chinese adults interviewed was higher than for any other group, including all types of ethnic minority, and the mainstream 'British European' group. None were 'in arrears' with housing costs; 15 per cent of Chinese reported 'some' or 'many' worries over money, the lowest amongst any minority group; the comparable proportion in mainstream 'British Europeans' reporting such worries was 27 per cent.

Neighbourhood and housing Ninety-one per cent of the Chinese respondents lived in a local authority ward in which the population contained no more than two per cent of their ethnic group. This was a unique pattern of settlement compared with all of the other ethnic minority groups surveyed, and fits the pattern of Chinese people moving into neighbourhoods not served by other Chinese businesses or restaurants. However, 20 per cent of the Chinese people surveyed said that would like half or more of the people in their neighbourhood to be of Chinese origin. But unlike other ethnic minorities, the lack of places to worship was not seen as a particular problem. Thirty per cent of the Chinese sample would like however to move from their area of current residence, seeing it as run down to a greater or lesser degree. This is compatible with the upwardly mobile trend for the Chinese community, and it is likely that the Chinese family of the future will leave the high street fish shop behind, as they acquire greater capital and qualifications.

Racial harassment This is a serious problem for ethnic minorities, and has been highlighted in successive Policy Institute Surveys. One per cent of Chinese people (both males and females) had been physically attacked in the previous year, but this was the lowest rate for all of the groups surveyed. Indeed, five per cent of mainstream 'British European' males, and two per cent of females in this group had been the subject of physical attack in the past year (attacks which did not occur across ethnic lines). Chinese people reported levels of property damage which were no different from those of the mainstream group, but did report levels of racial harassment in access to employment, housing or services which were *higher* than those of any other ethnic group. This could relate to a 'glass ceiling' for an upwardly mobile group, although the survey was not detailed enough to allow this as a final conclusion.

However, when the mainstream British European group was asked to list ethnic groups against whom they expressed racial prejudice, 'Asians', 'Caribbeans' and 'Muslims' were disliked by more than 20 per cent (Muslims were most disliked, by 28 per cent); but Chinese people were disliked or rejected by only nine per cent. While this proportion is disturbing enough, it does appear that British-Chinese people have greater verbal acceptance amongst the mainstream, 'British European' population.

Culture and identity Chinese people when asked this question tended not to describe themselves in terms of country of origin, physical characteristics, or religion. Their overt identity was relatively uncrystallised, compared with that of other ethnic minorities. More than three-quarters spoke a Chinese language (66 per cent spoke Cantonese, 10 per cent Mandarin, 11 per cent, Hakka). By their actions, Chinese people had closer ties with the country of their ancestors than any other ethnic minority, 60 per cent having visited their country of origin in the previous years. Of all the ethnic minorities, the Chinese people shared with those of Caribbean origin a tolerant view of marriages mixed by ethnic group. Ethnic mix did not influence whether Chinese people saw a school as desirable or not, and they were not concerned about access to religious instruction or special places of worship. Unlike some other ethnic minorities, the Chinese sample had no objections to coeducational schools. The Chinese people surveyed were more likely than any other ethnic group to see themselves as 'British'. However, on the basis of several attitudinal variables, the survey described most Chinese people as having an 'acculturative' strategy to living in Britain, retaining a strong element of traditional identity whilst accommodating to some major features of life in Britain.

Recent Sociological Studies

In comparison with other groups from the former Commonwealth who have migrated to Britain, there is a relative dearth of studies of Chinese people. Nevertheless, some worthwhile sociological studies have begun to emerge. The two studies we mention here were both part of research for doctorates. David Parker, beginning research on identities in Chinese youth in Britain could find few studies, but did find some studies published in diverse areas, and produced a useful annotated bibliography (Parker, 1994).

Parker, who is of mixed European and Chinese descent, admits that in the interviews he undertook with Chinese youth (people of his own age) he was handicapped by his lack of facility in Chinese language; inevitably, he approached the accounts of cultural identities from his own understanding and experience of identity. The title of his book *Through Different Eyes* (Parker, 1995) is drawn, ironically, from a statement by the late Enoch Powell who in one of his inflammatory speeches (in Southall, in 1971) declared that: 'It is truly when he looks into the eyes of Asia that the Englishman comes face to face with those who would dispute with him the possession of his native land.'

One of Parker's major findings is the importance of Hong Kong popular culture, having a central place in the cultural identities of young, Chinese Britons. Cantopop and Cantosoap are ubiquitous and easily accessible from local Chinatown markets, and from satellite and local radio stations. But unlike Canada (where the writer of this chapter is currently resident, and is listening, as he writes, to a Cantopop station) in Britain Cantopop music has not informed popular culture in Britain to the same degree as Caribbean, and latterly Indian subcontinent music. Parker observes:

> Rather than a fusion of elements that interpenetrate, Chapter 7 shows how Hong Kong culture remains a separate presence in Chinese identity here [in Britain], there is no further transformation or syncretization as yet. This pattern is matched in the sense of identity among many young Chinese people. The confinement of Chinese culture and identity largely to the domestic sphere can act as a defence against racism (p. 208).

This leads Parker to conclude that in the 54 young people he interviewed there is a sense of '... guarded Chinese identities, held in the private domain with a certain enforced innerness. The formation stems from the very specific forms of racism and discrimination young Chinese face' (p. 233). In part this is reinforced by the ecological scattering of the Chinese community because of work in the catering trade (take-aways are not close to one another, for obvious economic reasons).

Parker makes the following astute observations:

> Identities in a multicultural context are strong only to the extent that they admit of internal diversity, allow breathing space, and cede a little of themselves to others. A conception of culture as inherently possessed by birth as Chinese, and the metaphor of roots often accompanying such a view, is too enclosed and confining. As Chambers suggestively phrases it, attention should be given to *routes* rather than to *roots* ... a more exploratory and pluralistic conception of identity formation (p. 237).

Parker suggests that with the passing of time Chinese cultural identities in Britain may become more public and more multifaceted: 'More fluid and pluralistic identifications could characterize the emergent generation of Chinese in Britain' (p. 248). This might involve greater involvement of young Chinese people in 'mixed' marriages.

The second study of note is by the Korean researcher Miri Song (who like Parker is a leading researcher on children and adolescents with 'mixed' ethnic heritage). In her doctoral thesis, (Song, 1997) a qualitative study, examined sibling relationships in young British-Chinese people. She points to differing types of role performance in young people who work in their parents' catering establishments, some acting like the 'good' child, others negotiating a more deviant identity with different scholastic aspirations and cultural identities than those desired by their parents. These are young pioneers, taking 'routes' in Parker's phrase, rather than being grounded only in 'roots'.

A number of these interesting themes are explored in Part III of the present book, which includes extended case material collected by Sylvia Sham for her doctoral thesis.

Conclusions

The Chinese population in Britain are well-settled, and relatively satisfied with their position in British society, according to the evidence which emerges from the Policy Studies Institute Survey (Mahdood et al., 1995). In terms of economic adaptation and upward mobility they are the most successful of recent immigrant groups in Britain. Traditional family values are maintained, with loyalty to parents and to elderly people in the culture of origin. Despite this, there is evidence from some qualitative studies of both isolation of traditional Chinese cultural affiliations from the majority culture, and the desires of young people educated in Britain to explore with more freedom the non-Chinese culture which surrounds them. This implies complex identity formation, but does not have clear implications for self esteem development. In theory however, strong rootedness in family tradition should imply stronger self esteem, despite the experience of demeaning acts racism outside of family contexts.

The sample of Chinese students accessed in this study were, because of the sampling methods (using GCSE entrants in Chinese Language, and attendance at Chinese language supplementary schools) likely to focus on the least acculturated (and potentially, the most recently arrived) group of immigrants from Hong Kong. They might not be as economically advantaged as the families described in the PSI survey.

3 Self Esteem and Cultural Identity

Introduction

Whereas the identity of individuals is dynamic and formed in the years leading to maturity, the identity of groups of people tends to be stable over time since it is an inheritance that has been selected and reinforced by many generations. The identity of such groups is commonly referred to as their culture and may be identified as a mixing of values, attitudes, beliefs and behaviours to which its members largely subscribe.

For the majority of people who grow up with the experience of a single culture, the relationship between their ethnic and personal identities presents few problems. The process of maturation and the development of personal identity are assisted by the consistency of the information about the nature of society, the privileges it confers on its members and the obligations it demands. However, as migration between countries has increased, large numbers of people are coming into contact with and in one way or another, are having to come to terms with cultural norms and values which are markedly different from those of their parents and grandparents.

The Present Study: Concepts of Cultural Identity

The primary purpose of this study was to explore the cultural identity of Chinese adolescents in Britain and for this purpose a modified version of Ghuman's (1991) cultural identity scale employed. This owes much to Wilpert's (1989) definition of identity – the sense of belonging expressed in the shared values derived from a common group membership. The intention behind using this approach was to see how closely the respondents related themselves to various aspects of Chinese culture and, therefore the extent to which they saw themselves as culturally Chinese rather than as culturally western European, or as a blend of the two cultures.

Of course, this in turn begs the question of the meaning of culture. Bullivant (1981) saw culture in its several definitions as relative to the environment.

> The first is the natural or geographical environment and habitat, with its biotic and natural resources. The second is the social environment consisting of other social groups with which a society comes into contact ... the third is more speculative, but is needed to explain the often elaborate nature of a culture which enshrines a religious world view. This is the 'metaphysical environment'.

In effect, Bullivant regards culture as a 'problem-solving device' which helps a social group to cope with its environment. Culture is therefore progressive and dynamic, constantly changing as it comes to terms with outside phenomena and the challenges they pose.

The dynamism of culture has been stressed by Verma with Ashworth (1986):

> Culture is not a static entity in the form of a fixed social heritage. It does not exist in a vacuum; it evolves and changes over time ... Many traditional cultural characteristics disappear or change when they are no longer able to meet the challenge of social, economic and technological changes.

Worsley (1984) has suggested that culture could be defined in four ways:

> ... the elitist, holistic, hegemonic and the pluralist. In the first, culture implies superior values, reserved for the dominant few; in the second, a whole way of life; in the third, a set of behaviours imposed by those who rule there. The last, a relativist sense, recognises that different communities in the same society have distinctive codes of behaviour and different value systems – which may even be opposed.

For the purposes of this study we adopted the holistic sense of the term and our concern was with a whole way of life within the social environment. We were also prepared from the outset, to discover that the culture of the young people who were the subject of the study was not necessarily that of their parents, still less that of pre-revolutionary China.

Concepts of Identity

Given the nature of this study, the terms 'self esteem' and 'identity' are widely employed. Since these are complex ideas and have been the subject of an extensive literature, it is sensible to offer a brief overview.

The problem of identity is one of the most difficult challenges for social science, and scholars have responded in various ways (Burkitt, 1991), which we review in this chapter. No single heuristic device is likely to encapsulate the whole dimension (Sarbin and Scheibe, 1983). The classical theory of identity is usually grounded in the work of the psychologist Erikson (1965, 1968) who regarded identity development as a cycle of 'crises' of development which offer challenges to the individual at different life stages, from infancy to old age. Each identity crisis, which all of us must experience if we are to move successfully to the next stage of development, presents the individual with various choices and commitments. These are not moral or even conscious choices; rather, the individual is propelled by aspects of his or her previous experiences, and is drawn forth by teachers, parents and community by sets of values which define and constrain the roles one has to perform. The identity crisis of adolescence is a crucial one, in which the young person has to recapitulate and integrate previous achievements within an identity framework which should (for the successful individual) incorporate an optimistic view of oneself as a child-becoming-an-adult who will soon try out a range of new roles.

Marcia (1966) derives from Erikson's schema of adolescent identity formation a fourfold classification describing the manner in which the adolescent faces and tries to solves these challenges to identity development.

a) *Identity Achievement*: individuals in this state have explored options and alternatives in the identity domain and have come to decisions to which they are comfortably committed, not by any great act of will but by the ease of the transition which their family and social system build for them. Families and communities in crisis may experience difficulty however in giving their adolescent the psychological strengths by which identity tasks can be achieved. When proper Identity Achievement cannot be made, then various alternative, temporary or permanent psychological states emerge.

b) *Identity Diffusion*: individuals have made no commitments in the domain of identity development, and show little evidence of trying to do so.

c) *Moratorium*: individuals in this state are currently 'in crisis', actively exploring amongst the alternatives in an attempt to form commitments.

d) *Foreclosure*: individuals in this state have clear commitments but show

> no evidence of having experienced a period of exploration of alternatives, largely due to extreme constraints imposed by external forces over which they and their families have no control. Hauser (1971) argues that oppressed minority groups (e.g. ghetto dwellers) may have this kind of identity formation imposed on them, and the only means of meaningful psychological development is through attendance at black colleges and other institutions which can raise ethnic pride.

The current status of Hauser's theory in the United States is unknown, and black people are rightly critical of the casual imposition of psychological theories which seem to condemn them to marginal status (Stone, 1981). If Chinese immigrants in Britain were subjected to extreme racism and forced to live in ghettoes (a fate which was imposed for example, on Chinese people in Indonesia in the present century, prior to the massive pogroms of the 1960s)[1] what would be their patterns of psychological adaptation?

The use of the four-status approach has led to the development of a number of important contexts for identity development including the home, family, peers, the media and educational experiences (Grotevant, 1987). However, not much is known about whether the experience of growing up as a member of a minority group within a dominant group is associated with particular patterns of identity development. Since about 1980 there has been a moratorium on these kinds of studies in the United States, as blacks successfully argued that they should no longer be the objects of study by majority group psychologists seeking (apparently) to prove states of psychological marginality and inferiority. Scientific racists in psychology have retreated into the field of 'intelligence', often using very old data to try and prove the intellectual inferiority of oppressed groups (e.g. Rushton, 1995).

A positive view of black identity development has argued that the black family is a powerful crucible for providing children with care and psychological sustenance in ways which can foster successful social and economic participation (Young and Bagley, 1982).

Social change may force an identity crisis upon a cultural group, just as the onset of adolescence may imposed an identity crisis upon an individual. A relevant example of social change is migration in which the old culture is left behind, and the adolescent has to face not only the usual demands of adolescent role development but also has to find ways of working successfully within his or her new culture. This could cause families to be more controlling and protective, including being particularly restrictive about choice of marital partners.

Identity stands at the pinnacle of psychological development both in terms of complexity and in terms of temporal development. Very young children have 'situated self esteem', seeing themselves as successful in one role (and therefore having good self esteem of themselves as, say, someone who can create colourful pictures) but poor in another (having a poor opinion of themselves as riders of a bicycle – a self-opinion likely to change rapidly). At the age of seven, a child's evaluation of ethnic identity and his or her self esteem are likely converge (Milner, 1997). The older the child, the more global self esteem becomes and, by the age of nine, children will think of themselves as generally good (or not) at school work, or at sport. Come adolescence, the roles in which self-evaluation are possible become both numerous and interconnected to the extent that the purely affective dimension of self esteem becomes intertwined with a cognitive concept of roles which are part of the individual's everyday status. Thus self-concept is formed, and at the stage of adolescence is often synonymous with identity.

The individual retains a measurable self esteem throughout life, which is known to be predictive of success in various roles, and vulnerability to various kinds of stressors. Although self esteem can be reliably measured as a valid concept in itself, it is also contained within an individual's *global identity*, the highest order concept involving both self-concept and self esteem in an integrated whole. Within global identity are the parts of the self, related to one another in particular configurations, representing various degrees and types of ego-integration. The complexity and the uniqueness of global identity are recognised by psychologists who, following Kelly (1955) elicit personal constructs from individuals. Each individual has a unique personal construct: the uniqueness of the construct makes comparisons between individuals difficult, although some scholars (e.g. Weinreich, 1979) have attempted to do this in the field of ethnicity. The technique requires lengthy individual administration, and was unsuitable for the present study which administered a relatively short self-completion questionnaire in classroom settings.

Wilpert (1989) defines identity in terms of the individual and his or her relationship to the collective (i.e. social structure). He sees identity as a sense of belonging which is expressed in the shared values, beliefs and symbols derived from common group membership, tradition, language and history. Breakwell (1983) regards identity as a dynamic social product residing in psychological processes which could not be understood except in relation to its social context and historical perspective. Weinreich (1989) defines identity as a process of continuity and gives central importance to the process of personal construal of self in relation to environment. One's identity is defined as the totality of one's self-construal, in which how one construes oneself in the present expresses the continuity between how one regarded oneself in the past, and how one construes oneself to be in the future.

Lange and Westin (1985) regard ethnic identity as falling into two main categories – identity as 'defined/perceived by others', and identity as 'self-defined/perceived.' Wallman's (1983) British research suggests that ethnicity is not a fixed, inflexible commitment; nor is it necessarily singular. Multiple ethnic identities often exist. Similarly, Weinreich, Kelly and Maja (1986) in their discussion focus on situated identities. They suggest that alternative states of identity might be engaged in by an individual cuing into different social contexts. Such alternative identity states might be regarded as aspects of one's overall identity in which how one behaves, presents oneself and experiences one's situated self differ according to social context. Identity, according to this view, is constantly changing as it is associated with new encounters and terminations of social interactions.

This view has a basis in Barth's (1969) seminal view of ethnic identity in which minority group individuals define their ethnic identity in terms of how they perceive the relationship of their ethnicity to the dominant cultural group. In this theorem 'ethnic identity' is not self-evident for any particular minority group person, but must be elicited through a series of qualitative interviews – one of the research strategies used with a sub-sample in the present study. A good example of identity research in the Barth tradition is Ullah's (1990) study of how second-generation Irish youth in Britain construct their ethnic identities, in a situation where 'passing' as English is a strategic possibility for virtually all of this group.

Werbner (1991) points out that the sources of personal identity and group affiliation conferred by migrants' past backgrounds can be of crucial importance in identity development. However, past backgrounds and experiences are only one source of personal identity. As Werbner argues, current residence and work are equally important. The migrant has to incorporate at least three sources of sometimes profound stress into identity formation: the loss of the old culture, for which the grieving may never end; the trials of learning the folkways and idiomatic language of the new culture; and, unfortunately, racist rejection when the migrant has prepared him or herself for full participation in the new culture, but is still rejected.

But ethnic identity (particularly so for the highly visible minority of Chinese origin) may have to incorporate a self-conception of one's physical self as a person with a particular kind of skin shade, hair type and features. This self reflection is forced upon the migrant who had never regarded himself as ethnically different before.[2] Thus Lange and Westin (1985) regard ethnic identity as falling into two main categories – 'identity as defined/perceived by others' and 'identity as self-defined'.

Wallman (1983) rightly observes that ethnicity is not a fixed, inflexible commitment; neither is it necessarily singular, since multiple ethnic identities and allegiances can also exist (this is particularly so for the growing population of 'mixed race' youth). Similarly, Weinreich, Kelly and Maja (1986) focus on 'situated identities'. They suggest (following Barth) that alternative states of identity might be presented by individuals cuing into different social contexts: an obvious example is the Chinese adolescent in his or her family, and at school. Such alternative identity states might be regarded as aspects of one's overall identity in which how one behaves, presents oneself and experiences one's situated self differs according to social context. Identity, according to this view, is constantly changing as is encounters new role demands and changing cultural values.

Werbner (1991) builds a useful model of migrants' identity, which incorporates elements of past backgrounds and language with new status and role relationships, and new forms of language required or imposed by the host culture. Bagley and Young (1991) combine these two elements – past identity and new challenges to role relationships – in commenting on the adaptation of immigrants in Canadian culture, arguing for a reciprocal contract between hosts and migrants: migrants should be allowed a guarantee of tolerance and nondiscrimination, including the practice and maintenance of 'private culture' (which includes those public behaviours relating to dress and religious observance); for their part, migrants as part of this contract should undertake to obtain relevant skills and education, pay relevant taxes, seek employment, and learn one of the national languages (English or French). This policy proposal offers a set of clearly defined roles for the migrant: in each he or she will have a certain self-concept, and the personal evaluation of performance in the collectivity of role behaviours will constitute a global identity. If discrimination is experienced, this too must be incorporated into identity with appropriate strategies, including action for political change.

The Social Dimension of Identity

The assertion that identity is the product of the interaction of the individual with influences of the physical and social world is not new. Phenomenological idealists and philosophers both described identity as a social product, even though they have focused on quite different social processes in its production (Breakwell, 1986).

In the sociological literature, the link between society and identity has been most directly addressed in the symbolic interactionist tradition, traced primarily to Mead (1934), Cooley (1902) and Thomas (1923). A key feature of the interactionist account of identity is its emphasis on the social situation as the context in which activities are established and maintained through a process of negotiation. The structural interactionists emphasise the concept of role – identities are viewed mainly as internalised roles. 'A person's identity is composed of a number of different roles located at different points in the status dimension. Role enactments vary in the degree to which the actor is involved in the role' (Sarbin and Scheibe, 1983).

In the worst-case scenario, the oppressed minority group will learn or internalise the symbolic identity imposed by the powerful majority group. Or, in a mode of political activism, the discriminated group will seek politically active ways of seeking to unmask the now exposed forces of alienation (Bagley, 1975). This is a model we applied to Afro-Caribbean youth in Britain (Bagley, 1997), but no model yet exists of how Chinese youth would react if they perceive that society discriminates against them to a profound degree.[3]

Breakwell (1986) usefully describes the social context of identity as structurally comprised of interpersonal networks, group memberships and intergroup relationships. Each individual is located within the matrix of these relationships, and each set of relationships provides roles for the individual to adopt. The process of social influence generates the ideological substance of the structure. Interpersonal networks and groups manipulate or negotiate their relative positions through attempts at influence and ideological change: the nexus of interpersonal relationships surrounding identity is rarely static. Each group (e.g. majority and minority ethnic groups) arrives at an interpretation of reality which suits its own interests and intentions, and then attempts to convert other individuals or groups to its view (Breakwell, 1986).

Rex (1991) outlines a theory of identity which has specific relevance for ethnic minority communities in Britain. He notes, as did Verma with Ashworth (1986), that the concept of identity implies a sense of continuity of the individual through various imposed and chosen roles: the nature of this ethnic identity is constantly under review and is changed both actively and passively by discontented ethnic minorities and by various types of macro-level cultural change. These could include demographic changes, in which a minority group gains enough social and economic power to enable a more secure structural position to be negotiated. Rex notes that despite many structural changes, the family system and its associated religious practices and beliefs are likely to form a more constant part of identity. He cites Geertz (1963) on what has come to be called the 'primordial' theory:

> The givenness that stems from being born into a particular religious community, speaking a particular language … and following particular social practices … One is bound to one's kinsman, one's neighbour, one's fellow believer … by virtue of some unaccountable absolute import attributed to the very tie itself.

What this serves to explain, as Rex puts it:

> … is why it is that, despite very strong pressure in complex societies for groups to be formed of congruence of interest, many individuals do, in fact, stubbornly continue to unite with those with whom they have ties of ethnic sameness, even though such alliances might run contrary to patterns of group formation determined by shared interests (Rex, 1991, p. 10).

Language and Ethnic Identity

Research has shown that ethnic identity is intrinsically connected with language. Language interweaves the individual's personal identity with his/her collective, ethnic identity. According to Lange and Westin (1985), there are five conditions promoting this connection:

a) existentially, language is significant to the individual as an instrument for naming the self and the world;
b) essentially, primary socialisation is a matter of linguistic interaction;
c) social representations, as the cognitive connective tissue of a culture, are expressed in language;
d) language is the medium of the ethnic group's mythological conceptions of its common origin;
e) of all ethnic markers, spoken language is one of the most salient.

For Chinese people in Hong Kong, there is an additional aspect of language that is an important part of identity, and that is the scripted form of the language. Each word is represented in Chinese by a pictograph, based on ancient pictorial symbols. By the age of three, the traditional Chinese child will begin to draw these symbols, with practice in the appropriate direction and thickness of the required pen strokes. For ordinary literacy, a Chinese person will need to recognise and draw at least 10,000 symbols (30,000 or more for university study) many of which, to the untrained Western eye, look very similar. Chinese people take great pride and pleasure in the correct mode of drawing each character, and for some the drawing of pictographs is an art form. For a person to be *Chinese* in a proper sense, he or she must also be a fully literate person. But for the Chinese child in Britain ordinary school will not impart these skills: they must be learned at home and in supplementary schools. For a Chinese child to become literate not only in spoken Cantonese (or Mandarin, Hakka or another of the dozen dialect groups – all have the same script), he or she must spend many hours of patient industry. This role as a student of language, faithful to the knowledge and teaching of the elders, must become part of a young person's identity. Not to become literature in Chinese involves an important, symbolic role transition to becoming a Westernised Chinese person. Newly migrated parents may wish their children to assimilate, and not teach them Chinese so that in the second generation their children have to recover these ancient skills of language by a more arduous route.[4]

Language, Lange and Westin (1985) argue, is important because it is used to name oneself, and other important people. In Hong Kong children entering secondary school are often asked to give themselves a Western name, and one is often chosen from the world of literature, music or sport. In Chinese the clan name (only about a hundred of these exist in Chinese) is presented first, with personal names second. Thus a girl is named, say Wong Siu-Ying and later becomes through her own choice Mary Wong Siu-Ying. She will present her Western name or her Chinese name (or both) according to context.

Her relatives are described by complex kinship names: not merely 'aunt' but for example 'aunt who is my mother's sister'. Imposing Western kinship names embodies a Western kinship system of honour in which all aunts are potentially equal: in Chinese kinship systems, aunts in the patrilineal line are accorded more status.

Linkage between mother tongue and identity is extremely complex and this complexity has led to many assumptions being made about the relationship between bilingual education and ethnic identity retention which have not been adequately tested. While there is a long history of general research into identity formation, the process is less well understood in relation to children growing up as members of a minority community in a dominant culture differing in a number of respects from their own. This is particularly true of Chinese children in diaspora who, often because they have not been perceived as a problem – or, as is the case of those growing up in Britain – have not attracted research interest.

A final comment in this section on how Chinese parents perceive their children's abilities: the idea of fixed, limited or finite intellectual potential does not seem to exist in traditional Chinese culture. The child who achieves poorly in school work is seen to be lazy or disobedient, but not stupid. The solution for those who can afford it is to enrol the child in private classes, or with a private tutor before or after normal school. The idea of *industry* in obedience to parental wishes is built in to many roles in Chinese culture. The underachieving child will not, as in many British schools, be taught at the level at which teachers expect him or her to achieve (buffering low self esteem which could result from poor academic results). These high educational expectations could be a factor causing some Chinese pupils to have low self esteem, relative to their British peers.

Is There a Hong Kong Cultural Identity?

This is an interesting and important question which does not permit an easy answer. First of all, those who have emigrated from Hong Kong tend to be the most successful and ambitious of the former Territory's residents and often, having established the right of residence in Britain, Canada, New Zealand or Australia return to high paying professional or business posts in Hong Kong. The large majority of Hong Kong's 6.5 million inhabitants belong to the Cantonese ethnic group, a minority within China. Although Cantonese has the same script as Mandarin (the official language, whose script is now being simplified), the two languages are pronounced quite differently, and verbal facility is not easily transferred. The learning of English was introduced into most schools at secondary level, and began with the formalistic study of grammar. But by 1998 all but a hundred secondary schools offered all tuition in Chinese. The majority of people in Hong Kong do not speak any English (having only primary school education, or having been educated in the PRC), while those who learned it in secondary school speak it with the same facility as the average English person speaks French.

The Special Administrative Region of Hong Kong is the eighth richest region in the world, yet some 20 per cent of its people live in crowded housing with very low incomes. Income inequalities are profound, probably more so than in any other region in the world (Bagley, Ko and O'Brian, 1997). Some 60 per cent of the population retain beliefs and rituals surrounding ancestor worship, which is expressed within their family as the principle of filial piety, in which sons honour their fathers, and wives and sisters support males in these sacred duties. The will of the father was, and sometimes still is, absolute. While the majority of the population hold beliefs linked to Buddhism, Taoism or ancestor worship, an important minority of the Hong Kong population are Christian. Baptist College was granted full university status in 1993; the Adventist Hospital (subvented by the Seventh Day Adventist Church) is an important health care provider, as is Baptist Hospital.

It is likely that migrants from Hong Kong are not only overweighted by the better educated sector, with those speaking some English also over-represented; they may also contain more people with Christian beliefs than would be expected from a random sample in Hong Kong.

For the Westerner in Hong Kong the Chinese scholar or business person has a public face, one of affability and good nature, curious about Western speech and customs. The British colonial presence was tolerated because of its temporary nature. This sometimes lulled the British colonial apparatus before 1998 into the false belief that British culture was actually respected and admired by Chinese people. British culture has been tolerated certainly, but the eyes and hearts of the majority of Chinese people of Hong Kong have been directed towards the Middle Kingdom, the central (and superior) region of the earth, standing above the Western and Eastern Kingdoms.

There is another aspect of Cantonese culture not readily appreciated by those who meet the scattered community of Cantonese people in Britain. This is their ethos of jollity and great sense of fun: in Hong Kong, public places and restaurants are always crowded by people and families enjoying themselves noisily and with laughter. There is an old saying: 'Mandarins will read anything; Cantonese will eat anything'. Certainly nothing pleases the Cantonese heart so much as a good meal eaten with family and friends.

Michael Bond, a leading scholar at the Chinese University of Hong Kong has wrestled for many years with the problem of understanding 'the Chinese face' (Bond, 1991). Bond and Pang (1990) in exploring Chinese values and identity obtained extensive data on responses to a value orientation scale, completed by adults in 21 countries, and identified two major dimensions along which most cultures differed. The first value dimension was labelled 'social integration versus cultural inwardness' marked at one extreme by tolerance of others, patience, search for harmony, and trust in others; and, at the other extreme, by a sense of cultural superiority, a desire for chastity in women and a control of their activity, and the frequent observation of rites and social rituals. Respondents in The Netherlands and Western Germany emerged as the most tolerant, with Pakistan, India and Bangladesh the most ritually and culturally inward. England fell towards the pole of tolerance, while Hong Kong fell towards the pole of ritual integration and traditional values, although the differences were not extreme – both English and Hong Kong respondents converged towards the middle of this value axis.

The second value dimension posed 'reputation and status-seeking' versus 'a sense of righteousness and morality.' The English sample had the *highest* score on this value dimension, being excessively concerned with being seen as a respectable and successful person, and a person of wealth and status. The Hong Kong sample had a *directly opposed* set of values on this dimensions, laying emphasis on the practice of social and moral purity, together with a subjective sense of righteousness in relation to metaphysical goals. On this value dimension, the English and the Chinese differ profoundly, the English face being coated, like the whited walls, with hypocrisy, while the Chinese face hides a search for inner spirituality.

Cheung, Lee and Chan (1994) found that neither wealth nor status in Hong Kong Chinese predicted the strength of traditional values (particularly those concerned with filial piety). However, affiliation with Buddhist ideals was associated with adherence to the values of filial piety, supporting Bond and Pang's (1990) finding of a strong spiritual element in the holding of traditional values. It may be however that those Hong Kong Chinese who migrate are those with the most acculturated values, which allow them to accommodate to the traditional fetish in British culture for visible status (Jowell, Findlay and Skeldon, 1995).

An additional element defines Hong Kong Chinese identity, setting it apart from the rapidly modernising culture of the People's Republic (Gransow, 1995). This is the idea of political liberalism which has developed a high profile in Hong Kong. According to Wong's (1996) survey, 60 per cent of Hong Kong people believed that freedom and human rights are more important than state and nation, and more then 40 per cent believe that Tibet (annexed by the PRC) should be freed; 37 per cent would, if possible, leave Hong Kong if the liberal traditions of Hong Kong were suppressed following its absorption in the PRC. This is an important point to remember: although the first wave of Hong Kong Chinese immigration had ceased by 1998, fresh waves are possible and it is important to develop knowledge in educational systems as to how best to meet the needs of these welcome immigrants.

Studies of ethnic identity in Chinese youth following migration to Australia and America (Rosenthal and Feldman, 1992) have shown that with the passage of time, youth and young adults showed increasingly successful participation in the wider culture, while retaining an allegiance to traditional Chinese values. These youth have, in Ghuman's (1991) term achieved 'the best of both worlds'.

Will Chinese youth in Britain achieve such a balanced state, or will their aspirations be frustrated by the British obsession with class and colour, which has traditionally underpinned much British racism (Bagley and Verma, 1979)? Certainly, in comparing Jamaican immigrants to Britain and to Canada (Bagley, 1997) we have argued that British racism has led to the alienation of many Jamaican immigrants, whilst Canada's more accepting policy has allowed the tolerant assimilation of most Jamaican immigrants.

Further comparative studies of Chinese immigrants to different Commonwealth countries are in order, to investigate these important issues.[5] Further work must also be undertaken on the impact of immigration as a disruptive and stressful process, with possible implications for mental health in migrant Chinese adolescents and adults. It is worth noting in this respect that a study of 'young elderly' Chinese immigrants (aged 60 to 75) in Canada found that they did not have impaired mental health, relative to those who had not migrated from Hong Kong, and compared with those who were long settled in Canada (Bagley, 1994). These immigrants who joined adult children were rapidly absorbed into existing Chinese networks. It will be interesting to replicate this study in Britain.

Conceptions of Self Esteem

Self esteem may be described as a facet of both personality and personal identity and is perceived as being of particular relevance to this study.

Morris Rosenberg (1965) defines self esteem as a positive or negative attitude towards a particular object – the self. High esteem means that the individual respects himself or herself, considers himself or herself worthy, recognises limitations, and expects to grow and self-develop (what Maslow, 1954, calls 'self-actualization'). Low self esteem implies self rejection, self dissatisfaction or even self contempt. Another major American theorist of self esteem, Stanley Coopersmith (1967 and 1975) defines self esteem as the evaluation which the individual makes, and customarily maintains with regard to self characteristics. It expresses an attitude of approval or disapproval, and indicates the extent to which the individual believes himself or herself to be capable, significant, successful and worthy.

Coopersmith found with his original normative sample that children could be divided into three groups whom he labelled as having 'high', 'medium' and 'low' self esteem. Those with 'high' self esteem had positive, realistic views of themselves, were confident, active, expressed positive emotions to others, were socially self-confident and well-liked, enjoyed taking part in social activities, were generally successful in their academic work and were not worried by criticism. The 'medium' group (the majority) had some of these qualities but were less secure in their social relations, less certain of their worth and were more conformist generally. The 'low' self esteem group he describes as isolated, passive, nervous, self-conscious, insecure and oversensitive to criticism. They constantly underrated themselves and were likely to underachieve in their school work.

Both Rosenberg and Coopersmith have devised self esteem scales for completion by adolescents, and these measures have established reliability and validity. The two scales correlate at around 0.70 (Bagley and Mallick, 1997) and are clearly measuring the same psychological domain. The validity and predictive power of the Rosenberg scale is demonstrated in the work of Kaplan (1975) who asked several thousand junior high school students entering the junior high school system in Houston, Texas to complete the Rosenberg scale. Scores predicted truancy and school dropout, delinquency and drug use, unwed pregnancy, and suicidal behaviours into young adulthood, suggesting that if self esteem levels could be enhanced, self-confident individuals would not fall into deviant pathways. Kaplan develops a theory of self esteem to explain these results: all individuals need a high level of positive self-regard in order to survive as healthy, autonomous individuals. When significant others (teachers, parents, mainstream peers) give the individual persistently negative feedback, new reference groups are sought. The most easily available are delinquent gangs, and in these new groups the young person at the threshold of delinquency obtains a new identity as a deviant person.

In Hong Kong, youth joining the secret Triad Societies is a well-marked social problem, since membership of such groups may involve a career of extortion, crime and corruption. In an important replication of Kaplan's (1975) theory of delinquent gang formation, Leung and Lau (1989) used a Chinese translation of the Rosenberg scale to show that low scores of the Rosenberg scale, reflective of poor relationship with school and parents, was a significant predictor of delinquency and gang membership in 13 to 15 year-olds.

Of particular interest because of its focus on academic achievement is the work of Brookover (1965, 1967) who reports studies extending over six years on 500 American children aged 13–18. A positive correlation was found between academic achievement and self esteem at all ages. Crucially, this work provides evidence that the relationship operated in two directions. Those with high self esteem were high academic achievers but when the self esteem of a group of 14 year-old underachievers with poor self esteem was enhanced by persuading their parents to give positive encouragement rather than making negative comments on their children's work, there were significant improvements to both their self esteem and their academic performance. In important British work, Lawrence (1996) also showed that enhancing self esteem through Rogerian-type counselling was significantly more likely to improve reading test scores than was remedial teaching alone.

A different (but not necessarily competing) theory of the importance of self esteem in the development of severe maladaption (taking the form of psychiatric illness) comes from the longitudinal work with young adults (Bagley and Young, 1990 and 1999). In this model, self esteem and global self-concept become impaired through stress and trauma in childhood and adolescence. The individual (who may not have successfully negotiated some of the crucial tasks in Erikson's identity schema) brings to young adulthood a vulnerability to new trauma and stress based on low self esteem, which in turn impairs the ability to elicit social and community supports. Such individuals are particularly likely to develop clinical depression when faced with new stress.

In British work using the Coopersmith scale with a national sample of young adolescents, Bagley, Verma, Mallick and Young (1979) showed that pupils with lower self esteem held the most prejudiced attitudes, and also had elevated scores on a number of scales measuring maladaption, neurosis, and conduct disorder. The Coopersmith and Rosenberg scales correlate at around 0.70 (Francis and Wilcox, 1995) so they are likely measuring the same underlying construct. In British work establishing norms for the Rosenberg scale, Bagley and Mallick (1999) show that the score is associated with negative perceptions of family life and various kinds of emotional and behavioural disorder. This finding holds in cross-cultural comparisons when Canadian, British, Pakistani, Hong Kong and Filipino samples are compared (Bagley et al., 1998). It is clear that impaired self esteem has a central place in personal adjustment, in adolescents in a wide variety of cultures.

Zimmerman, Copeland, Shope and Dielman (1997) in an American study studied scores on the Coopersmith Self Esteem Inventory (CSEI) in 1,160 young adolescents at several points in time through high school, and found that the adolescents fell into four groups, independently of ethnicity: those whose self esteem was consistently high over a four-year period; those with moderate but rising self esteem levels; those with steadily decreasing self esteem levels; and those with consistently low levels of self esteem. Youth with poor or declining levels of self esteem were also those most likely to report high levels of alcohol use and drug misuse. Although there is no direct evidence, youth with consistently low or declining levels of self esteem could be youth who have failed to achieve some of the crucial identity tasks presented in adolescence (in Erikson's model) or have 'foreclosed identity' in Hauser's (1971) term.

In Canada, Bagley, Bertrand and Bolitho (1997), using the Rosenberg Self Esteem Scale (RSES) with 2,100 randomly sampled adolescents, found that low self esteem at all ages (13 to 18) was associated with family disruption, conduct disorder, and drug misuse, a finding replicated in Britain Hong Kong and elsewhere (Bagley and Mallick, 1998).

In sum, self esteem is now a well established facet of personality which underlies important aspects of adaptive behaviour. Those with poorer self esteem tend to be those who experience most difficulty in the academic environment, have the most problematic behaviours, are most vulnerable to stress, and are those most likely to develop depression in the face of stress.

Measuring Self Esteem in Chinese Adolescents

Cross-cultural psychologists often distinguish between *emic* (culturally specific) and *etic* (culturally universal) psychological traits and processes. In work of profound importance in this field, Yang and Bond (1990) and Yik and Bond (1993) replicated the work of American psychologists of the 1930s in collecting all words in the Chinese language which could apply, evaluatively, to a person. Large samples were then asked to rate themselves on dimensions implied by these adjectives, and the results subjected to factor analysis to extract principal components or clusters of variables. The main or higher order clusters were similar to the six personality types (emotional stability; conscientiousness; openness to experience; extraversion; intellectual curiosity; agreeableness) which have emerged in Western studies of personality; nevertheless, there were some lower order components which were emic, or culturally specific for Chinese populations. These were termed 'restraint' and 'helpfulness'. Bond's ultimate argument is that many psychological instruments can be safely back-translated[6] into Chinese, although some aspects of personality and behaviour may require culturally specific instruments. Self esteem measures are most likely to be predicted by the six higher order facets of personality.

There are specific elements of Hong Kong Chinese identity, including values which involve a strong orientation to traditional rituals and religion, and deference to the wisdom of elders. Another aspect of Chinese presentation of self is that of shame at loss of face; this is not merely a surface trait, but one which involves genuine feelings of guilt at failure in role performance (Bond and Pang, 1990). This may be one reason why youth suicide has such prominence in Hong Kong (Tse, Bagley and Mak, 1994).

Conclusions

The study of cultural identity is an important way of understanding ethnicities, and how these change in relation to new social pressures and roles, including those imposed by migration which involves pressures to conform to the values and folkways of a new culture, along with various negative pressures such as intolerance of the migrant's traditional culture, and of more basic and cruder types of racism.

Self esteem is contained with global identity (which emerges in the crucial identity resolution stage of adolescence) and indicates the degree to which an individual evaluates self characteristics negatively or positively. At the core of self esteem is an existential evaluation of self, which often colours how the individual evaluates personal role performance in various areas. Impaired self esteem in adolescence is a significant predictor of later adjustment problems, and appears to make individuals more vulnerable to external stressors.

Hypothetically at least, racist pressures, as adolescents struggle to achieve a balance between the demands of two cultures, might affect self esteem in negative ways.

Adolescents (and their parents) in and from Hong Kong have a particular form of unique cultural identity, which reflects the cultural values and social organisation of Hong Kong. While adolescents from Hong Kong are likely to have personality profiles which are similar, in general, to those of adolescents in Western cultures, there are unique aspects of Hong Kong cultural identity, which may survive the process of cultural migration.

Notes

1. Ironically, at the time of writing (February, 1998) Chinese people in Indonesia were once again the subject of racist attacks during a time of economic crisis. Like Lebanese and Jewish emigrants, Chinese people have filled economic niches in many world countries, but have also, like these groups, become the subject of pogroms and racist scapegoating in times of economic down-turn.

2. One of the authors of this chapter who is physically white, taught for some time at the University of the West Indies in Trinidad. One day at a committee meeting at which he was the only white man, he looked at his watch and caught sight of strange looking white flesh appearing below his short-sleeved shirt. Brief, subjective panic occurred: 'My God, I've turned white,' he thought. Recovering, he began to realise his physical, ethnic identity with some curiosity, and a certain distaste.
3. The popular stereotype of Westerners is that Chinese people when discriminated against, will simply work harder and obtain more capital or educational qualifications. But Chinese people, as oppressed minority groups have adopted the role of radical insurrectionists, in the case of Malaysia.
4. One of the authors of this chapter, a European-Canadian undertook a university extension course in Cantonese prior to spending three years as an academic in Hong Kong. Three-quarters of the class of 20 were young Chinese adults wishing to learn the tongue and the script which their parents had felt they should ignore.
5. Wayson Choy, the Chinese-Canadian novelist addresses the issues of being both Chinese and Canadian in his writings. 'I'm a banana and proud of it,' he asserts (Choy, 1997).
6. Back-translation is a necessary first step in cross-cultural research. The instrument is translated into the required language, and than back-translated into the original language by a new translator who has not seen the original instrument. Differences in the original and back-translated versions are then compared for conceptual or substantive errors. The need for this was borne upon one of the present researchers who in work with a Japanese colleague using the Coopersmith SEI found that the item 'I often get fed up an home' back-translated as 'I get lots of good food at home'. All of the instruments in the present study have successfully survived back translation!

4 The Design of the Study and Sample Characteristics

The Focus of the Study

As Chapter 1 explained, the primary focus of the study was to explore *the cultural identity, self esteem and identity issues encountered by Chinese adolescents growing up in Britain*, their experiences and relationships within the family and within society at large. In order to locate the findings ecologically and give them greater meaning, it was decided that similar samples would be drawn from Chinese youngsters living in Britain, the European British[1] community and those from Chinese young people living in Hong Kong. It was also assumed that differing factors (for example, the social context and environment) would contribute to the development of identity in differing ethnic groups.

In adopting this strategy we aimed to make comparisons between the cultural identities of three groups, by means of statistical comparisons and narrative case studies drawn from personal accounts. The European British and the Hong Kong Chinese would be part of dominant cultures whilst the third, the British-Chinese, would be a minority group, caught perhaps in the tensions between the cultures of their parents and the society in which they were growing up, and therefore under pressure to make adaptations to their cultural inheritance.

A secondary focus of the study was *the educational aspirations of the British-Chinese,* again making comparisons between them and their European British and Hong Kong Chinese peers.

Finally it was thought timely, in the light of the 1990 British Nationality Act (Hong Kong), to offer profiles of the *social backgrounds and educational needs and aspirations of young people in Hong Kong* who had emigrated to Britain up to 1997.

Research Questions

In Chapter 1, we gave an account of the assumptions and initial thinking which preceded the study. These effectively gave rise to a series of research questions which seemed to require answers. In the course of discussions within the research team, they became:

- how are the personal and cultural identities of Chinese adolescents affected by growing up in Britain and the fact of their attending British schools? Is there evidence of conflict arising from the differing cultures of home and school? If they are subject to conflicting expectations, how effectively are they coping? Is there evidence that racism is adversely affecting their self esteem?;
- what are their educational aspirations?;
- how do they differ, if at all, from their European British peers as well as from young Chinese people growing up in Hong Kong?;
- what appropriate measures should be adopted by schools, Local Education Authorities, community organisations and other agencies to meet the needs of British-Chinese adolescents?;
- are such measures also likely to be appropriate for those Hong Kong Chinese who might enter Britain after 1997? If not, what other kinds of responses might be appropriate?

These questions seemed to outline the research areas for investigation whilst remaining firmly located within the study's aims – the nature and process of cultural identity of Chinese adolescents in Britain and Hong Kong. At the same time, it seemed that the answers would be useful or of interest to teachers, educational advisers, social workers, educational researchers and others engaged in the work of related disciplines.

Methodology

Every research has its own significance depending on the subject investigated and the sources of data collected. Educational or social psychological studies employ different techniques to tackle different issues or problems. There is not one single standard methodological package which can fit all human inquiries, but there may be one strategy common to all research processes (Fox, 1969; Tuckman, 1972). This common approach includes the need for identification, research design strategy, implementation and result evaluation (Verma and Mallick, 1998; Walker, 1985). All these phases are interrelated, although according to the nature or interest of each research area, they may have different emphases.

It is generally recognised that in some studies a single method may not be adequate to generate the data required. Consequently, such studies will require a combination of approaches. Burgess (1984) stressed that the researcher should pursue a range of methods and be flexible in approach when dealing with complex issues. Cohen and Manion (1985) also argue that a combination of qualitative and quantitative approaches could lead to a greater flexibility, thus increasing the validity and generalisation of the data. According to Cook and Reichardt (1979), such techniques can serve as a means of monitoring research findings and of increasing confidence that one's data are sound.

The nature of the present study may be regarded as an empirical one incorporating a variety of methods. It is a multi-technique approach, drawing its methodological basis mainly from survey, descriptive, empirical and historical research methods. It employed both quantitative and qualitative approaches, in combination, and hoped through these to acquire complementary data, thus reducing the possibility of unsubstantiated findings (Olafson, 1991; McFee, 1992).

The main techniques used in the study were self-completion questionnaires and interviewing. The tools and their administration are briefly described in the following section.

Questionnaires

The fact that access to the respondents was dependent on the good will of schools both in Britain and Hong Kong meant that questionnaires had to be capable of completion in a reasonable time. We took this to be an average school period of about 40 minutes. This had to include the time required for the researcher to introduce him or herself, distribute the questionnaires and collect them after completion.

Within this constraint, questionnaires were designed which included four main sections. The first of these sought to provide biographical data. The second, third and fourth sections were devoted to instruments which are described in some detail below.

The instruments Three major instruments were used in this study: a cultural identity scale, a self esteem inventory, and an educational experience scale.

The cultural identity scale was originally developed by Ghuman (1991) and was modified, reworded and adapted by the research team. Ghuman's original scale consisted of 30 items which had been devised for 465 British Asian adolescents aged 14–15. It was concerned with Asian and English culture and took as its issues food and clothes, the role of women, religion, entertainment and community life. Following discussions within the team and a pilot study, revisions were undertaken to make it applicable in the context of British-Chinese adolescents. Relevant items were retained, those which seemed inappropriate were deleted and some statements were inserted. As a result, the final scale presented in the British-Chinese questionnaire consisted of 33 items.

The final list of items was as follows: 1) sexual equality; 2) festival celebration; 3) Chinese customs; 4) the return to the homeland; 5) meeting with English boys and girls; 6) Chinese food; 7) living with grandparents; 8) women and jobs; 9) Chinese medicine; 10) making friends with Chinese; 11) Chinese language; 12) English food; 13) naming system; 14) learning Christianity; 15) going to youth clubs; 16) neighbours; 17) visiting English friends; 18) Chinese films; 19) ignoring Chinese language; 20) relations with English people; 21) mixed marriage; 22) marriage arranged by family; 23) Chinese women's behaviour; 24) grandparents' advice; 25) Chinese music; 26) moving away from parents; 27) boys and girls in higher education; 28) worshipping ancestors; 29) significance of working hard; 30) parents and homework; 31) group and individual decisions; 32) supporting parents; 33) the responsibility of elder sons or daughters for parents.

These issues were appropriate to British-Chinese adolescents but it was recognised that they might not be suitable for use with European and Hong Kong Chinese adolescents because of their different cultural background and experiences. For the samples taken from those two groups, some items mentioned above were either omitted or modified whilst preserving comparability as far as possible.

The second instrument used in this study was the 23 item Coopersmith Self Esteem Inventory (Coopersmith, 1967; Bagley, Verma and Mallick, 1982; Bagley, 1989a). It provided measures of evaluative attitudes toward the pupils' self, and was described more fully in the previous chapter. The Coopersmith scale covers three areas: self esteem in the context of the home and the family; self esteem in relation to school and peer group; and a general evaluation of the self. Pupils' responses, according to their feelings, were 'like me' or 'unlike me' to descriptive statements in those three areas.

In the original normative and validation work in America, Stanley Coopersmith (1967 and 1975) found that high scores (indicating poorer self esteem) correlated significantly with sociometric isolation, being a listener in group discussions, being compliant to group norms, being sensitive to criticism in group discussions, having an inability to confide in parents, coming from a home where there was considerable emotional tension, having poor physique, coming from a home with few and poorly defined limits for behaviour, and harsh and autocratic methods of control. Several of these findings were replicated in English work (Bagley, Verma, Mallick, and Young, 1979).

The shorter version of the Coopersmith Self Esteem Inventory was designed for use with British children or adolescents (Bagley, Verma and Mallick, 1982). It is based on the result of factor analysis in which two main factors were found – termed 'I am a failure' and 'lack of social confidence'. For this analysis 23 items with the highest loadings at .30 or above, for both sexes were selected for a short form (Bagley, 1989). This 23-item scale has satisfactory validity for both sexes in the age range 11–15, and perhaps for different ethnic groups (Bagley, Verma and Mallick, 1982).

In a study measuring racial attitudes in adolescents in multi-ethnic settings (Bagley and Mallick, Young and Verma, 1979), the 23 item scale correlated at 1 per cent significant level in both sexes with the Cattell HSPQ measurement of ego strength, guilt proneness, alienation from school authority, and a jaundiced view of life. For test-retest correlation, the scale achieved 0.681 over a six-month period. This scale also strongly correlated with the Piers-Harris Self-Concept scale on subjects drawn from a number of British ethnic groups, including Asian, Cypriot, English and West Indian (Bagley, Verma and Mallick, 1982). Since then the scale has been widely used in the British samples and has achieved a satisfactory validity in a number of ethnic groups.

The scale has been translated into Chinese and its validity and reliability demonstrated in studies with Hong Kong adolescents (Yang and Bond, 1980; Cheung and Lau, 1985; Lau and Cheung, 1987; Chan and Lee, 1993). Since the Coopersmith scale has been validated in several other cultures in various translations, it is safe to assume that it measures pancultural aspects of personal adaptation.

The third instrument used was an educational experience scale based on existing material and modified by the research team to make it more relevant to the populations being studied. Five attitude scales were included in this study: school life; academic achievement; activity participation; teacher relationships; and, praise and blame. These scales, each containing four statements, were mixed with positive and negative attitudes and were applied to all three groups. Other specific items contained in the scale were in association with 'prefer to work on my own ideas', 'prefer examinations to projects', 'like to be told what to do by teacher' and 'important to respect teacher'.

Scoring was based on assigning weights from one to five for each position on the scale. Favourable statements were weighted five to one (Strongly Agree to Strongly Disagree) whereas unfavourable statements reversed from point 1 to 5 (Strongly Disagree to Strongly Agree); the higher score indicated a favourable attitude The items of each scale are as follows: schooling (Items 1, 6R, 11R, 17) , academic achievement (Items 3, 8R, 15, 19R), activity participation (Items 4, 9R, 13R, 20), teacher relationships (Items 2, 7, 14R, 16R), praise and blame (5, 10, 14R, 16R).

Interviews

A little more than 10 per cent of those who completed questionnaires were interviewed. Interviewing is an interactional procedure in which both interviewer and respondent contribute to the communication process (Kahn and Cannell, 1967). It is a basic mode of inquiry to record the different life experiences of human beings. The adequacy of interviewing depends on the purpose of the research and the questions being asked. In many cases it provides access to the context of people's behaviour and provides a way in which researchers may understand its meaning (Mishler, 1979).

Cohen and Manion (1985) suggested that an interview has three purposes. First, it serves as a means of gathering information from the subject's mind. Second, it is used to test a hypothesis or to suggest new ones, or to identify variables and relationships. Third, it is used in conjunction with other methods in a research undertaking. Kerlinger (1970) suggests that it might be used to follow up unexpected results, or to validate other methods, or to go deeper into the motivation of respondents and the reasons behind their responses.

A research interview is a meaningful conversation which has a specific purpose and focuses on certain specific content objectives. The development of specific objectives for an interview depends not only on the application of techniques but also on the ingenuity, insights, and experience of the interviewer (Verma and Mallick, 1998). The determination of interview objectives is primarily a matter of obtaining insights into the explored issue. There are no set rules or procedures for obtaining such insights.

There are three main types of interview in educational research: 'structured', 'semi-structured' and 'unstructured'. The structured interview is one in which respondents are asked a series of questions with fixed wording and sequences. The content and procedures are organised in advance. Since the wording of the questions is determined by means of a schedule, the interviewer is left little freedom to make modifications. In addition, such interviews may produce a great variety of data and result in coding difficulties if complex information is being sought (Mason and Bramble, 1978).

Having greater flexibility, the semi-structured interview begins generally by asking highly structured questions and follows up by probing more deeply through open ended questions. The unstructured interview is an 'open' situation with the greatest flexibility and freedom for the interviewer. In the unstructured interview, through topic guides the interviewer asks questions in a manner which leads the respondent towards producing the type of information being sought. During an unstructured or semi-structured interview, a conversational style is mostly adopted. The sequences and wording of questions can be modified and probed where necessary. Ambiguous questions or responses can be clarified and both the interviewer and interviewee can ask the other to expand on a particular point of interest.

It is well recognised that both semi-structured and unstructured approaches are highly useful for investigating complex issues or sensitive feelings because people are more likely to disclose themselves in an unstructured situation than in a structured one (Stenhouse, 1975; Measor, 1984; Hammersley and Atkinson, 1983). Lasting from a half hour to an hour, these kinds of interview are frequently used in qualitative research (Spradley, 1979; Hammersley and Atkinson, 1983).

Since the design of a semi-structured interview lies between structured and unstructured methods, it enjoys the advantages of covering the specific subject matter written in the schedule in advance on the one hand, and of providing greater flexibility for researchers to ask probing questions when appropriate on the other. As a research tool, the main weakness of the interview is its potential bias. Interviewers may take their own bias along to the interview and tend to seek answers which fit their preconceptions. Though interviewers attempt to remain objective, they may nevertheless give verbal or nonverbal cues that influence the respondents' replies. Respondents may seek to satisfy the interviewers by giving desirable answers. Where questions are felt to be too searching, respondents may engage in 'cognitive avoidance'.

The personal experience, gender, age, social status, race, language and ethnicity of the interviewer can influence the interaction between interviewer and interviewee – the respondent in attempting to please the researcher may give socially admirable but misleading answers (Oakley, 1981). In order to reduce the possibility of bias during interviews, careful construction of the questions asked, awareness of the social interaction, cautious promotion of the pleasant and trustful environment, and sound training of the interviewer are all advocated.

This study employed three sets of semi-structured interviews, with the British-Chinese, Hong Kong Chinese and European British. The main issues in all interview schedules included the following seven topics: 1) school experience; 2) culture and ethnicity; 3) relationships with parents and other adults; 4) friendship; 5) racial discrimination; 6) career ambitions; 7) religious beliefs. Following discussions within the research team, these elements emerged as those most likely to throw light on the main concerns of the study. The topics were common to all groups, with the exception of the topic concerning racial discrimination, where the questions were raised only of the Chinese in Britain.

During interviews, conversations with interviewees were tape recorded only after having obtained their permission. The analysis of collected interview data was selective as to which major features and patterns would be interpreted and certain passages would be grouped into certain categories. Since the procedure of transcribing tape recordings is time consuming and its effectiveness is questionable, the recording tapes, gathered from interviews, were used only to check the wording of the quoted statements and to validate the notes (Bell, 1989).

Statistical Tests

A number of statistical tests were applied to the data generated by the questionnaires. They normally served to establish the reliability of the data. Where they were used, a note is added to the relevant table. Most common was the Chi-squared (X^2) test and where, as is the usual case in the findings, a table is accompanied by a note which states, for example, $p<0.01$, this means that the probability of the distributions displayed being as they are purely by accident, is less than one in a hundred.

The Samples

The samples employed in this study were drawn from three groups of adolescents: British-Chinese, European British and Hong Kong Chinese. The optimum sample size for reliable population estimates to be made for the British-Chinese group of the relevant age range was calculated at 360, using a formula published by the National Education Association. The overall design of the study required similar numbers from the other groups so that the total sample size was 1,080.

The data on the British-Chinese adolescents were collected in Manchester, London and Liverpool. Through contacts with local authorities, schools, community language schools and an examination board which offered a Chinese language examination, students of Chinese origin were identified and invited to participate in the study. European British data were obtained from three schools in Greater Manchester: one in Wigan, one in the City of Manchester and one in Stockport. Data on Hong Kong Chinese adolescents were collected from four schools: two situated in Hong Kong Island and two in the New Territories. All these schools were run by Local Education Authorities and all but one were coeducational.

In practice, the combined sample sizes of the three groups amounted to 1,107 young people, made up of 362 British-Chinese, 381 British Europeans and 364 Hong Kong Chinese. The personal interview sample was 121 youngsters: 40 British-Chinese, 38 British European and 43 Hong Kong Chinese.

Table 4.1 gives the ages of the three samples and shows that three quarters of the respondents in each group were between 13–16 years old. Of those outside that range, there was a fair balance in the British-Chinese and European British groups whilst in the Hong Kong Chinese group, the majority were either 17 or 18 year-olds. Table 4.2 shows the gender balance to be even for all three groups.

Table 4.3 shows that the majority of British-Chinese (65 per cent) were born in Britain. Most of those born elsewhere were born in Hong Kong (20 per cent) or Vietnam. As might be expected, virtually all (98 per cent) the European British group were British born. Of the Hong Kong group, 78 per cent were born there and a further 21 per cent were born in China. Table 4.4 provides information on the respondents' length of stay. More than three quarters (77 per cent) of the British-Chinese group had lived in Britain for more than 10 years with the remainder having done so for less than five (10 per cent) or between five and 10 years (12 per cent). Of the Hong Kong Chinese group, 85 per cent had lived there for more than 10 years. On the basis of the data on their place of birth, it is reasonable to assume that those who had lived there for shorter periods had previously been living in China.

Although the tables which follow, giving information on the place of birth and education of parents, might not to be strictly relevant to the biographical details of the respondents, it was decided to include them at this stage for the light they cast on family backgrounds.

Table 4.1 Age by country of residence

Age	UK Chinese *N=362* %	UK European *N=381* %	UK Chinese *N=364* %
11	2	2	0
12	9	17	1
13	18	19	12
14	26	30	20
15	19	15	18
16	12	14	24
17	7	2	14
18	4	1	9
19	1	0	2
20	1	0	0
Missing	1	0	1

Table 4.2 Gender by country of residence

Gender	GB Chinese *N=362* %	GB European *N=381* %	HK Chinese *N=364* %
Male	44	50	46
Female	55	50	54
Missing	1	0	0

Table 4.3 Place of birth

Place of birth	UK Chinese *N=362* %	UK European *N=381* %	HK Chinese *N=364* %
Britain	65	98	0
Hong Kong	20	0	78
Vietnam	9	0	0
Other	6	2	22
Missing	1	0	0

Table 4.4 Length of stay

Length of stay	UK Chinese *N=362* %	UK European *N=381* %	HK Chinese *N=364* %
Less than 5 years	10	1	5
5 to 10 years	12	2	10
More than 10 years	77	87	85
Missing	2	11	0

Table 4.5 makes it clear that for all practical purposes, all the British-Chinese respondents were the children of first generation settlers in Britain. Disregarding the slight differences between mothers and fathers, some 40 per cent of parents were born in Hong Kong and a further 30 per cent were born in China or elsewhere. Only 1 per cent were British born. In the Hong Kong Chinese group, a third of their fathers and approaching half their mothers were born in Hong Kong. It is of interest to note that more than half the parents of this group were born in China, which suggests a substantial internal migration a generation ago. As expected, 95 per cent of European British respondents' parents were British born.

Table 4.5 Parents' place of birth

Parents' birth place	UK Chinese *N=362*		UK European *N=381*		HK Chinese *N=364*	
	Father %	*Mother* %	*Father* %	*Mother* %	*Father* %	*Mother* %
Britain	1	1	95	95	*	*
Hong Kong	41	45	*	*	31	45
China	34	25	*	*	62	46
Other	19	22	4	5	6	7
Missing	6	7	1	1	1	2

* This item was not included in the questionnaire.

Data on parent's education given in Table 4.6 are less helpful than might have been because of the relatively high numbers of British-Chinese and European British respondents who did not know what their parents' educational experience had been, compared with the Hong Kong Chinese. Clearly, if they had been able to respond, it would have made a significant difference to the numbers recording known educational achievements. However, it seems reasonable to infer that in terms of formal education, the parents of both Chinese groups were less well educated than those of the British European group.

Table 4.6 Parents' education

Education level	UK Chinese N=362		UK European N=381		HK Chinese N=364	
	Father %	*Mother* %	*Father* %	*Mother* %	*Father* %	*Mother* %
Never went to school	6	11	*	*	3	6
Up to primary	11	14	*	*	31	43
Up to secondary	36	32	42	46	48	37
University level	10	7	22	23	7	4
Don't know	36	36	34	29	11	10
Missing	2	1	2	2	0	1

* This item was not included in the questionnaire.

Of the British-Chinese group, most parents were born in Hong Kong (father, 41 per cent; mother, 45 per cent), some were born in China (father, 34 per cent, mother, 25 per cent) and very few born in Britain (1 per cent each for father and mother). For the European British, the vast majority (95 per cent) of their parents were born in Britain. In the Hong Kong Chinese sample, a significant number of the parents came from China (father, 62 per cent, mother, 46 per cent) and less than a half were born in Hong Kong (father, 31 per cent, mother, 45 per cent).

Finally, in this brief description of family backgrounds, we provide data on parental occupations in Tables 4.7–4.12. Unfortunately the data are not as useful as might have been hoped. Substantial proportions of all three groups were unable to supply any answer to this question. Many more were so vague that their answers were not very helpful. 'Worker' or 'Businessman' for example might mean anything from director of a major company to a self-employed door-to-door salesman. However, a few cautious observations are possible.

Our data confirm what some other studies have found: about six out of 10 British-Chinese fathers are engaged in catering or allied trades. If 'shopowner' is taken to mean 'take-away' or 'fish and chip shop' owner, three out of 10 of their mothers were in the same business, as well as an unquantifiable number who helped their husbands as well as being 'housewives'. Another approach was to see how many parents were engaged in professional or managerial employment. This suggested that just over 5 per cent of British-Chinese fathers and less than 4 per cent of mothers fell into these categories. These figures compared with over 13 per cent of European British fathers and nearly one in four of their mothers. For Hong Kong Chinese parents, the figures were over 6 per cent of fathers and 4 per cent of mothers. Those occupations which we took to qualify for inclusion as professional or managerial are marked with an asterisk in the tables which follow.

Bearing in mind the caveats expressed above, particularly the uncertainty about the meaning of 'worker' and 'business' in the Hong Kong Chinese fathers' occupations, it seems safe to conclude that something like three times as many European British parents were engaged in management or the professions as either of the two Chinese groups. It is also apparent that six times as many European British mothers as Chinese mothers could be included in these categories. It appears then that the parents of the British Hong Kong teenagers are rather less likely to occupy middle class roles than the Chinese adults in the British Sample Survey of ethnic minorities (Modood et al., 1997). This could be due to the fact that parents with several adolescent children (who were more likely to get into our sampling frame) contain fewer professionals. Or the bias against professional parents in our sampling could reflect the fact we recruited many adolescents from Chinese language classes. Or it may be that Manchester and Liverpool where our samples were mainly drawn, contain fewer middle class, Chinese parents. Whatever the reason for bias, it should be borne in mind that we are addressing the least advantaged sector of Chinese adolescents in Britain.

Conclusions

The three samples of adolescents who completed questionnaires in classroom settings (and the sub-samples who were personally interviewed) are both similar and different. The occupations of the Hong Kong Chinese are more varied than those of the Chinese parents who had migrated to the United Kingdom. The concentration of this latter group in the catering group may be a form of occupational ghettoisation rather than rational choice, just as earlier generations of Chinese immigrants in North America had to concentrate on laundries and in the dangerous and demeaning tasks of railroad construction. Future research will establish the degree to which the children of these Chinese immigrants break out of the occupational ghetto of the take-away, with its drudgery of long hours and hard work serving the English customers who care to patronise them.

Table 4.7 British-Chinese: fathers' occupations

Occupation	N	%
Missing data/unemployed/dead/retired	76	21.0
Chef/Cook	99	27.3
Waiter	32	8.8
Works at home	1	0.3
Restaurant/shop-owner	78	21.5
Works in a casino	3	0.8
Helper	1	0.3
Business	22	5.1
Sewing	2	0.6
*Teacher	7	1.9
Part-time jobs	2	0.6
Engineer	4	1.1
Self-employed	1	0.3
Police	2	0.6
*Doctor	1	0.3
*Researcher	1	0.3
*Lecturer	2	0.6
*Designer	1	0.3
Electrician	4	1.1
*Manager	2	0.6
Tailor	1	0.3
Officer	3	0.8
*Accountant	1	0.3
Food supplier	3	0.8
*Consultant	10	0.3
Student	1	0.3
*Computer analyst	1	0.3
*Nurse	1	0.3

* Presumed middle class occupation.

Table 4.8 British-Chinese: mothers' occupations

Occupation	N	%
Missing data/don't know/retired/ unemployed/pensioner/died	67	18.5
Housewife	138	38.1
Waitress	33	9.1
Works at home	3	0.8
Shopowner	55	15.2
Cashier/shop assistant	19	5.2
Cook	11	3.0
Cleaner	1	0.3
Sewing	4	1.1
Looking after Temple	1	0.3
Business	3	0.8
*Interpreter	2	0.6
Physiotherapist	3	0.8
*Teacher	5	1.4
Self-employed	1	0.3
Pub-owner	1	0.3
Designer	1	0.3
*Doctor	1	0.3
Technician	2	0.6
Secretary	3	0.8
*Nurse	6	1.7
Baby-sitter	1	0.3

* Presumed middle class occupation.

Table 4.9 European British: fathers' occupations

Occupation	N	%
Missing data/unemployed/retired	56	14.7
Landlord	3	0.8
Plumber	5	1.3
Businessman	59	15.5
Skilled worker	18	4.7
Engineer	19	5.0
Electrician/technician	22	5.8
Builder	31	8.1
*Author	1	0.3
Driver	29	7.6
Technical demonstrator	1	0.3
*Lawyer	2	0.5
*Director/executive	2	0.5
*Instructor/lecturer	10	2.6
*Accountant	4	1.0
*Manager	16	4.2
Cleaner	4	1.0
Self-employed	3	0.8
Gardener	1	0.3
Butcher	1	0.3
Factory worker	13	3.4
Police/security/army	6	1.5
Postman	2	0.5
*Computing	6	1.5
*Teacher	9	2.4
Catering/chef	4	1.0
Civil Servant/Clerk	18	4.7
*Consultant/Doctor	2	0.5
Shopowner	5	1.3
*Social worker	4	1.0
*Geologist	1	0.3
*Editor	1	0.3
Hair stylist	1	0.3
Farmer	2	0.5
Foreman	1	0.3
*Paramedic	1	0.3
*Designer	1	0.3
Disk Jockey/Clubman/Bartender	3	0.8

* Presumed middle class occupation.

Table 4.10 European British: mothers' occupations

Occupation	N	%
Missing data/unemployed/retired	46	12.0
Landlady	4	1.0
Housewife	63	16.5
Housing Officer	3	0.8
Industrial/Factory worker	13	3.4
School Helper	27	7.1
Sales	2	0.5
Outdoor Instructor	2	0.5
Shop/Warehouse Assistant	15	3.9
Cleaner	14	3.7
*Nurse	45	11.8
Catering	9	2.4
Shopowner	10	2.6
Production Operator	4	1.0
Chemist	2	0.5
*Manager/Director	8	2.1
*Optician	1	0.3
*Teacher	33	8.7
Clerk	34	8.9
*Architect	1	0.3
Dead	1	0.3
Self-employed	4	1.0
Laundry	1	0.3
Child worker	10	2.7
*Social Worker	2	0.5
Civil Servant	6	1.6
Voluntary Organisation	1	0.3
Student	2	0.5
Business	4	1.0
Police/security	2	0.5
Hairdresser	3	0.8
Bank worker	2	0.5
*Accountant	3	0.8
Cinema	1	0.3
Librarian	1	0.3
Computing	2	0.5
*Psychologist	1	0.3

* Presumed middle class occupation.

Table 4.11 Hong Kong Chinese: fathers' occupations

Occupation	N	%
Missing data/unemployed/retired	40	10.4
Business	44	12.1
Clerk	18	4.9
Artist	1	0.3
Driver	12	3.3
Transport worker	12	3.3
Worker	131	36.0
Civil Servant	14	3.8
*Manager	9	2.5
Catering/cook	14	3.8
Sailor	1	0.3
Street Seller	4	1.1
*Editor	2	0.5
*Engineer	7	1.9
*Systems Analyst	2	0.5
*Administrator	1	0.3
*Accountant	1	0.3
*Doctor	1	10.3
Salesman	6	1.6
*Social Worker	1	0.3
Police/Security	9	2.5
Driver	18	4.9
Hair Stylist	2	20.5
Dead	2	0.5
Estate Worker	5	1.4
Shopowner	1	0.3
Skilled Worker	1	0.3
Pianist	2	0.5
Nurse	2	0.5
Fireman	1	0.3

* Presumed middle class occupation.

Table 4.12 Hong Kong Chinese: mothers' occupation

Occupation	N	%
Missing data/unemployed/retired/dead	67	12.1
Housewife	140	38.5
Clerk	26	7.1
Shop Worker	8	2.2
*Accountant	8	2.2
Civil Servant	4	1.1
Worker	66	18.1
*Nurse	2	0.5
Business	16	4.4
*Manager	2	0.5
Waitress	10	2.7
*Teacher	2	0.5
Secretary	3	0.8
*Editor	1	0.3
Skilled Worker	1	0.3
Administrator	1	0.3
*Social Worker	1	0.3
Cook	2	0.5
Street Seller	3	0.8
Beautician	1	0.3

* Presumed middle class occupation.

Note

1. The generic term 'European' refers to the original British inhabitants of the British Isles who have absorbed through intermarriage of successive waves of European immigrants: Celts, Romans, Saxons, Engles, Jutes, Vikings, Normans and others from Europe in more recent times. We prefer the term 'European British' to describe this group rather than the term 'White', with its unpleasant overtones of racial classification.

5 Identity and Migration Experience in Chinese Adolescents

Complex Identities

This chapter focuses on Chinese respondents in Britain who were asked to select which of three descriptions, 'Chinese', 'British-Chinese' or 'British' they felt best defined their ethnicity. Table 5.1 sets out their responses. It is a matter of interest that 36 per cent described themselves as 'Chinese' whilst 60 per cent described themselves as 'British-Chinese' and three per cent felt themselves to be 'British'. Thus, 96 per cent of these young people recognised their Chinese inheritance, though its meaning and significance to their lives and their perceptions of themselves varied considerably.

Table 5.1 Adolescents' self description of ethnic status

	British-Chinese *N=362* %
British-Chinese	60
Chinese	36
British	3
Missing	1

Although Table 5.1 gives the numbers of respondents who described themselves as 'British', 'British-Chinese' or 'Chinese', it provides no underlying reasons for their choices. Indeed, there was no evidence that these were anything but arbitrary choices, made on the spur of the moment and having no real significance.

In an attempt to get below the surface, we turned first to the interviews to see what light they might throw on the matter. During the interviews we asked

'Do you sometimes feel that you have to live in two worlds: an English one when you are at school and a Chinese one when you are at home? Which one do you feel more comfortable in?' and 'Is it important to you that you are Chinese?' Not surprisingly their answers were very varied, but fell into three broad groups.

Firstly, there were those who felt that they were neither simply Chinese nor British, like the 13 year-old from Liverpool who said:

> I feel in-between Chinese and English. I feel Chinese with my mum and my father, I feel English with my friends. In school I feel more English. Once I go back home I feel more Chinese. Being a Chinese it helps me to get along with my parents, understand them and my other Chinese friends.

Similarly, another 13 year-old observed,

> When I'm in school I think I am English but at home I think I'm Chinese because my mum speaks Chinese to me ... I think I am Chinese, but when it comes to outside with English and Chinese friends ... I think I'm a bit of both.

The conversations above indicate that these Chinese youngsters and others like them had a sense of cultural belonging to 'a bit of both': Chinese and English. While 'Chinese' related to home and parents, 'British' related to school and friends. For them, the term 'British-Chinese' thus meant the environment and the people.

For others, 'British-Chinese' related more to language. Although the question asked in interviews was not exactly the same as in the questionnaire, it was thought that there was likely to be a close link between youngsters' 'two worlds' experience and the 'British-Chinese' self-description category. Karen, a 13 year-old, born in London commented:

> It does [seem] a bit strange. Because in school I am English and sometimes Chinese, but at home I normally speak Chinese, it is different from school. I talk to my brothers and sisters sometimes in English, but mostly in Chinese.

A 14 year-old, born in Hong Kong who came to England at four months, clearly expressed how she moved from one culture (which, significantly, she associated with their respective languages) to another – and seemed at home in both – when she said,

> Sometimes I feel I live in two worlds. When I am in school, I think I am an

> English, when I am at home I feel I am Chinese. In school we talk English but at home Chinese people are around me. I feel more comfortable at home with my parents and family, but in school it is easier to use the English language.

Language is widely recognised as an important indicator to distinguish cultural belonging. For these youngsters, the term 'British-Chinese' seemed to revolve around the English language they spoke in school and the Chinese language they spoke at home. It would appear as they spoke to us that they were using the language as a kind of synonym for culture.

Secondly there were those who, during their interviews, were in no doubt about their Chinese identity. Thus, for example, a Manchester-born 14 year-old who went to Hong Kong when aged four and returned to England aged six focused very much on *physical* characteristics.

> I am Chinese because I have yellow skin and dark hair. We speak a different language and our physical appearance is different from the English people who are taller than us. I enjoyed learning Chinese. I am proud of being a Chinese.

For others it was more a *social definition* and included the importance of friendship with other Chinese youngsters and the physical sense of belonging to a Chinese community – perhaps even living in Chinatown or close to other Chinese families.

Thirdly there were those who in interviews revealed very complex feelings concerning their sense of cultural belonging and group identification. As conversations developed, the contradictions often involved in trying to come to terms with belonging to two (or more) communities emerged.

Daan, aged 15, was born in Vietnam and came to Britain aged three years:

> I am not a Chinese really. My mum is Chinese and my dad is Vietnamese. Obviously I know things about my being brought up. It is good in a way if I decide to live in here. If I live in Hong Kong, I obviously want to know about the country.
>
> I know myself deep inside I am Vietnamese. No one can take away from me. The way I am behaving and my life as now I am an English. I speak English every day and talk to English people every day. At home I speak English to my brother. I am afraid I would become more English by the way of Westernised or whatever. My parents do like me to learn about the Chinese language and culture and they afraid us becoming English people.

A number of respondents were keen to distinguish between being Chinese and 'HongKongese'. Martin, for example, who was aged 16 and had come to

Britain three years earlier, had this to say:

> I think I am between Chinese and HongKongese. For English, I have a little feeling, everything a little bit. However, I think I have a sense of belonging as a HongKongese rather than belonging to others.

Nellie who was 17 and had come to England 4 months earlier was largely in agreement:

> I think I am HongKongese. When I contact people from China, I feel that we come from a different Chinese culture and different Chinese society. As a result, our thinking might be different. Although we seem to be quite the same, we actually have a lot of differences, such as with those Taiwanese and Singaporean, we have differences.

Like most ethnic minority settlers, the Chinese in Britain have to manage multiple identities. On the one hand they find themselves in a position where they feel they have to accept their status as bi-cultural – Chinese and English at the same time. On the other hand it is possible for them to confirm their sole Chinese status. Some youngsters seemed to be affected by two cultural elements such as: 'Vietnamese' and 'English' together; 'British-Chinese', 'Chinese' and 'English' together; or 'Chinese' and 'HongKongese' together. While the first two categories involve a sense of Englishness and with it a tendency to become assimilated in the society, the last one indicates inter-cultural group differences among 'Chinese' and 'HongKongese'. Those newcomers from Hong Kong might identify with their 'Hong Kong' status more strongly than with their 'Chinese' status.

Again, as is the case of all migrant communities, *length of stay* was a significant factor in the development of degrees of association with the host country. The development of cultural identity is a developmental, dynamic and complex process. Although youngsters believed that no one could take away their 'Chinese' identity, they recognised that if they lived in England for a long time, there was a real danger that they would become increasingly Westernised. There was concern that, with greater involvement in British society, regularly speaking the English language and making English friends, they might themselves become more 'English' and so, as they saw it, less 'Chinese'.

Thus, interview data confirmed what common sense would indicate: the motives which impelled these young people to assign themselves to one ethnic group or another were varied and complex.

We then returned to the data obtained from the questionnaires to see whether there were connections in the minds of the respondents between the categories they chose and the answers to questions concerning specific aspects of their lives, culture and activities.

We found significant relationships between their self descriptions and their place of birth, age on arrival in Britain, length of stay, the choice of language used with parents, brothers and sisters and friends, the language they felt they spoke best, and the people they felt it was most important to please. The Tables which follow set out these findings.

Not surprisingly, respondents born in Britain, or under three years of age when they arrived, were more likely to describe themselves as 'British' or 'British-Chinese' than those who arrived later in life (Tables 5.2 and 5.3). Table 5.4 shows quite clearly that new arrivals see themselves primarily as members of their community associated with their place of birth but that this changes substantially with length of stay in Britain. This is particularly interesting in relation to the 'British-Chinese' category, which clearly has meaning only for those who have lived in Britain for a substantial time. Even so, 62 per cent of those describing themselves as 'Chinese' had been here for more than 10 years.

The crucial link between language use and choice of cultural identity is well illustrated by Tables 5.5 to 5.8. They show that those respondents who described themselves as 'British' used English exclusively in their conversations with their brothers and sisters and friends and that 90 per cent of them believed that they were more fluent in it. They were also more likely than those in the other groups to use English when speaking to their parents. Similarly, the 'British-Chinese' used English rather than a Chinese language more frequently with their friends and brothers and sisters than those who described themselves as 'Chinese'. Conversely, the 'Chinese' group were more likely to use Cantonese on those occasions. Finally, and, in the light of the above, unsurprisingly, those who described themselves as 'British-Chinese' felt less competent in English than those who described themselves as 'British', and of those who described themselves as 'Chinese', nearly half felt that they were more competent in Cantonese, Mandarin or some mixture of these.

Connections with other characteristics strongly associated with Chinese culture also seemed worth investigating. These included the need to please parents as an aspect of respect for them. As part of the questionnaire, respondents were asked to indicate who they felt it was important to please.

Table 5.9 indicates that the 'British' category had relatively a stronger desire to please their teachers but a weaker desire to please their parents than

Table 5.2 Self described ethnic status and place of birth

Place of birth	Self-described ethnic status British *(N=11)* %	Chinese *(N=128)* %	British-Chinese *(N=217)* %
Britain	64	53	73
Hong Kong	0	28	16
Vietnam	27	9	8
Other	9	10	3

Note: X^2, p<0.01.

Table 5.3 Self described ethnic status and age on arrival in Britain

How old were you when you came to Britain?	Self-described ethnic status British *(N=9)* %	Chinese *(N=126)* %	British-Chinese *(N=215)* %
Born in Britain	67	50	70
3 or younger	22	14	20
4-6	11	9	3
7-11	0	17	5
12 or older	0	11	1

Note: X^2, p<0.05.

Table 5.4 Self described ethnic status and length of stay

Length of stay	Self-described ethnic status British *(N=11)* %	Chinese *(N=127)* %	British-Chinese *(N=214)* %
Less than 5 years	0	21	4
5 to 10 years	18	18	9
More than 10 years	82	62	87

Note: X^2, p<0.01.

Table 5.5 Self described ethnic status and language normally used with parents

Language normally used with parents	Self-described ethnic status British (N=10) %	Chinese (N=124) %	British-Chinese (N=210) %
English	30	10	15
Cantonese	40	68	70
Hakka	20	10	10
Mandarin	0	4	1
Other	0	5	3
English and Cantonese	10	0	2
Cantonese and Mandarin	0	1	0
Cantonese and Hakka	0	1	0

Note: X^2, not significant.

Table 5.6 Self described ethnic status and language normally used with siblings

Language normally used with brothers and sisters	Self-described ethnic status British (N=11) %	Chinese (N=125) %	British-Chinese (N=212) %
English	100	60	85
Cantonese	0	30	13
Hakka	0	2	1
Mandarin	0	4	0
Other	0	1	0
English and Cantonese	0	4	1
English and other	0	1	0

Note: X^2, English versus all other language usages, $p<0.01$.

Table 5.7 Self described ethnic status and language normally used with friends

Language normally used with friends	Self-described ethnic status British (N=11) %	Chinese (N=125) %	British-Chinese (N=215) %
English	100	63	76
Cantonese	0	30	17
Hakka	0	0	0
Mandarin	0	0	0
Other	0	1	0
English and Cantonese	0	6	7

Note: X^2, English versus all other language usage, $p<0.01$.

Table 5.8 Self described ethnic status and best spoken language

Best spoken language	Self-described ethnic status British (N=10) %	Chinese (N=129) %	British-Chinese (N=217) %
Cantonese	10	33	16
English	90	57	78
Hakka	0	3	9
Mandarin	0	1	5
Vietnamese	0	0	1
Other	0	2	0
Cantonese and English	0	2	3
Cantonese and Mandarin	0	1	0
Cantonese and other	0	1	0

Note: X^2, English versus all other language usage, $p<0.05$.

the 'Chinese' or 'British-Chinese' groups. However, for all groups, eight or more out of 10 identify parents as the group most important to please. Indeed, the unanimity across the groups was the most significant finding.

Finally, in this exploration to find the significance underlying their decision to assign themselves to one or other of these three categories, we looked in some detail at their responses to the cultural attitude scale contained in the

Table 5.9 Self described ethnic status and those important to please

It is important to please ...	Self-described ethnic status		
	British *(N=10)* %	Chinese *(N=126)* %	British-Chinese *(N=212)* %
Your friends	10	11	6
Your teachers	10	2	3
Your parents	80	84	87
Myself*	0	1	2
No-one*	0	0	1
Teachers and parents*	0	2	1

Note: those marked * were not included in the questionnaire but were written in by the respondents. They are included for the sake of completeness. X^2, not significant.

questionnaire. These were re-analysed to see if there were significant differences in the responses provided by the three groups and the results are set out in Table 5.10.

Although the data in Table 5.10 are complex, it is possible to discern a pattern which repeats itself in several of the nine items. That is to say, for items 3, 4, 6, 11, 18, 20, 24 and 28, the group who described themselves as 'Chinese' are more likely to agree with statements supporting traditional Chinese cultural attitudes than those who described themselves as 'British-Chinese' or 'British'. In item 21 which dealt with marriages between Chinese and English people the pattern is less clear though the numbers of those declaring themselves to be 'Undecided' suggest that the same trend emerges.

Members of minority communities live constantly with the tension created by belonging in some degree to two communities. It was thought possible that this might lead to the rejection of one culture, or at least some elements of it, in favour of the second. We therefore asked respondents if they sometimes felt that they did not want to be Chinese. This section is concluded by considering the responses of the British-Chinese sample to that question. A summary of their responses appears as Table 5.11.

It can be seen that one in five of the youngsters either 'often' or 'sometimes' felt they did not want to be Chinese. More significantly, however, the majority have never or hardly ever had a such feeling.

Analysis of variances showed significant differences between members of the self-assigned categories and the above responses (see Table 5.12). In the absence of information gathered during the study, it is not possible to

Table 5.10 Self assigned category and cultural attitudes

Item	Group	SA+A %	U %	D+SD %	Total *N*
3. Chinese customs and traditions are best for us	Chinese	57	35	9	129
	British-Chinese	36	48	15	216
	British	9	73	18	11
4. I prefer to live in Britain rather than the place where my family came from originally	Chinese	43	30	28	129
	British-Chinese	44	39	17	216
	British	65	27	9	11
6. I would rather eat Chinese food all the time	Chinese	36	33	31	129
	British-Chinese	22	39	39	218
	British	36		55	11
11. We should learn to speak and write the Chinese language	Chinese	82	15	3	129
	British-Chinese	78	15	6	217
	British	46	36	18	11
18. Chinese films are more entertaining than English and American films	Chinese	47	31	23	129
	British-Chinese	32	45	23	218
	British	0	60	40	10
20. I feel very uneasy with English people	Chinese	13	21	66	128
	British-Chinese	6	16	77	215
British		0	0	100	10
21. There should be more marriages between Chinese and English people	Chinese	16	64	20	128
	British-Chinese	33	54	14	218
	British	30	30	40	10
24. Advice given by grandparents is always good advice	Chinese	39	39	23	129
	British-Chinese	22	49	29	218
	British	36	46	18	11
28. Worshipping ancestors special festivals is important	Chinese	62	29	8	127
	British-Chinese	47	40	12	217
	British	27	55	18	11

Note: SA= Strongly agree; A= Agree; U= Uncertain; SD= Strongly disagree; D= Disagree. Differences on Items 3, 21, 24 and 28 are significant beyond $p<0.05$ by Chi-squared.

Table 5.11 Desire not to be Chinese

	British-Chinese *N=362* %
Often	3
Sometimes	17
Hardly ever	24
Never	56
Missing	1

Table 5.12 Self ascribed ethnicity and the sense of not wanting to be Chinese

		Often/ sometimes %	**Hardly ever/ never** %	**Total** *N*
29. Do you sometimes feel that you don't want to be Chinese?	Chinese	10	90	129
	British-Chinese	25	75	217

Note: distribution of differences is significant at the 5 per cent level, by Chi-squared test.

comment here on what might have been the reasons for not wanting to be Chinese among the minority in each group who said they 'often' or 'sometimes' experienced this feeling. What is worth noting is that most Chinese youngsters whom we surveyed were quite happy with their Chinese identity.

The Experience of Racism

Clearly, there are cultural experiences and attitudes – factors, that is, within the Chinese community – which, when exposed to the external influence of the dominant culture, might create tensions in the minds of youngsters growing up in Britain and lead to feelings of dissatisfaction at being Chinese. Experiences of racism, however, might equally cause young Chinese to wish that their ethnic origins did not make them targets. In an attempt to discover whether racism was widely experienced, it was explored both in the questionnaire and the interviews, with the British-Chinese and it is perhaps appropriate here to present our findings. Tables (5.13 and 5.14) show the pattern of responses on the issue.

In the questionnaire we asked the British-Chinese youngsters to say if they ever felt they had been badly treated because they were Chinese (Table 5.13). More than seven out of 10 reported that this had been their experience at one time or another. Nearly half (Table 5.14) said that it had happened to their friends. We would also note the very high proportion of 'missing' data in Table 5.14. Whilst there may be a number of possible reasons for this, it is our opinion that respondents did not answer when they did not know or were unsure about their friends' experiences. It might be, therefore, that Table 5.14 understates the extent of the problem.

In any event, racism or perceived racism was a fact of life for most young Chinese in Britain. Although some significance can be attached to the frequency of the experience – in both tables, respondents were asked to record it in terms of 'often', 'sometimes' or 'hardly ever' – we would argue that it is the *experience* of racism that is important. Even if it happens 'hardly ever', its impact on the self-image and confidence of a young adolescent can be powerful, long-lasting and harmful. Merely to be aware of its existence can be damaging. It can be compared with the fear that many people – particularly women – have of becoming a victim of theft or violence, even though they have never been victims and know that the chances of their ever being a victim are small.

Interviews confirmed the widespread experience of racism. It took a number of forms. Commonest, perhaps, was name-calling, particularly in relation to language and colour. Many of the youngsters we interviewed reported that they tried to ignore such name-calling, but others were less accepting:

> In the street they picked on us and call us 'Chink'. In school, the same. I told the teachers. They don't care. Some pick on us, they are a bit racialist. We told the teacher but they don't do anything. They just let it happen. The way they call out our names is racism, 'Chink'! We are shouting at them, 'What you are calling us for?' Sometimes we ignore them.

A 12 year-old reported on the strain of such experiences:

> When you play out, all the kids just recognise you at games. They just call you. So I don't want to play out any more. I don't like it. You just don't want to stay out, people horrify you sometimes.

Table 5.13 Experiences of racism

	British-Chinese *N=362* %
Often	5
Sometimes	34
Hardly ever	33
Never	28
Missing	1

Table 5.14 Friends' experience of racism

	British-Chinese *N=362* %
Often	5
Sometimes	30
Hardly ever	12
Never	11
Missing	42

At other times, name-calling was allied to what might be described as low-level bullying:

> Sometimes my classmates have discriminated against us, particularly laughing at us while we speak English. At dinner time, we were in a queue. Most English girls pushed us and stand in front of us. They never picked on other English girls or pushed or stand in front of them. We can't do anything to stop them because they are mostly very strong and taller then us. In school, some pupils are always laughing at us and pointing at us. They call us 'Chink'. Although I am angry and upset, I have never told my teachers. I am scared and worried about things in school, like people laughing at me when I speak English wrongly.

Sometimes they spoke of more than bullying and name-calling and described events of racially motivated violence. A 13 year-old reported:

> Always [racial harassment] ... Sometimes at school and sometimes at home. They always knocked at my doors and smashed the windows ... They are neighbours ... Police are doing nothing.

Thus racism (as is the case with many other ethnic minorities – see for example Verma, Zec and Skinner, 1994) was the cause of real suffering for many Chinese youngsters. Their experiences culled from the interview data revealed that, for at least some of them, racism had strongly affected the quality of their lives. People threatening them and calling them names was part of their social experience as they grew up in British society. Unwillingness to report such experiences and the lack of confidence expressed by some in teachers and the police to deal adequately with them must be cause for concern.

Conclusions

Drawing these findings together, it seems possible to say that these young people, particularly those who were not born in Britain, were going through a process of adjustment in relation to their cultural identities. For them, what they perceived as their culture was often closely entwined with language, so much so that for some, the two were indistinguishable. Their present state of mind was strongly related to their length of stay, but there was some evidence to suggest that they had, or were coming, to terms with being culturally Chinese in a western European society.

However, the numbers of those who were apparently unhappy with their ethnic identity, were sufficiently large to be a matter of concern. We therefore looked next at the possibility that experiences of racism might have some part to play.

6 Language and Identity

Introduction

Language is a powerful force in establishing, forming and preserving a person's cultural identity. We were therefore particularly interested in the linguistic practices of the British-Chinese group. Information on their use of languages are set out in Tables 6.4–6.7.

Table 6.1 shows that the language most youngsters said they spoke the best was English (67 per cent) followed by Cantonese (22 per cent). Other languages such as Hakka, Mandarin and Vietnamese accounted for a small number – not more than three per cent of the sample. Some youngsters (3 per cent) said they were bilingual in both Cantonese and English. We should add that this last option did not form part of the original question but was written in by the respondents.

Table 6.1 Language spoken the best

Language spoken best	**British-Chinese** *N=362* %
Cantonese	22
English	67
Hakka	2
Mandarin	1
Vietnamese	1
Other	1
*Cantonese and English	3
Missing	2

* This response was not offered by the questionnaire but was written in by respondents.

One approach which seemed worth taking was to attempt to discover if there were elements in their personal biographies – their place of birth, age on arrival and length of stay – which affected their language selection. Chi-square tests were used in order to find out the possibilities of such associations.

Tables 6.2 and 6.3 present these results. They seem to suggest quite conclusively that being born in Britain or arriving when young (under three years old) or having lived for more than 10 years in Britain are, singly or in combination, likely to result in English being the favoured language. The case of those who said they spoke Cantonese best is not nearly as clear cut. They tended to be born in Hong Kong and to have been living in Britain for more than 10 years, but the effect of their age on arrival was, at best, inconclusive. It seems reasonable to conclude that other factors, not so far identified, were having an impact.

Table 6.2 Language spoken the best and place of birth

Place of birth	Language spoken the best	
	Cantonese *N=78* %	English *N=252* %
Britain	39	74
Hong Kong	46	12
Vietnam	9	9
Other	6	4

Note: X^2, $p<0.01$.

Table 6.3 Language spoken best and age on arrival

Age on arrival	Language spoken the best	
	Cantonese *N=78* %	English *N=252* %
Born in Britain	36	71
3 or younger	13	18
4–6	8	5
7–11	24	3
12 or older	18	0
Missing	1	3

Note: X^2, $p<0.01$.

Table 6.4 Language spoken best and length of stay

Length of stay	Language spoken the best	
	Cantonese	English
	N=78	*N=252*
	%	%
More than 10 years	45	90
5–10 years	22	8
Less than 5 years	30	2
Missing	4	1

Note: X^2, p<0.01.

Evidence provided by studies of other ethnic minorities (for example, Smith and Tomlinson, 1989) has suggested that children are likely to be functionally bilingual and draw on their abilities in the language most suited to their circumstances. Questions 7–9 in the survey sought to test this pattern for Chinese young people. Table 6.5 gives information on the respondents' use of language when they communicated with friends, brothers and sisters as well as their parents.

The evidence it provides is very clear. When speaking to their parents, 68 per cent used Cantonese and a further 16 per cent used some other mother tongue. Only 13 per cent of parents and children used English as the customary language. However, when speaking to siblings and friends, over 70 per cent normally used English and barely 20 per cent used Cantonese or a mixture of English and Cantonese. Chinese languages clearly remain important to young people as a means of communicating with their parents in addition to any value they perceive in them as part of their cultural identity.

Outside the home, British-Chinese youngsters have to use English to communicate with others as a matter of survival. However, it was interesting to discover whether they wanted to learn Chinese since to do so would suggest that they were concerned to retain one of the major components of their cultural identity.

Of our sample, 86 per cent had attended a Chinese Community School, Language Class or Sunday Language School and 75 per cent were still doing so on a weekly or monthly basis. This may not be typical of the total teenage population as some of our sample was accessed through Community Schools with the result that attendance at such schools is high when compared with national figures as estimated by the Hong Kong Government Office.

Table 6.5 Language mostly used with parents, siblings and friends

Language normally used	British-Chinese, N=362 When you talk to your ... parents %	brothers & sisters %	friends %
English	13	74	71
Cantonese	68	18	21
Hakka	10	1	0
Mandarin	2	1	0
Other	4	1	0
English & Cantonese	1	2	6
Missing	3	3	2

Also of interest were the motives which caused these young people to attend the classes. It would, for example, be a bad omen for the future if it turned out that they were going simply to please their parents. In fact, as Table 6.6 shows, the wishes of their parents were either important or very important for half of them in their decision to attend. However, to put an alternative gloss on the figures, half of them said that their parents wishes had little to do with their decision. Of greater significance was the fact that, for 94 per cent of those surveyed, the opportunity to learn the Chinese language was either an important or very important consideration for them. Either way, the significance of parental pressure can be overestimated: many children acquire knowledge and skills of many kinds which they come to value for their own worth because their parents insisted on it in the first instance.

However, in interviews, some youngsters indicated that parental pressure was the *only* reason they went and this inevitably led to some resentment. Julie, for example, said,

> My mum and dad tell me to go to Chinese language school. I don't want to go because it's boring. I have been there for about five years.

Lu Denh similarly,

> I go to the Church Sunday [language] School. I don't like it but my mum ask me to go. It is hard.

Others had more positive attitudes towards learning Chinese. For these youngsters, there were significant benefits. Of particular interest were those

Table 6.6 Reasons for attending Chinese community school or equivalent

	British-Chinese, N=362		
	Very important/ Important %	Not very important/ Not at all %	Missing %
To learn the Chinese language	94	5	1
To find out more about Chinese history and traditions	65	31	4
To meet friends	63	33	3
Because your parents say you should go	52	45	3
To join in sports and other cultural activities	36	61	3

who, like this Hong Kong-born 14 year-old, with increasing maturity, were becoming more interested in Chinese culture.

> As I grow older, I think about Chinese culture a lot, because my parents do involve Chinese ways of living, such as they celebrate Chinese New Year. It encourages you to know more about Chinese culture, like English celebrate Christmas.

Others, like 13 year-old Kargan, saw the acquisition of Chinese as valuable because it enabled him to maintain contacts with friends living in Hong Kong.

> I studied in the Chinese language school. I have been there for four years. I want to do it because I got many friends in Hong Kong and I don't know most of the words they know, so I want to learn it.

Although many youngsters said that learning the language was 'boring' they often admitted that doing so had a long term value. Others, however, gave up learning Chinese due to its difficulty or their other commitments. Karen, aged 13, reported:

> I used to go to the Chinese language school, not any more now. I give up because I don't like it. My parents do want me to learn more Chinese and write everything, but it is hard.

And Steven, aged 15, told us:

> I used to go to Chinatown Chinese language school, but I stopped now because it clashed with my work in another school. About three years ago, I stopped. I have been there for two or three years.

Although many Chinese youngsters attended the Chinese classes, many encountered considerable difficulties. Lack of qualified teachers and pupils' frustration about progress seemed to be common in some Chinese language schools. As Daan aged 15, said:

> Why is it boring? It's just the method of teaching. I am not critical or anything, but the teachers are not real proper and qualified teachers.

With no 'proper' teachers and limited resources, it was interesting to discover how the pupils achieved. Based on the questionnaire data, Table 6.7 below shows youngsters' self-assessment of their reading ability in Chinese. It indicates that one in 20 cannot read Chinese at all; more than a quarter (27 per cent) read very little Chinese; 56 per cent read Chinese less well than English and one in 10 (11 per cent) read Chinese language as easily as they can read English.

Table 6.7 Ability to read the Chinese language

British-Chinese	*N=362*
	%
As easily as you can read English	11
Less well than English	56
Very little	27
Not at all	5
Missing	1

Of course, academics have come to accept as self-evident the central importance of language in having access to and understanding a culture. About half of our respondents seemed by their actions to have taken a pragmatic view of the preservation of a culture and learning its language which was voiced in this extract from an interview:

> I don't think learning about Chinese culture can help me in daily living. My parents are not good at English so that when I learn Chinese it can help me to communicate with my parents and understand them more. Most of my friends speak Chinese most of the time. I only have a few English friends from school.

Language and Cultural Identity

It can be argued that supplementary schools are an artificial means adopted by minority communities to preserve their culture. We were therefore interested to discover the extent to which Chinese youngsters participated in the wider cultural events of their community. Indications from the survey are that few did so to any great extent (Table 6.8). Whether the reason for this lay in the absence of opportunities for participation, or the barriers of language, the indications are that involvement outside the formal supplementary school provision was uncommon. If nothing else, it demonstrated the importance of such schools in preserving and passing on Chinese culture to future generations.

What should not be overlooked, however, was the close association in the minds of our sample between language and culture. Indeed, for many of them, the language was not the medium through which culture could be accessed, it held within itself the essence of Chinese culture. A 13 year-old Chinese girl who was born in Liverpool put it this way:

> When I was five, I started to go to Chinese Sunday school. I learn Chinese language, history, the Great Wall and the Chinese New Year, Chinese festivals and religions there.
>
> Because my parents speak Chinese, I don't know what they are saying sometimes. I speak little Cantonese, but I get on well with my Chinese friends. I am not good at reading but I just can manage to write a bit Chinese. My parents mostly speak Cantonese, they can't speak English. When they came to England, they had no education. They told me about the life of Chinese people and that I should learn more about it rather than play outside.

For her, learning the Chinese language seemed to be at the core of her Chinese cultural identity.

Table 6.8 Frequency of attendance or involvement in Chinese cultural activities

	British-Chinese *N=362* *%*
Often	4
Sometimes	17
Not very often	37
Never	41

Perhaps it is tempting to read too much into the fact that 41 per cent of our respondents said that they 'never' attended or were involved in Chinese cultural activities. (It is also tempting to wonder whether or not European British adolescents would give similar responses and what conclusions might be drawn from their answers about the continued survival of western European culture as a consequence.) Another way of looking at it would be to say that 59 per cent of them, in varying degrees, did so. For those who did, it could be a meaningful experience as this 13 year-old made clear:

> When I grow older, I think about Chinese culture a lot, because my parents do involve [me] in Chinese ways of living, such as they celebrate Chinese New Year. It encourages you to know more about Chinese culture, like the English celebrate Christmas. Christmas is their big day ...

It is also possible to overemphasise the significance of high culture in the lives of many people, not least for adolescents. More significant for them is what might be called 'domestic' culture and this aspect is dealt with in later chapters.

7 Demographic Factors in Cultural Identity

Inter-group Differences

Our interest focused on whether matters such as birth place, length of stay in Britain, gender and age might have consequences and if so what they were. Tests were employed to determine whether these independent variables resulted in a range of attitudinal responses. The results presented below are those where the statistical differences shown reached a one percent level of significance.

Place of Birth

Whilst the effect of place of birth did not, on the face of it, seem likely to be significant, we none the less tested it against a range of responses relating to relationships with parents, schooling and culturally induced attitudes. The results of those tests showed that place of birth had little or no significant effect.

Length of Stay

As might be expected, length of stay was an important contributing factor to inter-group differences. Table 7.1 shows the results in this aspect. The first two items were about academic abilities. It was found that fluency in English increased significantly for those who had spent more than five years in Britain as did their sense of growing mastery over the language. The same could be said of their experience of school work generally: increasing length of time in British schools led to a greater sense of ability to cope with it. Notably also, responses to item 13 showed that increasing length of stay was positively related to their interest in school outings.

The second aspect shown in the table is that the under five years group were likely to have a more positive attitude in their school life than other, longer stay, groups. They felt that they had more interesting lessons in school (item 17).

Thirdly, significant differences were found in the youngsters' preference between having examinations and doing projects. The longer stay group, i.e. more than 10 years, exhibited a growing preference for doing projects rather than taking examinations and tests than their shorter stay counterparts.

Table 7.1 Length of stay and educational attitudes

Item	Length of stay	SA+A %	U %	SD+D %	Total *N*
3. I speak and write English fluently	<5 yrs	40	17	43	35
	5–10 yrs	80	19	2	42
	>10 yrs	91	7	3	275
8. I feel I have difficulty in mastering English	<5 yrs	49	31	20	35
	5–10 yrs	26	14	66	42
	>10 yrs	8	16	76	277
13. I am not interested in joining school outings	<5 yrs	23	26	51	35
	5–10 yrs	12	17	72	42
	>10 yrs	11	15	74	277
17. We have interesting lessons in school	<5 yrs	74	14	12	35
	5–10 yrs	43	31	26	42
	>10 yrs	40	38	22	277
19. I find that a lot of school work is difficult	<5 yrs	31	37	31	35
	5–10 yrs	14	26	57	41
	>10 yrs	21	25	54	274
23. I prefer examinations and tests to doing projects.	<5 yrs	37	40	23	35
	5–10 yrs	38	41	21	42
	>10 yrs	26	32	42	277

Note: SA= Strongly agree; A= Agree; U= Uncertain; SD= Strongly disagree; D= Disagree; differences are significant beyond $p<0.01$; Kruskal Wallis one way analysis of variance was calculated with two degrees of freedom.

Table 7.2 indicates the young people's personal feelings about different aspects of their lives. Item 2 indicates their satisfaction with their school work. The longer stay group tended to feel better than shorter stay groups – they were prouder of their school work than their shorter stay counterparts.

Apart from item 2, the rest of the statements relate to happiness or its associated attitudes. Happiness grows with length of stay (item 6). The proportion of those whose stay exceeded 10 years who felt 'pretty happy' was high as 92 per cent. Conversely, those whose length of stay was less than five years were much more likely to wish they were someone else. Although the questions do not ask for reasons, it might be thought reasonable to suppose that it may be connected to the cultural challenge of their early years in Britain.

It is interesting to note in item 13 ('There are many times when I'd like to leave home') that the percentage of those in the five to 10 years group who related to the statement was notably higher than those in the less than five years and more than 10 years groups. Again, one can only speculate on the reasons for this. It may be that it was the result of responses to finding themselves in a new environment. When they were new arrivals, exposed to all the stresses and uncertainties that this implied, they were on the whole grateful for the security of the home. Later, as the stress of being new settlers diminished, perhaps also as they were able to compare the relative freedom enjoyed by their European peers, the delights of leaving home became more attractive.

Then, as the years rolled by, they reassessed their situation relative to their parents and their own sense of Chineseness and came to recognise that leaving home meant not only an escape from the petty restrictions of parental domination that might attract any adolescent but also the rejection of their ethnicity and all that that implied. Those considerations might well weigh more heavily with them than the illusory attractions offered by notions of relative freedom. In a sentence, it perhaps reflects the process of coming to terms with the reality of their new life in Britain.

Length of stay also affected the respondents' sense of cultural identity as Table 7.3 reveals. Those who had stayed longer in Britain tended to prefer to live there more than those whose stay had been shorter (item 4). The same trend is observable in the other items in the table. Their preference for Chinese food diminished with time (item 6); their belief that boys and girls should have greater freedom to meet increased (item 15); their sense of ease at the prospect of meeting English people grew (item 20); and there was an apparent reduction in their sense of responsibility towards their parents in old age (item 33). It should be noted, however, much of the effect of length of stay in item 33 is accounted for by the increase in numbers of those 'undecided' rather than who rejected the proposition. That having been said, the general trends were undeniable and seemed to support the view that many traditional cultural values were modified as length of stay increased.

Table 7.2 Length of stay and self identity

Item	Length of stay	Like me %	Unlike me %	Total N
1. I often wish I were someone else	<5 yrs	49	51	35
	5–10 yrs	38	62	42
	>10 yrs	28	72	276
2. I'm proud of my schoolwork	<5 yrs	62	38	34
	5–10 yrs	74	26	42
	>10 yrs	83	17	276
6. I'm pretty happy	<5 yrs	79	21	34
	5–10 yrs	71	29	42
	>10 yrs	92	8	277
13. There are many times when I'd like to leave home	<5 yrs	29	71	35
	5–10 yrs	54	46	41
	>10 yrs	29	71	275

Note: all differences are significant beyond $p<0.05$; Kruskal Wallis one way analysis of variance was calculated with two degrees of freedom.

These findings might well be accounted for by the process of settling down as a migrant community. By this we do not wish to assert that what was being recorded was the process of acculturation or assimilation but rather a form of accommodation or adaptation to a new cultural environment.

Age and Sex Differences

Data from two age groups, 13 and 16 year-olds, were selected to see if there were significant differences in educational and attitudinal variables provided by the questionnaire. Having regard to the importance generally of increasing maturity, the results of this investigation were surprisingly inconclusive. Such differences as were found to be significant had to do with relationships between parents and children and were very much what might have been expected – having to do with the tendency of teenagers becoming more aware of themselves and less tolerant of parental authority.

Gender is (in a society which still discriminates in its sexual ascriptions) likely to be a significant factor in identity development and self-perception.

Table 7.3 Length of stay and cultural identity

Item	Length of stay	SA+A %	U %	SD+D %	Total N
4. I prefer to live in Britain rather than the place where my family came from originally	<5 yrs	14	40	46	35
	5–10 yrs	38	31	31	42
	>10 yrs	44	35	21	276
6. I would rather eat Chinese food all the time	<5 yrs	46	34	20	35
	5–10 yrs	29	38	33	42
	>10 yrs	24	37	39	278
15. Boys and girls should be allowed to meet each other in youth clubs	<5 yrs	71	23	6	35
	5–10 yrs	71	19	10	42
	>10 yrs	85	15	1	277
20. I feel very uneasy with English people	<5 yrs	32	20	49	35
	5-10 yrs	5	19	76	42
	>10 yrs	6	16	78	275
33. Elder sons or daughters should take responsibility for parents when they are old	<5 yrs	69	11	20	35
	5–10 yrs	79	12	7	41
	>10 yrs	56	24	20	279

Note: SA= Strongly agree; A= Agree; U= Uncertain; SD= Strongly disagree; D= Disagree; all differences are significant beyond $p<0.05$; Kruskal Wallis one way analysis of variance was calculated with two degrees of freedom.

Using the data collected through the questionnaire, the Mann Whitney U test was used to explore gender differences in the sample when applied to the cultural identity scale.

Table 7.4 reveals some quite marked differences between girls and boys over a range of aspects to do with cultural identity. The greatest difference (over 20 percentage points) was over the issue of arranged marriage: 86 per cent of the girls and adolescent women thought that marriages should be arranged by the family but only 63 per cent of the boys agreed. Other items on which there was a 10 per cent or greater difference between girls and boys were: item 3, 'Chinese customs and traditions are best for us', item 33, 'Elder sons or daughters should take responsibility for parents when they are old', which were supported by more boys than girls, and items 10, 23, 27 (respectively, 'I only like to make friends with Chinese', 'I would not like Chinese women to behave like English women', and 'It is more important for boys than girls to go on to higher education') which were supported by more girls than boys. There was little difference between them over the proposition that 'Girls and boys should be treated the same' and for this it is interesting to note that, not only was there a large measure of agreement (girls 97 per cent, boys 90 per cent) but very few were uncertain or disagreed with it.

Item 18, 'Chinese films are more entertaining than English and American films' aroused little passion either way: 40 per cent of boys and girls were undecided, which might suggest that they were prepared to treat the films on their merits as entertainment. It might also be that there is an indication here of the pervasiveness of 'youth' culture crossing the ethnic and traditionally defined cultural boundaries. This item was not unique in the level of uncertainty it evoked. Although we have already noted that item 23 ('I would not like Chinese women to behave like English women') was one over which there was a considerable difference of opinion between girls and boys, it should be added that it also was an issue over which 40 per cent of girls and boys were undecided, and the same could be said of items 24 and 31.

The items over which there were low levels of uncertainty were 1, 8, 10, 22, and 27 and it is perhaps noteworthy that they all had to do with aspects of equality.

Finally, and most significantly, whilst there were identifiable differences (boys, for example, tended towards the more traditional Chinese views where there was some benefit in it for them) what was more significant were the generally low levels of dissent between the sexes.

Table 7.4 Gender and cultural identity

Item	Gender	SA+A %	U %	SD+D %	Total *N*
1. Girls and boys should be treated the same	Girls	97	2	1	200
	Boys	90	6	4	160
3. Chinese customs and traditions are best for us	Girls	37	49	14	199
	Boys	51	38	11	159

Table 7.4 cont'd

Item	Gender	SA+A %	U %	SD+D %	Total *N*
5. I would like to see Chinese boys and girls going out with English boys and girls	Girls	54	36	10	198
	Boys	44	39	16	160
8. Chinese women should have jobs outside of their home	Girls	5	12	84	199
	Boys	12	16	73	160
10. I only like to make friends with Chinese	Girls	89	7	4	196
	Boys	75	14	11	159
18. Chinese films are more entertaining than English and American films	Girls	31	41	29	199
	Boys	26	39	45	160
22. Marriages should be arranged by the family	Girls	86	10	5	200
	Boys	63	20	17	160
23. I would not like Chinese women to behave like English women	Girls	42	44	14	200
	Boys	29	43	29	160
24 Advice given by grandparents is always good advice	Girls	31	50	20	200
	Boys	22	39	39	160
27. It is more important for boys than girls to go on to higher education	Girls	64	11	26	200
	Boys	49	18	33	159
31. Decisions made by groups are usually better than decisions made by an individual	Girls	33	47	20	197
	Boys	43	43	14	160
33. Elder sons or daughters should take responsibility for parents when they are old	Girls	56	22	21	200
	Boys	67	19	13	159

Note: SA= Strongly agree; A= Agree; U= Uncertain; SD= Strongly disagree; D= Disagree; differences on items 3, 10, 22, 23, 27 and 33 are significant beyond $p<0.05$; Mann Whitney U test was calculated.

8 Cultural Identity in Cross-Cultural Perspective

Introduction

In earlier chapters we focussed very specifically on the perceptions of the British-Chinese young people. We now explore the experiences of European British (i.e. Britons of Celtic, Anglo-Saxon and other European origin) and HK Chinese adolescents, in which their senses of cultural belonging are put into perspective. Based on interview data obtained from 160 young people, questions about the meaning of being 'British' and 'HongKongese', and the issue of Hong Kong's return to China in 1997, are highlighted in this section. It concludes with some data obtained from the questionnaires. We begin by reporting on interviews with European British youngsters.

What Does it Mean to be British?

A conventional or traditional answer to this question might define 'Britishness' as some being part of an island nation, and its good fortune in enjoying the privilege of nearly a thousand years of self-government uninterrupted by invasion. Would Britain's imperial past come to mind in responses, as well as Britain's (sic) literary and dramatic heritage? In fact, as the following extracts make clear, none of the markers of historical identity was called on by the European British youth in their attempts to respond to our question: what does it mean to be British? It was, of course, an exceedingly difficult question to answer – one that might present problems to much more mature minds – but one that we felt had to be asked.

Language was a factor which was often identified as salient, and there were as well some passing references to the royal family and an imperial past. The significance of religion was also touched on but mostly the young people spoke of the present – of crime and racism, poverty and oppression and the need for social justice which many clearly felt was lacking. References to high culture were notably absent as also were any real calls on history as defining Britishness. Even relatively recent history went unnoticed. It might be a matter for surprise, for instance, particularly having regard to the timing of this study, occurring as it did during the lead up to the celebrations of VE Day, that Britain's part in World War II went unmentioned.

All that having been said, many spoke of a feeling of pride in being British even though they felt unable to point to the sources of their pride. Some thought that being British meant being white. Of them, Steven (aged 14, British European origin) was a typical example when he said, 'British? White, isn't it?'

Most tried to embrace wider perspectives and link up the concept of Britishness to the people, their lifestyles and culture. For some, 'British' meant those people who were living in Britain. Danielle, aged 16, said,

> I am not a huge follower of the Royal family. I am British because I live over here. I follow the culture but not in a great strict way. It is very hard to pick up the culture you live in, other people can see it. But you can't see it for yourself. I can see bits like celebrating Christmas and things like that. I think it is only the language difference and the beliefs and the way you live. You don't think about the culture that you live in, you just accept [it].

Danielle's interpretation of being 'British' was characteristic of many others. Culture was something which you followed and lived in. As she rightly observed, sometimes you can't see it or be aware of it for yourself, any more, she might have added, than you could see or be conscious of the air you breathe.

Catherine, talked about religion and said,

> Being British don't mean a lot these days. It can be anything you like. 'British' – you can go into other cultures you like, you know. All Christians, a lot of British are Catholic. ... British are patriotic. Times have changed. A couple of hundred years ago people who were living in Britain were Christian or Protestant, but now you've got whatever you want. British can be Christians or Catholic or ... I think, Chinese or Christian, they don't have to believe in whatever, and the background they have to be. I think it is different now. To a certain extent I am proud of being British. People say, 'You are British?', you say 'Yes'. It is not something really good to me but suppose you get to the Olympics, you might have something to be proud of.

In her eyes, being 'British' once related to Christianity or the struggle between Catholics and Protestants. Unconsciously perhaps, she compared that time with the present when religious beliefs are perceived as irrelevant. National heroes were sportsmen, a view taken up by Stephen, aged 15:

> I am certainly proud of being English. Personally I am interested in sports. Certainly I would be proud to represent England as a sportsman or something.
>
> ... You can learn a lot from the third world countries. Sometimes you learn a lot from them and it's quite important to learn about the other country so you know whereabouts you are in the world, you are not in other area, or you are lucky in the area ....

Britain was seen as not being alone. 'Being British' meant relating to the world's affairs. The British were people who should be aware of social justice, e.g., should help the homeless people and fight against crime. Thus Sheridan remarked:

> I am proud of being British. I don't know, ... I think there is something different. I never got any thought on it. I am English and that is the way I am.
>
> I don't see why people should make statues. Government is a different thing. For the royal family, I don't think the people should fight for them. British are modern people, ain't they? I think the Government and the people should be sensitive towards homeless people, ethnic minority people and disabled people and people who might be depending on social security, who haven't got enough money. I am unhappy about the way some white people frighten people, break into houses or steal things, or something like that.

For Rachel, being British was a source of mixed feelings. Like many others, she seemed unable to distinguish between ethnic and cultural identity. There were aspects of society that worried her and she singled out racism as one of them. It seemed that the word had associations (perhaps picked up from its usage by organisations such as the British National Party) which she distrusted.

> I feel I am an English. Sometimes ... it depends. I feel proud of it but sometimes I dislike to be British when I hear all the stuff about rape and racism in the news. It makes you feel horrible to be part of such a society. I don't know what it means to be English. The place? I don't know. There is not really any difference between us. It is only the way we speak and the way we look that make us different.

Michelle, like Rachel, had problems over the difference between cultural and ethnic identity which contributed to her sense of puzzlement. One can see how she has a sense that historical markers, like being white, going to church and having roast beef for lunch on Sunday no longer had any significance. After struggling with the question, she came up with an interesting distinction when she spoke of the difference between being *happy* to be British but not necessarily *proud* to be British.

> I don't know what it means to be British ... It is different now. Everyone's from different places. You can't say I am British because I am White because many different coloured people come from Britain. They are born in Britain. I am British. I don't know what it is. There are traditions like going to Church on Sunday and roast dinner on Sunday and go to football matches on Saturday. I go with my brother – shopping, ice-skating. What's different with Germans? Are they German because they speak German? They speak their language and we speak ours ....
>
> I don't feel all the time being proud of being British because of the things like we have done killing people and stuff like that and hooligans going to Dublin, whatever. I don't think that [it] is right [to be] proud. I am not proud. Sometimes I am happy to be British but not proud to be British. I don't like the way that we had different Empires. British had Empires and we had control over Hong Kong. I don't like that. I don't see why she should have control. Everyone should have their own thing. We should not have control over others just because we are a rich country.

The concept of being 'British' was not seen as being one that could be defined in isolation. Many youngsters thought that it should be seen in relation to other cultures and that to do this, it was necessary to know more about both 'ours' and 'theirs' and to adopt the best of both. It was interesting to come across the perception that British culture could be dynamic in its response to other cultures rather than something that had to be protected from change. Thus, for example, Anna, aged 13:

> I think it is very important to learn your own culture or things like that. It helps you to know how things were happened ... I like to learn other ethnic minority cultures because they are a part of our culture.

Mark, aged 15, was rather less certain about this. He felt the need to know more about his own history and culture but he too recognised the importance of knowing more about others. He also voiced the sense that religion was somehow important in defining a culture as did Carla:

> British, from Britain really. … It is quite important to know about the country rather than the others. It is also important to learn about others. … I think it is good to do something about different religion, apart from Catholic. We do not really learn much other religions and subjects.

> We don't learn much cultural things because we just have religious education only once a week, so we don't have that much about different cultures.

While many talked about culture in a wide social perspective, we conclude with Emma, aged 14, who spoke of her sense of being English although her father was American. Her closing thoughts are a salutary reminder of the struggles adolescents have to come to terms with the immediate and personal reality of their lives. For her, and no doubt many others, these are more important than abstractions like 'culture' and 'being British'.

> I think of myself as English because I was born here and when I was 18 months old we went over there. I think of myself as English but there's still a lot of American in me. I was growing up there and my dad is American, I go there once every year … I try my hardest. It has been a bit difficult for me because my mum got married in July and I have been alone with her for six years. I like the person that she married but, I don't know, there's something else and I don't really like him. It's as if he is trying to separate my mum from me in my eyes. We weren't very close anyway. But it seems the gap is getting wider and wider between us.

Thus, for these young people, their sense of being British did not derive from any powerful sense of being inheritors of cultural traditions. It had much more to do with their country of birth and their language. Much of the time, when they were trying to arrive at their personal definitions of Britishness they were struggling to come to terms with what they saw of society about them and testing those perceptions against their sense of fairness and decency. A good deal of what they saw about them – poverty, racism, intolerance, lack of care for the disadvantaged – did nothing to make them feel proud. Their concerns were firmly rooted in the present and their culture had more to do with youthful idealism than a mindset constructed out of the past.

Chinese Cultural Identity in Adolescents in Hong Kong

Hong Kong at the time of these interviews was a British colony on the threshold of being merged with a great nation with a past rooted in profound cultural achievements, and a present and future based on revolution and economic development, which may one day dominate the world stage, in comparison with the offshore island of Britain with its small population and declining economic development. Hong Kong's long history as a British Crown Colony resulted in some confusion in the minds of some young people, arising from differing senses of ethnic and cultural identities. The extracts from interviews illustrate this ambiguity. While some Hong Kong adolescents perceived themselves (in the Chinese language interviews, with the Chinese authors of this book) some preferred to select the term 'HongKongese' to describe the group which they belonged to. Examples which selected Chinese as their cultural group are given below. Ming Sai had this to say:

> I admire the economic achievement of Hong Kong, and its many facilities and social system. I think that Hong Kong is better than China in terms of economic achievement, therefore I want to be a HongKongese. On the other hand, I feel that China is my root place. She has her own culture and I think that I was born in China and I am one of the Chinese people. I hope my country would be growing all the time. I belong to China.

Similarly, Ka Man:

> I am a Chinese, because I was born in China, and I came to Hong Kong at the age of seven. ... I am proud of being Chinese. I think the Chinese culture is very special. The other countries do not have the cultural characteristics. ... I do not feel unhappy at being a Chinese. I do not have any feeling about the returning of Hong Kong to China. I do not think there is any influence on me and my family.

For these two adolescents, ethnic inheritance was a more powerful factor in constructing their sense of identity than any cultural distinctions that might be made between Hong Kong and China. For others, the reverse was true. For Ka Li the fact of being born there was important but she also felt a cultural difference: Hong Kong people set about the business of making a living in a different style from the mainland Chinese:

> I think I am a HongKongese. Because since I was young, I have lived in Hong

> Kong. The difference between the people in Hong Kong and China is great, e.g. the methods of the people who do things is different. For instance, the people in Hong Kong who built houses are more stable than the people in China.

Yuen Wai shared her belief in the superiority of Hong Kong's economic prosperity but also felt that it was less prone to natural disasters:

> I think I am a HongKongese. As a HongKongese I am very fortunate. The reason is that we do not [suffer from] disasters, good economics, and worthy ... I do not have anything that I do not like about being a HongKongese. For example, now the floods in the Southern part of China: people there are dying and having a lot of suffering. I think that I am very blessed.

Yu Kai goes some way towards recognising the difference between the claims of ethnicity and culture but, more interestingly, echoes the English girl in her distinction between being 'happy' and 'proud' of being HongKongese:

> I think I am a HongKongese, because I was born in Hong Kong and grew up in Hong Kong ... I do not have the feeling of being proud of that. I am happy to be a HongKongese because I have a lucky family. I do not have anything to be unhappy about ... I think that the land of Hong Kong originally belonged to China. I think it is quite appropriate that Hong Kong returns to China. We have not thought of migration. I have not thought of studying overseas and I would not like to study overseas.

Some found the distinction between 'Chinese' and 'HongKongese' meaningless. Ka Min, for example, thought they were the same, as did Kam Siu, though with a different emphasis:

> I think HongKongese and Chinese are the same because HongKongese belongs to China. ... I do not feel in particular that I am proud of being a Chinese.

> Because the land of Hong Kong belongs to China. We all belong to the family of China, of course, we are Chinese. I don't like people to make the distinction that you are a HongKongese or Chinese. HongKongese is Chinese. I am a Hong Kong person so I am Chinese. I have a yellow skin and dark eyes.

By 1997, the numbers of newcomers from mainland China to Hong Kong had increased, both in terms of legal and illegal immigrants. Some interviewees whose parents had made the move spoke of discrimination by the local Hong Kong young people: Yip Kin for example talked about being bullied:

> I think that many Hong Kong people look down on people from the mainland. In Primary School, pupils bullied me and said 'mainland boy'; this stopped when I went to secondary school. At that time I felt unhappy, and showed a hard face to them. If they still continued to bully me, I ignored them. In Hong Kong, you cannot run away. I have not talked to my teachers about it, because they did it verbally and I am used to it.

> I was born in China and I live in Hong Kong. I like Hong Kong, but I came from China. I do not know which group (HongKongese or Chinese) I belong to.

The passage of 1997 and the absorption of Hong Kong as a special administrative region within the People's Republic of China affected not only the political and economic situation in Hong Kong, it also made for higher levels of stress in the lives of many Hong Kong young people. The feelings and attitudes of some of them are explored below.

As Ching Ha spoke, he was worried by the prospect of cheap labour driving down wages but behind his comments was the perception that there was a cultural difference between Hong Kong and China:

> I think that Hong Kong people do have an influence caused by the issue of 1997 whatever we study or work. Because there is competition, the Chinese people come here to work, and they are quite capable.

Much the same could be said of Choi Yue. She too was worried by the possible economic ill-effects of the change but believed that, on balance, the reunification of Hong Kong with China was a good thing:

> I came from China and I was born in Hong Kong. I came here in 1989. I think that the thinking of Hong Kong people is very strange. I think that they do love their country. They admire foreign things. They like to work closely with foreign countries ... In terms of (?)patriotism, Hong Kong returning to China is good. In practice, from an economic point of view, Hong Kong will step back and not be as successful as now. But I like 1997. Hong Kong eventually belongs to China. Hong Kong has been a leased land and it is not good. I think that Hong Kong returning to China is better.

Reunification with China was also welcomed by Ming Sai. He was worried about the possibility of change to the political climate and the loss of freedom that might result from it, but his concern about this was outweighed by his pleasure at the thought of Hong Kong being one with China again:

> After 1997, if China does not play the political game, that would be good. It is certain that the politic climate has less freedom. At that time the economic situation might be better because of the close relationship between China and Hong Kong. Hong Kong returning to China is a very happy thing. I think that it is a shame that Hong Kong was ceded to the British.

Ka Man expressed her opinion from a personal stance. Her concern was about the impact it might have on her studies and future career. For her, the prospect of continuing her studies among strangers was sufficiently daunting to have made her reject it:

> I do not think that 1997 will affect my learning or career. I have not thought of going overseas for further study. Because foreign countries are different from Hong Kong, and I do not know about the places and the people, so I have not considered study overseas.

Yuen Wai was clearly troubled by the prospect of change. She anticipated a period of instability and had heard that communism was 'bad' and something to fear. She saw little prospect of leaving Hong Kong because she did not think her parents could afford it:

> The issue of 1997 influencing Hong Kong is a definite matter. As a matter of fact, I don't know what will happen after 1997. I think that there will be a lot of instability. I've always heard from people how bad communism is. Maybe I have not experienced about it and I do not know how to be afraid of it. ... When 1997 comes, I think my parents will stay in Hong Kong. Because the financial situation at home is not that good, we have not thought of migration.

Ka Li's parents had thought about migrating – her father wanted to move to Australia. She was worried about the effect of 1997 on her studies and subsequent career and, like others, was concerned about the effect of cheap labour from the mainland:

> About 1997, my father has thought about migration. My father is doing business in electronics. He wants to migrate to Australia. I do not want to have the change because of 1997. Because Hong Kong is used to being governed by the British Government. China and Hong Kong originally are separated ... 1997 will have an effect on me in studying and work. For example, the workers from China are cheaper than the workers in Hong Kong.

Ho Bond's optimism at the prospect of the family's planned move to

Canada was coloured by all sorts of regrets. He was going to miss his friends. Even more, he was going to miss Hong Kong itself and foresaw difficulties in adapting to a new environment. Given the chance he planned to return to Hong Kong eventually:

> I am optimistic because my parents will leave Hong Kong. We will migrate to Canada. We have decided and will leave after my GCSE examination. I have a brother and we will move as a whole family. I don't like it. I have never gone out of Asia. I don't want to migrate because I have many things I like to remember, e.g. friends. I have a sense of belonging because I have lived in Hong Kong for more than 10 years and the lifestyle of a foreign country will be totally different. I will have difficulties in adapting to the environment there and the fact that they are not Chinese people, so it will be difficult to live with. This will influence my study and work. If I have chance, I would like to return back to Hong Kong. After studying, I would like to return back to Hong Kong.

Yee Ki said she was not worried about the change but her parents were going to leave and she would go with them, either to Canada or the USA. She thought she might return to Hong Kong when her studies were completed: it would depend on how things had turned out there.

> I am not afraid, but my parents will leave. I will follow them to migrate. After studying, I will return back to Hong Kong. It depends on what happens. If it is good, I will return back. They will migrate to a foreign country, either Canada or United States, but for the time being we will remain here.

It appeared that Kam Siu was one of those likely to remain in Hong Kong and regretted the changes that were in store. He too was saddened by the loss of friends:

> ... the issue of 1997 means that I will lose some of my friends. The issue of 1997 may influence a lot of things that affect me, but the time has not come yet. I don't know what the effects will be. Now I think that the British govern Hong Kong better than the Chinese. That is what I think.

Yip Kin's response was one of uncertainty about the future and powerlessness in the face of change:

> I do not know what the society will be. I cannot resist the changes to the society. I can only recognise the changes and let them happen. Eleven billion people in China live there as a matter of course. I am not the only one.

Wing Man would have preferred Hong Kong to remain under British rule. She was depressed by the prospect of having to speak Mandarin and change to a simplified script:

> I prefer that Hong Kong belongs to Britain. My feeling towards China is that I will have to speak in Mandarin and to write in simplified Chinese. And I think that the system in China is not good. I like the British system.

Ka Min feared the changes which she was sure were inevitable. Perhaps they would migrate, perhaps not. Her cousin was to be sent to Canada to study and it was possible that she would follow him, though the lack of any relatives there was something that worried her. For her, the future was very confused:

> I am afraid of 1997. I am afraid that Hong Kong will be like China, without any freedom … My parents said, if we have the opportunity we would migrate to somewhere but it depends on prospects: we do not have to migrate. My aunt wants to send my cousin to Canada to study; my mother is now thinking about this. We do not have relatives there. It all depends on what happens. I think I would continue to study.

Taken together, these extracts taken from interviews present a picture of young people who were facing a future which they saw in many ways as, at best uncertain, often threatening, and fraught with actual or potential loss. Moreover, whilst they were all secure in their ethnic identity, there was a widespread sense, imprecise though that might have been, that the cultures of Hong Kong and China were far from being identical.

As with the European British youngsters, their cultural identities were formed from their perceptions of the immediate past and the present. Unlike the British, however, they were facing a time of traumatic change and we were left with an impression of rootlessness – though we accept that this may have been more apparent than real, growing out of the nature of the interviews rather than their deeply held feelings.

To test this, we turned to the responses given by all three groups, each numbering some 360 persons – British-Chinese, European British and Hong Kong Chinese – to the cultural identity scale which formed part of their questionnaires.

Respondents in all three groups, British-Chinese, European British and Hong Kong Chinese were asked to complete a cultural identity scale which formed part of their questionnaire. Whilst it was not sensible to give each group identical propositions (for example, 'We should celebrate Christmas as we celebrate the Chinese New Year' was for British-Chinese respondents only with a variation on the theme for European British respondents and omitted for Hong Kong Chinese) the majority in each case were the same. Their responses are to be found in Table 8.1.

With an array of propositions as extensive as this, many of them with responses by three groups, the data present a complex picture. Our first resort in an attempt to detect useful patterns was to search for propositions which elicited responses from the British-Chinese and Hong Kong Chinese groups which had more in common with each other than those of the European British group. These turned out to be items 1, 18, 22, 25, 27, 32 and 33 which dealt with issues of equality between boys and girls, marriage, the duty of children towards their parents and forms of entertainment. The most clearly defined of these differences were to do with the obligations of children towards their parents in which the two Chinese groups (unlike their European peers) were strongly of the opinion that they should provide financial support throughout their lives and generally hold themselves responsible for their care when they were old. However, and we would be inclined to attach some importance to this, although both Chinese groups felt stronger filial obligations than the European British group (see items 32 and 33) in both cases the British-Chinese scored lower than their Hong Kong counterparts. Thus, to the proposition 'When I earn money, I will give some to my parents until they die', 89 per cent of Hong Kong Chinese said they would, as against 77 per cent of British-Chinese. Similarly 86 per cent of Hong Kong Chinese but only 61 per cent of British-Chinese said that they thought 'Elder sons or daughters should take responsibility for their parents when they are old'. On the matter of equality between boys and girls, the differences were less pronounced. Both Chinese groups were less likely to think that they should be treated the same and thought that it was less important for girls to go on to higher education than boys. Items 18 and 25 asked for responses to films and music by country of origin as a way of defining their cultural content. In both cases, the Chinese groups showed little preference either way. This might be interpreted in a number of ways but it suggests that these forms of entertainment can cross cultural boundaries and make themselves attractive with relative ease.

Since language had emerged as a significant factor for the British-Chinese group in the interviews, it seemed sensible to see what the responses had been to the questionnaire. Items 11 and 19 ('We should learn to speak and write the Chinese language' and 'We should ignore the Chinese language if we want to get on in this country') had been included. The strength of the responses to these two items left no doubt as to the significance of language in their minds. Almost eight out of 10 of British-Chinese respondents thought that they should learn to speak and write the Chinese language and almost nine out of 10 rejected the proposition that they should ignore the Chinese language if they wanted to get on in Britain.

Although (with the exception of a few Chinese Christians) religion as normally understood had seemed in the interviews to be of little consequence to the British-Chinese, item 28 ('Worshipping ancestors during special festivals is important') showed that for them, no less than for the Hong Kong Chinese, this remained important. In both groups, half said it was and a third were undecided. However, it was noteworthy that the questionnaire (item 14, 'It is good for us to learn something about Christianity') showed that for both Chinese groups, four out of 10 agreed, nearly four out of 10 were undecided and only one in five disagreed.

We also looked at items common to British and Hong Kong Chinese to see if they provided any evidence of differences to suggest that the British-Chinese were being affected by the dominant culture. For this, we inspected responses to items 7, 8, 9, 24, 29, 30 and 31. These proved to be largely inconclusive. Item 7 suggested that the British-Chinese were less tolerant of the idea that grandparents should form part of the family household than the Hong Kong Chinese and marginally less likely to think highly of their advice (item 24). On the other hand, they were more likely to think that traditional Chinese medicine was better than Western medicine. (Any explanation for this can only be speculative. It may be accounted for by the generally low levels of parental education, or by the tendency observed in other recently arrived groups to cling on to traditional beliefs and practices.)

Whilst both groups believed that hard work was the only way to succeed, the British-Chinese scored higher (86 per cent as against 75 per cent) and there might be some connection between this and the fact that more British-Chinese parents complained about insufficient homework than their Hong Kong peers. It is also a characteristic of first-generation settlers to perceive education as the key to social and economic mobility for their children. In this group of responses, item 31, which had to do with the relative virtues of group and individual decision-making, was perhaps the most interesting since it showed the British-Chinese to be less likely to support group decision-making than the Hong Kong Chinese. However, it has to be said that the significance of this finding was obscured by the high proportion of those who were uncertain.

What broad conclusions can be drawn? On the basis of this evidence, it appears that in certain, what might be described as 'core areas' having to do with the family, Chinese youngsters in Britain are likely to retain in large measure their traditional cultural attitudes. Crucially also, they perceive language-retention as very important, even though they know that facility in English is the key to their success in Britain. In the field of entertainment, it seems as if there is a youth culture which affects all three groups more strongly than traditional cultures. Finally, there was some evidence, notably in the area of responsibility towards parents, to suggest that traditional cultural attitudes were undergoing some modification. It is difficult not to conclude that this might be a result of their growing up in a society in which these responsibilities are taken less seriously or are discharged not through personal commitment but through institutionalised care.

Table 8.1 Culture and ethnicity

Item	Group	N %	SA+A %	U %	SD+D
1. Girls and boys should be treated the same	UK Chinese	362	74	4	3
	UK Euro	380	89	4	7
	HK Chinese	364	77	12	11
2. We should celebrate Christmas as we celebrate the Chinese New Year	UK Chinese	362	79	17	4
We should celebrate the festivals from other cultures as we celebrate Christmas	UK Euro	381	43	34	23
3. Chinese customs and traditions are best for us	UK Chinese	360	43	44	13
English customs and traditions are best for us	UK Euro	380	46	38	13
4. I prefer to live in Britain rather than the place where my family came from originally	UK Chinese	359	40	35	24

Table 8.1 cont'd

Item	Group	N %	SA+A %	U %	SD+D
I prefer to live in Britain rather than any other country	UK Euro	381	42	29	30
5. I would like to see Chinese boys and girls going out with English boys and girls	UK Chinese	360	50	37	13
I would like to see English boys and girls going out with boys and girls from other cultures	UK Euro	379	57	30	13
6. I would rather eat Chinese food all the time	UK Chinese	361	27	36	37
I would rather eat only English food	UK Euro	379	19	14	67
7. Children should live with their parents on their own and not with grandparents and other relatives	UK Chinese	361	34	33	34
	UK Euro	378	17	24	58
	HK Chinese	364	19	23	59
8. Chinese women should not have jobs outside their home	UK Chinese	361	8	13	79
Women should not have jobs outside of their home	UK Euro	381	10	4	85
	HK Chinese	363	7	11	82
9. Traditional Chinese medicine is better than English medicine	UK Chinese	358	30	51	17

Table 8.1 cont'd

Item	Group	N %	SA+A %	U %	SD+D
English or Western medicine is better than Chinese or African traditional medicine	UK Euro	379	15	59	26
Traditional Chinese medicine is better than Western	HK Chinese	363	9	55	37
10. I only like to make friends with Chinese	UK Chinese	357	6	10	82
I only like to make friends with English people	UK Euro	378	7	9	83
11. We should learn to speak and write the Chinese language	UK Chinese	361	78	16	5
We should learn to speak and write other languages such as French and German	UK Euro	380	71	13	15
12. Sometimes we should cook English food at home	UK Chinese	357	13	4	1
We should sometimes cook Chinese or Asian food at home	UK Euro	379	67	22	10
13. We should use English names so that our teachers can say them easily	UK Chinese	359	45	29	25
	HK Chinese	363	33	34	33

Table 8.1 cont'd

Item	Group	N %	SA+A %	U %	SD+D
14. It is good for us to learn something about Christianity	UK Chinese	362	43	35	21
	HK Chinese	363	40	39	21
It is good for us to learn something about religions other than Christianity	UK Euro	378	57	25	18
15. Boys and girls should be allowed to meet each other in youth clubs	UK Chinese	360	81	16	2
	UK Euro	378	93	4	3
16. I would prefer to live in an area where there are families from the Chinese community	UK Chinese	359	49	37	14
17. We should visit the homes of our English friends	UK Chinese	360	78	18	4
We should visit the homes of friends from other cultures	UK Euro	379	66	26	9
18. Chinese films are more entertaining than English and American films	UK Chinese	361	36	40	24
English and American films are more entertaining than films from other countries	UK Euro	377	55	23	22

Table 8.1 cont'd

Item	Group	N %	SA+A %	U %	SD+D
Hong Kong film are more entertaining than Western films	HK Chinese	364	24	39	37
19. We should ignore the Chinese language if we want to get on in this country	UK Chinese	360	5	8	86
20. I feel very uneasy with English people	UK Chinese	357	8	17	73
I feel very uneasy people from other cultural backgrounds	UK Euro	379	12	26	62
21. There should be more marriages between Chinese and English people	UK Chinese	360	27	56	16
There should be more marriages between English people and people from other cultures	UK Euro	378	41	45	13
22. Marriages should be arranged by the family	UK Chinese	362	10	14	76
	UK Euro	378	16	11	73
	HK Chinese	363	4	12	84
23. I would not like Chinese women to behave like English women	UK Chinese	362	21	43	36
I would not like English women to behave like Chinese or Asian women	UK Euro	379	26	40	34

Table 8.1 cont'd

Item	Group	N %	SA+A %	U %	SD+D
24. Advice given by grandparents is always good advice	UK Chinese	362	28	45	26
	UK Euro	377	34	38	27
	HK Chinese	364	33	41	27
25. I prefer to listen to Chinese music than English music	UK Chinese	361	45	24	31
I prefer to listen to English and American music than from other cultures	UK Euro	377	59	18	23
I prefer to listen to Hong Kong pop music than Western music	HK Chinese	364	41	30	30
26. Nothing in life is worth the sacrifice of moving away from parents	UK Chinese	359	26	46	28
	UK Euro	377	40	35	25
It is important to me to live with my parents	HK Chinese	364	64	23	13
27. It is more important for boys than girls to go on to higher education	UK Chinese	361	29	14	57
	UK Euro	377	22	8	70
	HK Chinese	363	19	17	63
28. Worshipping ancestors during special festivals is important	UK Chinese	358	52	37	11
	HK Chinese	363	49	34	17
29. Working hard is the only way to succeed	UK Chinese	361	86	10	4
	UK Euro	379	77	11	10
	HK Chinese	363	75	13	11

Table 8.1 cont'd

Item	Group	N %	SA+A %	U %	SD+D
30. My parents always complain that I do not get enough homework	UK Chinese	360	35	21	44
	UK Euro	378	34	17	49
	HK Chinese	362	24	23	53
31. Decisions made by groups are usually better than decisions by an individual	UK Chinese	359	37	45	16
	UK Euro	378	41	36	21
	HK Chinese	361	50	28	22
32. When I earn money, I will regularly give some to my parents until they die	UK Chinese	360	77	16	6
	UK Euro	378	39	33	28
	HK Chinese	363	89	8	3
33. Elder sons or daughters should take respons-ibility for parents when they are old	UK Chinese	361	61	21	18
	UK Euro	378	48	25	27
	HK Chinese	364	86	6	8
34. I would like to learn to use a language of one of the ethnic minorities living in Britain	UK Euro	375	29	47	23

Note: SA= Strongly agree; A= Agree; U= Uncertain; SD= Strongly disagree; D= Disagree.

We have referred elsewhere to what might be described as youth culture. It seemed interesting to discover what these young people did in their spare time. We asked them what they mainly did when they were out with their friends in the evening or at weekends. Table 8.2 sets out their replies. What it shows is the very high level of conformity between the three groups. They all spend a lot of their free time talking to each other, looking round shops, engaged in sports and going to the cinema, visiting the homes of friends and playing games there. Few went to discos and pop concerts and fewer still to the theatre.

Table 8.2 Spare time spent with friends

	UK Chinese *N=362* %	UK Euro *N=381* %	HK Chinese *N=364* %
Never go out with friends	6	1	9
When with friends:			
just talk	53	51	43
go round the shops	59	56	60
pop concert/disco	14	21	10
sports	40	43	39
cinema	60	52	45
theatre	6	2	7
go to town	65	69	*
visit friends' home and play games	56	49	43
other	10	21	16

* Item not included in the questionnaire.

9 The Experience of School and Educational Aspirations

Introduction

For most young people, the home and school are the two most important formative influences on their lives. We therefore turn now to report on experience of school. We begin this section by using extracts from interviews we recorded with some 40 young people from each of the three groups in which we hear of some of the particular difficulties encountered by the British-Chinese and of the pleasures of friendship and the pressures they all felt. We then use their responses to questions in the questionnaire to explore further their attitudes towards schooling, academic achievement, participation in school activities, relationships with teachers, experiences of praise and blame and their preferred working methods.

The School Experience

Of particular interest were their perceptions of and reactions to the different teaching and learning processes employed. This emerged most clearly in conversations with British-Chinese youngsters who had had an experience of Hong Kong schools but were now living in England and attending British schools. Martin, for example, was 13 when he came to Britain. At the time of the interview he was 16 and had this to say:

> I do not feel it is hard to study here. First, I feel that I do not have much pressure and the homework is less serious than Hong Kong. In my beginning years in Britain, the school work is earlier than the Hong Kong level; but in upper forms, it is quite the same as in Hong Kong. In the primary school, pupils here play a lot. They do not look like the Hong Kong pupils who always concentrate in their study ... Hong Kong students have greater pressure because universities there have only a few places and students struggle to get a place to study. Students have less chance to obtain a place in higher education than students in Britain. Here you do not have much pressure and it is easier to study. Hong Kong students

> have greater pressure and they need to struggle for better achievement. Also Hong Kong students need to memorise things very hard from books while British students do not need to memorise so much.

His perception that there was greater pressure to do well in Hong Kong than in British schools was echoed by Nellie. She however, was able to identify the significant difference: there was less emphasis on memorising in Britain than in Hong Kong: in Britain the emphasis was on understanding – and by implication, she seemed to approve of this:

> I think that studying in England is better. For the education in Hong Kong, you need to study a lot of knowledge in a short period of time. It tests your memory rather than understanding. The education system in England has a lot to learn. It is step by step. When I came to England, I found that I study for my understanding, not only for examination. In some aspects, I like Hong Kong's convenience, such as transport. But in terms of studying, I like England.

Of course, life in British schools was not entirely stress-free. There was a general recognition, voiced here by Daan who came to Britain aged three, that as they moved up through the school, they came under increasing pressure – though in his case, as with many others, there was a job to do as well. None the less, school, he thought, was 'quite fun.'

> I think the school is quite fun, a matter of life. I do enjoy it but sometimes I get a bit bored. I used to have a lot of friends. When you grow up you find more work and more pressure, so you would have stress. I find the school life now a bit boring because of the pressure from home, from the work I have. I work in a Chinese restaurant, just one night a week.

Problems of communication were often referred to:

> When I just arrived in England, language was a barrier. ... When I came, I dared not to speak English and did not use it. Hong Kong people are used to be shy and are afraid other people laughing at you. When you came here longer, you know other people would not laugh at you, you then learn the language faster ... Now it is quite all right. Although I might not have the accuracy in English language, I understand what other people say, so it is quite O.K.

Even for youngsters who had spent a number of years here, the problem could persist. Simon, for example, had lived in Britain for eight years but still felt disadvantaged by what he felt was his inadequacy in English:

> I find it is very difficult to keep up my English. I just try to keep up my school work. Every Tuesday, we have a Chinese teacher to help us. I think it is a good idea because she speaks Chinese to us. My teachers told me that my English is quite good, but I still feel that it is not good enough.

There was also more than a hint of loneliness:

> The school has only a few Chinese people. The Chinese people and the teachers are O.K. But I like to have more Chinese people in the school.

Allied to this feeling of loneliness was the fact that nearly all these youngsters were the children of first-generation settlers which meant that they could not look to their parents for help with their homework or, if it came to that, any real understanding of what the schools were trying to do:

> I don't have difficulties in my homework. My parents do not teach me because they do not know about it.

Not surprisingly, some found the transition to a British school bewildering and felt that they were not getting the kind of attention they needed. Sally, for instance, aged 13, who had lived in Britain for three years, had this to say:

> It depends on teachers. When I put up my hand to ask questions, they just ignore us because some teachers do not like Chinese. If we did the work well, some would give us encouragement ... It is always noisy in my class. I can't hear what the teacher said in the lesson. Few teachers spent most of the time to tell pupils off and shouted to them. We don't have much homework to do. It does not seem like the schools in Hong Kong.

It is worrying to observe her perception that she was ignored because 'some teachers do not like Chinese'. She could, of course, be correct though it seems possible that her teacher's apparent rejection of her request for help had more to do with the problems of controlling a badly behaved class than with racial discrimination, particularly when, in another part of the interview, Sally had this to say:

> ... In the school we celebrated the Chinese New Year. I felt very happy because the Western World celebrated our Chinese New Year. A teacher asked us to bring something about the Chinese New Year and we made Chinese decorations on the blackboard. Some pupils also asked questions about the Chinese New Year.

To provide an alternative perspective, we cite some responses made by European British youngsters to the same questions during their interviews. Typically, the following interviewee said that her parents were there to provide help when needed. She took a fairly relaxed view of the 'minority groups', observing that they tended to stay together. However, underlying her attitude of what might be described as 'lazy tolerance', she thought it unreasonable that the school should be expected to make too many concessions to minority cultures. On the other hand she seemed to have no problems with coexisting with other cultures.

> I do pretty well in normal subjects, they're not too difficult ... Some subjects I don't like as much as the others ... Fine, I am fine in my school. You get arguments in the school, but I get on well with everybody ... I don't really need help a lot, but if I need help, my parents will help me. I do not really get so much pressure from my parents, but they just want to make sure you do this and make sure you do that and work hard ....

> Teachers give the same attention to everybody and treat everybody the same ... The minority groups always hang together, some of them are really mixed up. You get quite a lot of them from other cultures. Everybody gets a little bit ... I think that the ethnic minority culture belongs to their own. I don't see why they have to be recognised in school. I mean, if they have their religion, that's fine, they are not here so they have had their religion ... I think it is up to them if they want something else ... I think everybody should be aware of what other cultures there are in the world. For learning about things, I don't think we have to take it to extremes; just to let you know what other things there are and then let you make a decision. Then it's fine.

Like the Chinese, they felt that they were under some pressure from their school work as they approached GCSE but this did not affect their liking for school. Sheridan said:

> I like the school here. I like the teachers in the school. ... I am quite happy in the school. ... I got a lot of examination pressure in my GCSE subjects. ... I get on well with most teachers.

and this theme was frequently echoed in one form or another:

> I generally enjoy the time I am in school ... I am reasonably good in my examinations but sometimes I feel under pressure in my school work.

> Teachers give everyone same attention. They don't have anything unfair, but I am not normally naughty and I am as good as others ...There is no racism in school.

A key difference was that of the pleasures of friendship in school – frequently mentioned by European British interviewees. Rachel and Danielle, for example:

> My friends make me feel happy in school, having a laugh and everything. What makes me unhappy? If something goes wrong at home, the school teachers get involved in it. I don't like that because it hassles me and I get stressed out and get worked up.

> I get on really well in my school. I miss it a lot when I leave on Fridays. When I finish school, I miss my friends and certain lessons such as drama, English and probably History. These are the things I like best.

The contrast between the pleasures of friendship they (and others) spoke of and the solitariness of many of the Chinese youngsters is particularly sharp.

To complete this section on the school experience, we turn to the responses of the Hong Kong Chinese. Again, friendship is one of the things to which they frequently refer. Thus, for example, Kam Siu:

> I think my school is not bad and it is quite good. I have a sense of belonging. Sometimes when I have a long holiday, I always want to return to school. I do not want to have a long break. Very often I want to finish the holiday soon. Perhaps my classmates and teachers are very good. I am very happy in the school and I learn a lot.

> ... if the schoolmates who I had known for a long time left, I would be upset.

They often talk of the pressures they feel themselves to be under to succeed. This pressure to succeed often seems inbuilt:

> The school rule is quite strict. We have to arrange my hair. Even though today is very hot we have to wear long trousers ... It is quite important to have a good result. We have a good result first, then we can find a job. I have very great pressure in examination. Sometimes I do not know about my homework. I have nobody to ask. My parents can help me only in a few subjects; like English, they could not help. My teachers can help me, they explain to me when I do not understand.

Similarly Yuen Wai, who admits to laziness but feels under an obligation to do well:

> I've got a lot of examination pressure. For this examination, for example, I've got a lot of pressure, because I am comparatively lazy, but I hope to maintain a reasonable standard, so I have great pressure about it. ...My parents have not given me much help in my homework. They received little education. Therefore I am responsible for my homework all the time and they seldom care about my homework.

For others it is peer pressure that is most important. It is also interesting how this interviewee insists that it is not from teachers or parents.

> The pressure comes from classmates. There is no pressure from family and teachers. Apart from the school work, other things are happy and everything is fine.

Ka Li, a 12 year-old, reflected on her school's teaching style and thought it ought to encourage more active learning methods:

> I found that when I come to school, all the days are study. I think that the school should provide more active learning methods, [that we] should not just 'sit to learn' ... I think that teachers should give pupils permission to walk around, not only just ask pupils to 'sit there'. For example, we should have more Physical Education lessons, and while teaching, games and active activities should be available.
>
> ... I found that if I had a good examination result, some classmates would think I am not with them. Some would ask you the things they don't know. If you originally got a good result and now have a bad result, classmates would laugh at you.

It was interesting to note her reference to classmates laughing at her when she got a bad result. That sort of observation cropped up frequently in these youngsters' replies and provides ample additional evidence for the peer-group pressure to succeed mentioned earlier.

It seemed, however, that ultimately it was the need to succeed in examinations (and fear of failure) that was the most potent influence on their academic studies. We conclude, therefore, with Yu Kai on this subject:

> The homework pressure is not that great but the examination pressure is very great. Before the examination, I am always very frightened. I am afraid that I will not get a good result. I don't know why. I think I give myself pressure.

Educational Aspirations

In the pages which follow we remain with educational aspirations and experiences but they are now revealed through quantitative data arising from answers provided in the questionnaires.

Table 9.1 compares attitudes towards schooling in the three groups. Whilst there are minor variations between the groups – British and Hong Kong Chinese are somewhat more likely to feel happy when at school than European British and are less likely to feel that going to school is a waste of time – it is the wide measure of agreement between the groups which stands out rather than the differences. Nevertheless, nearly twice as many British European (at 29 per cent) as British-Chinese (at 15 per cent) *disagreed* that they always felt happy at school.

Table 9.2 shows attitudes towards academic achievement. On all four items, the British-Chinese and European British scores were much more nearly aligned with each other than with the Hong Kong Chinese scores. This was not surprising for items 3 and 8 which have to do with fluency in English. However, the same was true of the other two items, on which the British-Chinese scores were higher than those of the European British and both were notably higher than the Hong Kong Chinese. Two factors may have influenced these results. First, they may be a reflection of the teaching methods in the two countries: the emphasis on memorising in Hong Kong schools referred to in the interviews may lead to poorer scores. The second is the cultural reluctance of Hong Kong Chinese to appear boastful about their personal achievements.

We were interested to discover what the perceptions of the three groups were so far as involvement in school activities were concerned. Table 9.3 shows their responses to four items relating to school activities. For three of the items, the same pattern as that noted in the previous Table recurred. The relationship between the British-Chinese and the European British groups was again quite close with the Hong Kong Chinese consistently scoring lower. Only on item 20 'I work and try very hard in school' was there a positive and consistent response from all three groups with the British-Chinese scoring highest.

Table 9.1 Attitudes towards schooling

Item	Group	N	SA+A %	U %	SD+D %
1. I always feel happy when I'm at school	UK Chinese	362	58	26	15
	UK Euro	381	40	30	29
	HK Chinese	364	64	28	8
11. Going to school is a waste of time	UK Chinese	362	4	9	87
	UK Euro	374	12	9	78
	HK Chinese	361	4	13	82
6. I feel really fed up on the first day of term	UK Chinese	356	43	19	37
	UK Euro	375	48	14	37
	HK Chinese	363	39	16	45

Note: SA= Strongly agree; A= Agree; U= Uncertain; SD= Strongly disagree; D= Disagree; only differences on Item 1 are significant beyond $p<0.05$ by Chi-squared test.

Table 9.2 Attitudes towards academic achievement

Item	Group	N %	SA+A %	U %	SD+D
3. I speak and write English fluently	UK Chinese	357	82	9	7
	UK Euro	377	78	12	9
	HK Chinese	364	7	28	65
8. I feel I have great difficulty in mastering English	UK Chinese	360	14	17	68
	UK Euro	376	11	17	70
	HK Chinese	362	66	14	20
15. When we have tests I get very good marks	UK Chinese	361	56	31	14
	UK Euro	378	43	33	24
	HK Chinese	364	17	51	33
19. I find a lot of school work is difficult	UK Chinese	356	22	26	51
	UK Euro	376	24	22	53
	HK Chinese	363	43	28	29

Note: SA= Strongly agree; A= Agree; U= Uncertain; SD= Strongly disagree; D= Disagree; all differences are significant beyond $p<0.01$ by Chi-squared test.

Table 9.3 Attitudes towards activity participation

Item	Group	N	SA+A %	U %	SD+D %
4. I am always active in school activities	UK Chinese	360	51	25	24
	UK Euro	381	54	24	22
	HK Chinese	362	29	26	45
13. I am not interested in joining school outings	UK Chinese	360	12	16	71
	UK Euro	379	8	11	80
	HK Chinese	363	20	18	61
9. I do not join in many school activities	UK Chinese	360	35	17	49
	UK Euro	375	29	17	53
	HK Chinese	361	47	16	36
20. I work and try very hard in school	UK Chinese	359	80	14	6
	UK Euro	380	69	19	11
	HK Chinese	363	72	17	10

Note: SA= Strongly agree; A= Agree; U= Uncertain; SD= Strongly disagree; D= Disagree; only differences for item 4 are significant beyond $p<0.05$ by Chi-squared test; other items, no significant difference.

Table 9.4 provides some insight into relationships with teachers. Here again the similarity of responses made by British-Chinese and European British respondents rather than difference was more evident. British-Chinese and European British respondents were of the opinion that their teachers liked them, more often than the Hong Kong Chinese. Conversely, Hong Kong Chinese were more likely to be afraid to ask their teachers questions and to be questioned by them but the differences, though statistically significant, were relatively small.

Table 9.5 shows perceptions of praise and blame in school. The first two items (5, 'Teachers have told me my class work is good' and 10, 'Teacher tells me I am doing well at school') again demonstrate the similarity between British-Chinese and European British who give strong positive responses. Responses to item 14 ('I have been told in class that my work is poor') produced different responses. The smallest number came from the British-Chinese, more from the European British and most (24 per cent) from the Hong Kong Chinese group. Responses to item 16 ('I am always told off by some teachers')

Table 9.4 Relationships with teachers

Item	Group	N	SA+A %	U %	SD+D %
2. I think teachers like me	UK Chinese	358	45	42	11
	UK Euro	380	36	44	21
	HK Chinese	364	18	65	17
12. I'm scared to ask questions of teachers when I don't understand	UK Chinese	360	24	21	55
	UK Euro	376	25	18	56
	HK Chinese	363	38	19	44
18. I feel scared when my teacher asks me questions about my work	UK Chinese	60	19	26	55
	UK Euro	378	21	23	56
	HK Chinese	363	32	25	43

Note: SA= Strongly agree; A= Agree; U= Uncertain; SD= Strongly disagree; D= Disagree; all differences are significant beyond $p<0.05$, by Chi-squared test.

suggested that this was most likely to be true of European British students (27 per cent) with both British-Chinese and Hong Kong Chinese at 9 per cent.

Differing teaching styles may offer some explanation for these variations. A worrying possibility is that few British-Chinese respondents were told that 'their work was poor' or were 'told off by teachers' because too little was expected of them or because, stereotypically, they were sitting at the back and making no trouble.

Table 9.6 indicates some preferences for working methods in school. There were few marked differences between the three groups and such differences as there were are difficult to interpret. If anything, all three groups favoured projects rather than examinations, though the numbers of those 'uncertain' rather obscured the result. There was a large measure of agreement over the importance of respecting teachers as there was over a preference for working to their own ideas. There was a similar response by all groups to being 'told what to do by teacher'. About a third of all groups either agreed to it, disagreed to it or were uncertain: perhaps, in the end, they were saying that it depended on which teacher was doing the instructing.

Finally, we asked respondents from all three groups what they intended to do when they left school. Did they intend, for example to go to a college or university? Their responses are remarkable in their similarities, with around three quarters in each group saying they intended to go on to further studies.

Table 9.5 Experiences of praise and blame

Item	Group	N	SA+A %	U %	SD+D %
5. Teachers have told me my class work is good	UK Chinese	358	80	14	6
	UK Euro	379	72	18	10
	HK Chinese	362	17	49	69
10. Teacher tells me I am doing well at school	UK Chinese	359	73	19	7
	UK Euro	378	61	23	16
	HK Chinese	360	11	56	32
14. I have been told in class that my work is poor	UK Chinese	359	5	13	80
	UK Euro	377	16	13	71
	HK Chinese	361	24	31	44
16. I am always told off by some teachers	UK Chinese	359	9	15	75
	UK Euro	375	27	17	53
	HK Chinese	362	9	23	67

Note: SA= Strongly agree; A= Agree; U= Uncertain; SD= Strongly disagree; D= Disagree; all differences are significant beyond $p<0.05$ by Chi-squared test.

We asked respondents from all three groups what they intended to do when they left school. Did they intend, for example, to go to a college or university. Their responses are set out in Table 9.7 and are remarkable for their unanimity. Around three-quarters in each group said they intended to go on to further studies.

Conclusions

These results point to a pattern of the general adaptation of pupils of Chinese origin in British schools. By and large there was much similarity in their attitudes to education when compared with their British European peers. There was thus a marked contrast in attitudes to education of the Chinese youth in Britain, in comparison with those of their Hong Kong peers. These results parallel those from the Coopersmith Self Esteem Scale: the more like British pupils these Chinese adolescents became in their educational attitudes, the better was their self esteem. Yet, as other evidence in this study shows, despite

Table 9.6 Preferred working methods

Item	Group	N	SA+A %	U %	SD+D %
23. I prefer examinations and tests to doing projects	UK Chinese	360	29	33	37
	UK Euro	378	21	18	61
	HK Chinese	364	30	28	43
24. It is important to respect teachers	UK Chinese	360	77	16	8
	UK Euro	378	69	17	14
	HK Chinese	364	80	15	5
22. I like to be told what to do by the teacher.	UK Chinese	360	37	31	32
	UK Euro	377	31	30	39
	HK Chinese	363	34	43	23
21. I prefer to work on my own ideas	UK Chinese	359	59	27	13
	UK Euro	379	66	21	13
	HK Chinese	360	54	33	13

Note: SA= Strongly agree; A= Agree; U= Uncertain; SD= Strongly disagree; D= Disagree; only differences for item 23 are significant beyond $p<0.05$, by Chi-squared test. Other items, not significant.

Table 9.7 Post-school aspirations: intentions to enter higher education

	UK Chinese *N=362* %	UK Euro *N=381* %	HK Chinese *N=364* %
Yes	78	72	73
No	6	7	9
Don't know	16	21	18
Missing	0	0	1

Note: X^2, not significant.

considerable acquisition of new language and educational attitudes, the Chinese youth when at home retained a strongly focused attitude on traditional Chinese values and family traditions. In a number of ways, they are getting 'the best of both worlds'.

10 Qualitative Study of Chinese Families in Britain

The Chinese Diaspora

According to Kleinman and Lin (1980), there were at that time at least 20 million Chinese who lived outside China, and the number has increased significantly as Chinese people have migrated in recent years from the People's Republic of China (PRC), from Taiwan, from Hong Kong, and from Macao (a former Portuguese colony close to Hong Kong). Chinese began to emigrate from the beginning of the 18th century. At least 15 million are spread throughout the countries of South East Asia, and more than five million are distributed over the rest of the world.

Most of the Chinese who are now living in Britain were originally from Hong Kong. Most arrived from the early 1960s, due to the collapse of traditional agriculture in the rural New Territories of Hong Kong and the links and opportunities which Britain offered.

Chinese people are dispersed in small groups across Britain and are mainly involved with the restaurant and catering trade. Chinese takeaways are to be found in most towns. It is not possible to find the exact statistics of the Chinese community in Britain because the Census reports only show country of origin. When we compare Chinese with other ethnic minorities in Britain, they are relatively small in number. To most people it does not matter what the numbers are, as 'The Chinese are not a burden on the community. They keep their heads down' (Garvey and Jackson 1975). Watson (1977, pp. 181–2) described the Chinese community as 'Undoubtedly the least understood of all Britain's immigrant minorities. They are hard working, shy, self-sufficient and 'invisible' as they are rarely seen to cause trouble.' Rack (reported in Pan and Goldberg, 1990) described the social image of Chinese in Britain as dominated by the popular view of the Chinese community which maintains a 'quiet position' and is a 'silent minority' within British society. It may be that these are the major reasons which have led to a neglect of studies on the Chinese community by educationalists in particular, and social scientists in general.

The most frequently recorded comments and beliefs about Chinese children and adolescents are from observers of schools. Head-teachers and teachers whom Sham (1990) interviewed commented:

> They seem to get on all right with the other kids in the class, never fighting or disturbing others.

> They work hard on their school work and don't cause any trouble. They are very quiet and polite.

> They seem a very self-contained and self-sufficient group.

> They seem to be doing well enough in their studies.

These views are supported by the research of Fong, who records the stereotypical British view of the 'good' Chinese pupil:

> She is a typical Chinese pupil. She is friendly and helpful, always well-behaved and does her best in school. She is a stable, well-adjusted pupil, most staff have mentioned her as a pleasure to teach(Fong, 1981, p. 17) .

In Simpson's (1987) short but illuminating study based on classroom research on 20 Chinese children in Leeds, he notes the same naïve comments by teachers about Chinese pupils in their class.

> I don't know much about them, they're cute little people. You wouldn't know they were in the room (p. 19).

It seems however that most teachers of British-Chinese pupils have a very positive image of them. Fong (1981) indicated that teachers enjoyed teaching Chinese pupils because 'they were seen as hard working, eager to learn, attentive in class and neat and tidy in their school work.' A typical comment was:

> He is a particularly hard working, intelligent person with special ability in mathematics. His oral English causes no problems, but he still has not mastered some points of grammar and so his written work is not always as good as it would otherwise be (p. 71) .

However, Garvey and Jackson (1975) reported that some of the teachers found it difficult and frustrating to teach British-Chinese pupils.

> He's bursting with enthusiasm. I just wish I knew how to help him, I really do. We just sit looking at one another (Sheffield primary school teacher).
>
> They're as anxious to learn as I am to teach them, but I've no idea where to begin (schoolmaster from Berkshire).
>
> You hardly know they're there.
>
> They're awfully well restrained. It's like another experience having to teach Chinese pupils.
>
> You can ignore them so easily, I mean, they don't ask for more than you want to give them. There is no clamouring, no trouble, but precious little learning either. This sort of behaviour is too tidy somehow, it's all right I suppose but it's not doing the kids any good.
>
> I don't like these impassive faces staring back at me. Sometimes I want to shake them and tell them to protest, react and do something dangerous for a change, but they never do. They look at you as if they're judging you. I've only two in my class, if I had a whole roomful, I'd go mad (Garvey and Jackson, 1975, pp. 28–9).

Fitchett (1976) and Ladlow (1980) noted that pupils of Chinese origin may take a long time to adjust to the English school learning environment. However, with skilful teaching, encouragement, patience and understanding of their cultural values, they can soon learn to participate in school life, enjoy it and perform well. As their confidence is built up, so their achievement levels will increase. According to teachers' assessments on the Bristol Social Adjustment Guide, reported by Taylor (1987), some 70 per cent of Chinese pupils were considered to under-react. This could be a result of shyness, quietness and timidity which inhibited them from interacting with others.

Discussion with teachers and pupils by the author of this section (Sylvia Sham) suggests that teachers often lack an awareness of British-Chinese pupils' cultural background, their language and home life in Britain. Teachers admit that they do not know enough about Chinese culture and even depend on Chinese pupils for this information (Lynn, 1982). Garvey and Jackson (1975) found that in some cases teachers ignored the one or two British-Chinese pupils who might be in their class, or indeed within the school as a whole. They tended to see them as a 'small temporary and insoluble problem which (if ignored firmly enough) will go away.' However, this is not likely to be the case.

Greater Manchester schools (the area in which the case study research was undertaken) experienced an increase of about 800 in the number of former Hong Kong Chinese pupils who enrolled in school for the Autumn term in 1997.

The Meaning of Education for Chinese People

For Chinese people everywhere, education is the 'golden rice bowl' to social mobility and wealth. The rewards for success can be considerable, but are sometimes limited to an elite few. There is a strong cultural tradition in Chinese families that their children should rise above their parents' given station in life. This applies to most Chinese families in Chinese societies all over the world. Suzuky (1980) has also pointed out that education in the Chinese family is associated with high emphasis on collectivism, which defines the academic success of the child as an important source of pride for the entire family. On the other hand, if the child fails in academic terms, that will act as stigma to the family. Therefore in the traditional Chinese family, whether working class or professional, poor or millionaire, there is the same philosophy and value of education.

According to Barker (1968) who undertook field data collection in the New Territories in Hong Kong, university graduates who are successful scholars were most respected on their return to their own village. A celebration would be organised by their families. Such a practice showed that people in rural areas also had high expectations of their children. This is one reason why Chinese society is so intense about education and why children struggle for school success. The pressure to succeed is constant and consequently costs Chinese students a great deal of emotional energy, depression and anxiety. Family pressure and authority force children to do endless homework.

Once we understand the Hong Kong Chinese educational system, pedagogy and the role of a Hong Kong teacher, we can be more aware of British Hong Kong Chinese pupils' educational expectations and aspirations, and particularly the expectations of their parents.

On becoming absorbed in the People's Republic of China in 1997, Hong Kong retains special status as a zone of capitalist free enterprise, and many schools retain their status as institutions of private enterprise. The private sector even after 1997 forms a major part of the Hong Kong educational system. There are three major types of schools. Firstly, there are schools run by the government; secondly, those operated by the voluntary sector but financially sustained by government, while the third type are run and financially supported by individuals or private institutions normally associated with Christian organisations.

Chen and Uttal (1988) describe two types of secondary schooling systems in Hong Kong: the Chinese schools are modelled on the Chinese traditions and the teaching language mainly used is Cantonese. The Chinese secondary schools traditionally represent only some ten per cent of the total number of secondary schools in Hong Kong. The rest are mainly English secondary schools, modelled on the western tradition, although the ratio changed rapidly after 1998, with only a minority of schools employing English as the principal medium. Despite the mode of language teaching, many Hong Kong students struggle with the English language when they enter university. Since most university lectures are still offered in English (by the many expatriate lecturers who have remained in Hong Kong post-1997) there may an increasing problem of academic communication in these tertiary institutions.

The two school systems, English and Chinese, differ in many respects particularly in curriculum design and practice, teaching style, extracurricular activities, and most importantly, educational principles. For example, one colloquial expression of intelligence in Chinese is 'Tsung ming', meaning good hearing and good sight. This is in agreement with the traditional practice among the Chinese that it is a virtue to think more, to use the senses more, and to speak less.

The traditional Chinese schools' teaching method has established a tendency for lessons to be conducted in a monologue by the teacher rather than a discussion between the teachers and pupils. The teachers encourage their pupils to work things out in their heads instead of expressing ideas verbally. Moreover, many researchers have suggested (Stevenson and Stigler, 1992; Bond, 1991) that Chinese pupils' performance on the verbal tests are lower than Western pupils and also that the Chinese pupils are suffering in verbal fluency because they are not trained to develop their debating skills with a superior. They struggle in persuasive argument in new situations because they have less opportunity to develop those skills.

Gibbons (1982) observed that in 90 per cent of Hong Kong primary schools the teaching language was Cantonese, English being taught (if at all) as a second language. If the pupils completed Chinese secondary school, they would have had at least 12 years of Chinese learning and therefore their English would be less proficient. Chann (1976) pointed out that to learn English is twice as difficult 'since it is completely alien to the average child in Hong Kong. English is hardly used or listened to outside the classroom and perhaps is often not taught by proficient teachers'. Lai (1976) and Lee in the ILEA English Centre (1979) show that Hong Kong pupils' spoken English is formal rather than colloquial, and their command is quite poor due to lack of exposure to everyday or conversational English, and the opportunity to practise outside the classroom.

Westcott (1979) pointed out that English has no everyday social function for the majority of the population in Hong Kong. The principal motivation for learning English is for educational and professional advancement. Due to the demands for places in Hong Kong schools the class sizes are often between 35–40 in secondary schools, which provides few opportunities for individual teaching in class.

Hong Kong's children face frequent examinations; at age three at kindergarten, followed by examinations at six years of age to enter the primary school, followed by examinations to enter five years of secondary education. There are school leaving examinations at the end of Form 3 in secondary schools and again at the end of Form 5, completing nine years compulsory schooling. Then there are of one or two years of sixth-form studies leading to the Higher or Advanced Level examinations for entrance to one of the universities. Thus there is clearly a nonstop battle of Hong Kong pupils to struggle through their educational life.

One famous Chinese proverb says 'On one mountain, there can not be two tigers' – only the best can survive and so competitive examinations are accepted as necessary. Another proverb tells 'With fire we test our gold' – children go through intense study and trial to achieve the highest prize. This is why Chinese pupils so often give an impression to the western world that they are highly competitive pupils even within their own group, both at home and in Western schools. Competition is considered a good way for the best pupils to climb to the top and it also produces the best educated and intelligent citizens. This is the logic which still drives much of the Hong Kong educational system.

According to Bray (1991), despite British colonial influence the educational system of Hong Kong has always been more strongly influenced by the cultural tradition of China. Although Hong Kong was for more than a century a British colony, and many aspects of the British educational system were filtered through colonial rule, there has also been an intense desire to continue Chinese tradition and practices. In the *Great Learning* Confucius declares:

> The aims of the great learning consists of illuminating the bright virtue, renewing the people, and resting only in perfection. Thus in ancient times those who

> wanted to illumine the bright virtue in the whole world first sought to govern the country well. Those who want to govern the country well first sought to manage their own families. Those who wanted to manage their own families first sought to control their own hearts. Those who wanted to control their own hearts first sought to purify their motives. Those who wanted to purify their motives first sought to extend their knowledge (Woo, 1985, p. 17).

The above quotation reflects how traditional Chinese thought has been influenced by the philosopher Confucius for over 2,000 years.

The Role of a Hong Kong Teacher

In Britain, discipline is a very topical issue. A Secretary of State for Education has shown his concern over poor discipline in schools and advocates the importance of the religious/moral values of the home in halting deteriorating trends (Ghuman, 1993). We hardly hear about vandalism and discipline problems in Hong Kong Schools. Hong Kong pupils treat their teachers as stern parents. They respond to them with silence, attention, fear and obedience. Questioning teachers or challenging the teachers' judgements is considered unacceptable behaviour (Morris, 1981).

Chinese culture places a great emphasis on respecting superiors' rule, whether this be a teacher or an employer. Pupils always respect and obey as if the teacher is a surrogate father or emperor. Within the Chinese culture, the teacher is a highly professional and well educated person, commanding the same respect as is due to one's father. The LIewellyn Report on Hong Kong education (1982) says: 'Many who become teachers often seem to be in search of an opportunity to raise their social and professional status.' 'Disobedience' in Chinese is composed of two characters, translated into English as meaning 'mouth back'. Thus pupils show their respect by keeping quiet. Stevenson and Stigler (1992) point out that Chinese pupils are traditionally self-disciplined.

In 1946, there was a great demand for teachers in Hong Kong. It was impossible to recruit highly educated teachers, therefore those who had completed a Form 5 education themselves were allowed to teach up to Form 5. No doubt, the quality and standard of teaching of some of these minimally qualified teachers tended to be low. It seemed at that time almost anybody could teach without qualification or training. Today Hong Kong teachers must have completed a certain level of higher education, but compared with Western standards and training they may still have questionable competence. In Fong's study (1981) into teachers and pupils' perceptions of teacher effectiveness she stated that 'Examination orientation is reflected in Hong Kong'. Teachers in Hong Kong 'are less concerned about their pupils as persons'. Hong Kong teachers seem to be autocratic and do not experience learning as a pleasure. They see themselves as imparters of knowledge. Teachers and pupils are self-sufficient, they do not wish to show their personal problems. In the early 1990s, the Hong Kong Institute of Education was founded, separately from the seven universities, and offers advanced courses in teacher training as well as post-qualifying courses for many of Hong Kong's teachers.

From ancient times in Chinese society, an educated person had to be a man who had memorised the classics. Even today, Hong Kong's educational philosophy still values the importance of memory work.

The Chinese teaching style is extremely formal, even from the earliest experience in the Kindergarten. Imagine entering a nursery age class – the 30–35 chairs and desks are arranged in uniform rows, nursery age children sit quietly or are holding a pencil trying to write their Chinese name, there are no toys or paint brushes.

In primary schools, a teacher talks and the pupils listen. A typical example is that of a teacher reading from a textbook and the pupil underlining the important sections or copying the notes from the blackboard. Occasionally the teacher asks questions of the whole class. Silence usually results because the children rarely volunteer answers. According to the Llewellyn Report: '... all was deadly earnest and students were seen taking notes, laboriously completing model answers and learning texts by rote' (Llewellyn, 1982, p. 15).

Role play, group discussion and games are not often used in class unless a visitor comes into a lesson. The teachers and pupils believe that games are not a serious way to learn and are a waste of time. Group discussion is thought to lead to indiscipline and noise. Several well documented studies by Wang (1982), Scovel (1983) and Oatey (1984) describe the reality of mainland China where pupils' attitudes in class are characterised by modesty and quietness and pupils refrain from spontaneously putting forward views and opinions.

Similar observations have been made by Morris (1981) who describes Hong Kong education as:

> A teaching and learning style which is characterised as being didactic, teacher-centred and theoretical. Rote learning, memorisation of passages, a strict adherence to the examination syllabus are the rule rather than the exception.

> The teacher's role is perceived as the provider of knowledge, defined in the sense of product rather than process. The pupil's role is that of a passive receiver of knowledge and diligence is perceived as the primary condition determining success (pp. 257–9).

Hong Kong pupils who have had a significant amount of education in Hong Kong before entering British schools face additional difficulties in their new environment not only because they lack information about their new life in Britain, but also because they come with a different cultural background and school experience in relation to their learning styles and preferred teaching styles. There is evidence which indicates that these cultural factors are persistent in the Chinese community, even after acclimatisation.

Problems Encountered During the Qualitative Study

Before approaching the specific methods and particular methodology chosen for gathering case study data, three main obstacles were identified. One was that the largest section of the Chinese minority group living in Britain could be described as family business people. From our personal experience many work unsocial hours, for example from 10:00 am until 12:00 am the following day, six days a week in their own 'take-away shops', and frequently seven days a week in restaurants and food catering businesses. They are usually very busy and also often suspicious of people asking questions. It was difficult to find families who would cooperate with the Chinese researcher.

Additionally, researchers have found difficulty in obtaining cooperation from the minority of educated Chinese professionals and politicians. Although they have become leaders and powerful people within the Chinese community, they appear unwilling to share their knowledge. Some previous researchers like O'Neill (1972), Cheung (1975), Lai (1975), Tsow (1984) and Taylor (1987) also experienced obstacles in gaining access to educated Chinese people in conducting research on Chinese communities in the Britain. Our recent research experience in China Town in Liverpool, London and Greater Manchester confirms these experiences

Finally, many Chinese people are reluctant to show or share their problems as they are afraid of 'losing face', having a strict belief in the ancient Chinese proverb: 'Every family has a skeleton in the cupboard' which should be kept within the family and not discussed outside. We accept this reluctance as a starting point for the qualitative research, since as Robson (1994, p. 26) argues, successful research develops from having 'real world value' with problems arising from the field.

Since the field researcher was of the same linguistic and ethnic group as the Chinese people studied, efforts were made not to take for granted a personal culture and experience, avoiding perceptions arising from a 'commonsense' interpretation of Chinese culture.

Case Study Interviews

This chapter concentrates on five case studies of British-Chinese families in the Greater Manchester area. The female researcher (Syliva Sham) had become friendly with the five Chinese families (all of whom owned 'take-aways'), and they invited her to meals and celebrations such as Chinese New Year, a traditional Chinese wedding party and birthdays. The researcher was often asked by Chinese parents to help with English, ranging from translating letters, going to school parents' evenings, visiting the doctor as a translator, writing letters and giving help to fill in forms.

All these informal and formal contacts enabled the researcher to establish a good network and firm relationships with a number of Chinese families. The researcher is accepted by most families as a friend and an adviser to the parents' generation and was thus able to identify suitable families and seek permission from those families for the study. In the context of each home, this study aimed to obtain data on a series of cultural practices which represented typical events, and which reflected the range of Chinese family living patterns in Britain. The researcher aimed to develop a confidence of approach by working with the wide age range of family members consistent with life history methods.

A Typical Weekday in Four of the Five Family Case Studies

In order to give the reader an overview of the life of several children whose parents own take-away shops, there follows a brief description of a typical week day in four of the five family case studies.

Four pm after school to most British children is the end of a busy day, but not for many Chinese children in Britain. For them, it is only the beginning of their working day. Many Chinese children go straight to the kitchen to eat their early supper, because normally their parents will have prepared some

Chinese noodles or fried rice which will be waiting for them as they return from school. After eating this supper and then getting changed, the work begins. The oldest brother or sister will switch on the potato peeling machine or the second elder sister or brother will switch on the huge chip pans to get the oil hot enough for deep fried fish and chips. The rest of the children know what to do. The whole family aims to be ready for six o'clock (opening time) or earlier in one example. One child will chop onions or mushrooms, another will beat eggs or soak noodles. Father is chef. He prepares the barbecued ribs or roast pork, mother will prepare the chicken, cut it in portions and cook the rice.

Sons or daughters between eight or 10 years of age each have their duties, which are often to look after their younger sisters or brothers as child-minders in the middle rooms or to work in the kitchen, washing the vegetables, sometimes standing on a stool because they are not tall enough to reach the sink. Most evenings are full of action and activities in the shop, the kitchen and the back or middle room. The telephone rings time after time from customers ordering from the take-away menus. The order forms are full of numbers indicating the different dishes which are passed to the chef. The older children help father (the chef) by stirring the fried rice and helping with other tasks in the kitchen. The little ones fill the containers, carry on chopping and those who understand some English answer the telephone. Their working day is well under way.

During business hours all the children will have their own favourite corner where they do their homework, for example, the top of the fridge or freezer, and their own chair or stool which they go to when they have no customers. This is their only opportunity to complete their homework. Sometimes on busy evenings, they do not have a chance to complete their homework before midnight.

Normally, meal time is about nine o'clock each evening or whenever the take-away has only a few customers. Mother will shout 'Supper ready!' Children lay the table with chopsticks; rice bowls and Chinese spoons are all placed in the correct position. One by one delicious meals such as steamed fish, fried Chinese leaves with dried shrimps and mushrooms, roast pork and duck are placed in the middle of the table. Every day they have different dishes and soups such as chicken with Chinese mushroom and dried scallop soup or Chinese herbs with chicken feet soup. Father cooks the dishes and mother, with another child, dependent upon how many children they have in each family, looks after the counter.

The researcher was always given the first bowl of rice. The children always gave the bowl of rice to the researcher with both hands, before filling up the rice in each of the other rice bowls for the rest of the family members. Others help to place dishes on the table. Each family member knows where they sit and how to behave during meals times. They try to eat as quickly as they can because the bell from the front door indicates customers, and they need to move quickly.

During the meal the atmosphere is one of silence with only the TV flickering and talking from the corner. Everybody has to concentrate on eating. There is no time to communicate at all. The ones who are helping mother at the counter always sit near the door to the counter, he/she would stand up immediately even though half way through eating a piece of roast pork. Father would be shovelling his rice very quickly into his mouth before getting the orders from the counter.

Finally, the parents serve the last of the customers and cash up the till. Everywhere has to be cleaned and made tidy. It is time for bed. It may be midnight or even 1:00 am.

In the morning mother and the eldest children will help the younger children get ready for school. Mother will prepare the breakfast. There is no sign of cornflakes or toast. Usually they have hot noodle soup or some Dim-Sum which would have been bought from China Town on the Sunday outing. Mother will most likely return to join father in bed for three hours until opening time at noon or thereabouts.

Over a period of eighteen months the researcher visited these five families in the Greater Manchester area on numerous occasions. There follows an account of each family, beginning with a brief description of the individual family background, followed by an account of specific cultural values and practices in the families. The first section is essentially the 'data base' from which the second is drawn.

Case Study 1	**The Mg family**
Origin:	From Hong Kong's New Territories
Family members:	Father
	Mother
	Two children:
	Ben (16 years old) son
	Ken (21 years old) son
General information:	Mr and Mrs Mg were immigrants to Britain nearly 20 years ago in 1975. They own their own take-away shop and live there.

Family Background

Mr and Mrs Mg married in Hong Kong in 1972. Wai Mg worked as a chef and Mrs Mg was a housewife. Their first son Ken was born three years later in 1975. When Ken was two, his father left for London's China Town to work as a chef. He returned to Hong Kong each year and in 1980 Ben was born. When Ken was seven and Ben two, they travelled to England with mother to be reunited with their father. After a while, mother, Ken and Ben were sent to Manchester's China Town to rent a take-away shop. They tried to set up their own business while father continued to work in London to earn more money to pay the rent for the Manchester shop which served as their home. After three years, they bought their own take-away business. Ken was seven years old when he arrived in England. He attended a primary school. Ben stayed at home with his mother and never went to nursery. Ben was seven years old when his mother took him to the local primary school.

Neither of their parents speaks or understands anything other than simple English. They did not know of any support services available for the early stages of their lives in Britain. They have employed Hong Kong overseas students to give private tutorials for their sons from the start of their schooling up until the present. Ken has now completed his secondary education and passed five GCSEs, including Physics and Mathematics. He was happy that he had eventually passed the GCSE in English. In order to fulfil his parents' expectation to achieve a degree level education, he tried twice to pass A-Level Physics, and it took three attempts before he passed the English at GCSE. He is now in the second year of a 2+2 HND and Bachelor of Engineering degree course at the local college.

Ben has spent most of his infant life at home, but he has had more opportunities to mix with English children than his elder brother. His performance at school was average. He was seen by his teachers as a passive and lonely pupil who did not cooperate with group work. He passed GCSE level in Mathematics and Computer studies with A Grades and GCSE English with a C Grade. Although he tried very hard to persuade his parents to let him leave school when he was 16 and then to go to college to study for a GNVQ and then to go to university, Ben's parents believed strongly that Ben was too young to go to college. They were concerned that he would mix with ill-behaved English students and not concentrate on his studies. Finally, Ben stayed at his sixth form. Both boys were expected to help out at the parents' take-away throughout their childhood and this is still the situation as this research progresses.

Language

During business time, when the telephone rang, Ben or Ken answered the telephone and took the orders. They both speak fluent English. The researcher noted that Ben and Ken's mother never had any inclination to answer the phone. One evening when Ben had just gone upstairs, Ken was busy cooking with his father in the kitchen and mother was in the shop at the counter near the telephone. The researcher was in the middle-room when the phone rang. It rang and rang again. Suddenly the voice came from the counter in Cantonese. 'Miss S____ Could you help me to take the order from the phone, I don't know what they want if they do not order by numbers from the menu.' She evidently spoke little English. Ken told the researcher later, 'My mother and father do not speak English at all. My mother doesn't understand but sometimes she talks English like "salt and vinegar?", "gravy?" My father's English is worse than my mother's. Father has been in England for 19 years and mother for 14 years.'

During the whole of the three-month period of visiting this family, the researcher never heard either parents or children speak English other than to enquire about salt, vinegar or gravy, or state the price of the food or to pass the time of day. The whole family speak Cantonese all the time. Ken and Ben told the researcher they felt more comfortable speaking Cantonese at home and using English at school. The mother of the two children told the researcher that Ben's knowledge of Chinese is limited. He does not have any problem in understanding or speaking in Cantonese but he cannot read or write in Chinese, not like his elder brother Ken who does not have any problem with Chinese at all.

A Sense of Respect

No matter what the situation, the researcher never heard the younger brother Ben address his older brother by his first name at all. He always called him *Di Lao*, that is big brother rather than Ken, whereas Ken called his little brother by his first name, Ben. Occasionally, Ken would tell the researcher that it would be better to ask '*my Xiao*' which means little brother. Everyone in the family always addressed the researcher as Miss S____. On every single occasion, when the researcher arrived at the take-away, Ben's parents told the sons to make tea. They always asked the researcher if she would like English or Chinese tea. The researcher heard Ken's father shout at them from the kitchen, 'Of course! Miss S____ likes Chinese tea! Chinese tea! for Miss

S____. Don't forget to give Miss S____ a cup of tea with both your hands this time! It is bad manners and very rough to give our guest a cup of tea with one hand!' Ben's mother asked the researcher, 'Will you stay for dinner tonight because Ken's father specially cooked Chinese mushrooms with dried scollop and chicken soup and Chinese roast pork?'

Respect for Elders and a Sense of Loyalty

Ken planned to go to Hong Kong for his summer holiday. He asked his mother, 'What do you want me to take back for grandmother in China this time? I will spend my first week in China visiting grandmother.' The researcher asked Ken 'Do you visit your grandmother every time when you go for a holiday?' 'Yes! I am the eldest grandson in the whole family. I will visit all the relatives from my father's side and then go to my relatives on my mother's side in Hong Kong. By the time I have done all the duties my holiday will be finished!' The researcher asked him 'Do you mind at all?' He replied that it did not bother him. 'I had a good time.'

Obedience

The researcher observed one day that when Ben was upstairs doing his homework and music was playing, that his father went upstairs and observed his son doing two activities simultaneously, homework and listening to music. Father became very cross and asked Ben's mother how Ben could do the homework and listen to music, 'He cannot really concentrate on his homework.' He called him down to chop onions and Ben came down immediately. There was no apparent anger or annoyance and he was instantly obedient even though the homework was needed for 9:00 am the next day.

During three months visiting Ben and Ken's family, the researcher never heard any arguing between sons and parents. The children in the family are always told what to do, and they do not ask any questions. They just receive the orders, and obedience rules in the family.

Tradition

The researcher was invited to a family wedding party. It was a brother of Ken's mother who was marrying a British-born Chinese girl. They had a very traditional Wedding Party. All the guests were picked up in Manchester's China Town by coach one Monday and were taken to a Birmingham Chinese restaurant to arrive at 3:00 pm. Most of the guests had a take-away or restaurant to run during the evenings and at weekends so the wedding was scheduled for Monday when most take-aways were closed. There were more than 200 guests. As in most traditional Chinese Wedding parties, each round table had 12 guests. Dishes were served continuously for four hours of nonstop eating. The bride wore a red and golden embroidered wedding dress and the bridegroom wore a dark blue suit. On that day Ken played the important role as the first eldest grandson in the family. His behaviour was very different. He was full of confidence, leading the guests and looking after the situation. He made sure that the drinks and food were well organised and the guests were looked after. At the end of the party, the bride and groom, and the close relatives such as the bride's parents and groom's close relatives, stood at the exit and shook hands, to say thank you and goodbye to the guests.

Reading and Writing

After two weeks of visiting Ken's family in the evening when they were busy, the researcher decided to plan visiting in the afternoon between 2:00 pm to 4:00 pm. This was the only time that the researcher could have the chance of talking to Ken's parents without disturbing their business and it seemed to be a more relaxed atmosphere. Ken's mother always invited the researcher to go upstairs to their lounge-room. Upstairs has the lounge-room, three bedrooms and a bathroom.

The impression the researcher gained from their living accommodation, even though this family has lived in England for a considerable time, was that the home in every way was typical of a Hong Kong household. There is a big television set with video-recorder, which they brought from Hong Kong, in the right corner, by the side of the television there is a huge book shelf, six feet tall and four feet wide which has row upon row of videos placed on it. There must have been more than 40 videos. There is a calendar displaying a beautiful Hong Kong night sky.

A few Kung Fu comedy books and some Chinese newspapers were placed upon a glass topped table which is in front of a leather sofa. Ken's mother showed the researcher around the house. Ken's bedroom is full of Manchester United football team posters and there are a few Manchester United football t-shirts hanging on the wall. His mother told the researcher that Ken is mad on football, but he has never been to a football match. The researcher asked why he did not go to football matches. The answer was that football is played in their working hours so they do not allow him to go. His desk was full of

Physics and Maths books but his book shelf was full of Kung Fu comedy books in Chinese writing. Ken's mother told the researcher that Ken only reads those rubbish Kung Fu comedy books. He buys some every week from China Town.

Ben's bedroom is full of drawing papers, computer magazines and boxes of computer games. He spends all his money on computer games. His father gets very cross because both boys spend their Saturday morning or after business is closed, playing computer games. Ken's mother says that they do not read much. Ken's father reads Chinese newspapers as does Ken, but not Ben.

Family Time: Entertainment, Television and Videos

Ken's father told the researcher that their two children always complained of being bored during their school half term, Christmas, Easter and summer holiday. They tried to do their best to take them to visit different friends and relatives or invited some of their relatives to come over to have big Chinese dinners. As he pointed out, they work all evening from 4:00 pm onwards to 12:00 pm, and asked where can they go? If they go further away, they need to rush back. He says that they do everything together as a family. They do not like their two boys hanging round with their English school friends. The boys themselves do not like to go out with their school friends either.

Ken's parents say that they watch videos most of the time, except that the boys also watch football. Most of the videos are recorded from Chinese Satellite Channel at night as often they are too busy or too tired to watch at the time of transmission. They go to China Town to do their grocery shopping, then go to the video shop to hire a number of Hong Kong films to watch for the week. Their children know all the Hong Kong films and pop singers and stars better than English stars.

Educational Expectations

Ben and Ken's parents told the researcher that they encourage their children to study as much as they want. Ken is now going to college to study for a HND in Engineering and then will take two more years to complete his degree at Manchester University. They believe that it is very important to have a degree or other qualification nowadays, but at the end of the day, 'We keep telling Ken that once we reach retirement age, this business will belong to him. It is a profitable business. Ken is the eldest son in our family. He should take this responsibility. He understands. However, Ken plans to go back to Hong Kong once he has completed his degree. Do you think he is silly? There are a million people in Hong Kong who want to come here because of 1997. My son! going back!, because he went back to Hong Kong for his summer holiday! He had a good time with my brothers and sisters. We do not think he realises once he works and lives in Hong Kong that it will be a different story. Truthfully, we do not think he will do that.'

Case Study 2	**The Lee family**
Origin:	From Hong Kong
Family members:	Father
	Mother
	Two daughters:
	Mei-Ling (15 years old) daughter
	Yuen Yuee (10 years old) daughter
General information:	The Lee family have lived in Britain for 25 years. They own a take-away shop and a Chinese restaurant.

Family Background

Mei-Ling (now 15) was born in Britain. When she was just one her parents sent her back to Hong Kong to be looked after by her father's parents. Then she came back to Britain at age seven. She lives with her younger sister (Yuen Yuee) who is ten, and who was also born in Britain. Their house is 10 minutes walk from their take-away shop.

Twenty-five years ago, Mei-Ling's father was a chef in a small restaurant in Hong Kong. He came to Britain because he wanted to build up his own business. At that time, his cousin was running a restaurant in Liverpool. His cousin paid his fare to enable him to work with him as a chef and offered to double his income. Mei-Ling's father thought that it seemed to be the only opportunity available to improve his income and there was also the chance to go abroad. Mei-Ling's father told the researcher that he cannot speak a word of English. He only completed his primary education and then went to his father's friends to work in a kitchen for eight years, to learn how to cook. He always wanted to have his own restaurant one day, to acquire capital, to have a good life. When he arrived in Liverpool he worked 20 hours per day and did nothing other than work most evenings and sleep every morning. The only way to spend his income was in supporting his parents in Hong Kong, and he saved the rest. He said he was very good with his money; no smoking, drinking or gambling in the casino. 'I kept working hard to hope that one day my dream would come true that I would have my own restaurant. Now I have got a restaurant and one take-away shop which is the result of all my hard work.'

After four years, Mei-Ling's father met his wife (Fung) in Liverpool. Fung had just come to Liverpool from the New Territories to help her father in their take-away because her mother was very ill. After a one year relationship, they decided to get married and moved from Liverpool to Manchester. Mei-Ling's father felt sufficiently independent to have his own take-away shop. He spent all his savings and bought a take-away shop from his friend in Manchester. One year after the marriage, Mei-Ling was born. Her parents found it difficult to run a business with a baby, so they took Mei-Ling back to Hong Kong to be looked after by her father's family. With both parents working and living on the premises of the take-away, one of them was able to fly back to Hong Kong every year to see Mei-Ling.

When she was seven years old, and had completed her first year in primary education in Hong Kong, she came back to Britain because her younger sister had just been born. Her parents needed her to look after the new baby, Yuen Yuee, who is now 10 years old.

Mei-Ling will take her GCSE examinations this coming summer. Then she wants to go to college to study A-Level Art or GNVQ in Art and Design. Yuen Yuee is still in her local primary school.

Language

Mei-Ling's family speak Cantonese as their first language and this is the dominant language in their home. Mei-Ling and Yuen Yuee were brought up speaking Cantonese as their first language. Mei-Ling's mother told the researcher that her children are so used to speaking English at school that they had to insist on their speaking English: Mei-Ling's father gets cross and shouts 'Speak to us in Cantonese.'

Mei-Ling's told the researcher that when she started primary school, she had to speak English for the first time and she became silent. She developed a dumbness. She was ashamed, even when she wanted to go to the toilet or to ask a simple question in front of the class, or ask the direction of a bus driver. She described how she stood frozen or she would hold up the line with back to front grammatical sentences. Friends or teachers kept asking her, 'What do you say?', ' What did you want?' The first two months of the time when she had just come to Britain, her parents bought a lot of English tapes for her to keep listening to and repeating sentences again and again. They believed that this was the way to learn English and employed an overseas student from Hong Kong who came to their house. Mei-Ling has a private one-hour tutorial in English and Maths every Wednesday and Monday after school.

Mei-Ling's mother told the researcher that Mei-Ling had done well in school, always getting a very good report, but she did not praise her in front of the researcher. She showed all Mei-Ling's school reports from the last four years. She said, 'You can read English, you know what the comments are? We need to depend on Mei-Ling's father's elder brother's son to translate the school report into Chinese for us. He's got a degree.' Mei-Ling also taught Yuen Yuee to write her Chinese name.

Mei-Ling and Yuen Yuee's parents seem to be particularly concerned about their two daughters since they often speak to each other in English. Their parents are deeply concerned that they will lose their fluency in Cantonese, especially Yuen Yuee who hardly ever speaks Cantonese outside home. 'We sent her to Sunday school to learn and write Chinese.' Mei-Ling's parents were more concerned that their two daughters were more and more becoming *Gweilo*. 'One day they may not be able to speak to us in Cantonese, so how could we expect them to speak Cantonese with their grandparents and relatives? I will be ashamed of being Chinese. Yuen Yuee will not talk to us. It may be she cannot put words together, but she can understand more than she can speak out in sentences.' They strongly believe that Cantonese is part of their cultural background. However, they have a conflict here, because being able to speak English is essential for a career in Britain.

Yuen Yuee told the researcher that her parents speak funny English. 'They don't pronounce properly. If I correct my parents the way they pronounce, my father becomes very angry. He just does not like me to correct his mistakes. He said that I am more like *Gweilo/Gweilpor* picking up his mistakes which shows there is no respect at all and I am cheeky.'

A Sense of Respect

Whenever the researcher was with Mei-ling's family, she always heard Yuen Yuee call her sister *Di Ga Jay* which means big sister. Mei-Ling calls Yuen *Yuee Xiao* which means little sister. They always address the researcher as 'Miss S____', as do Mei-Ling's parents. The researcher suggested they should call her by her first name, but they both replied that their parents would be cross, 'We can not, we must call you Miss S____ because you are older than us and you are a teacher.'

The researcher asked Mei-Ling if she knew why her parents sent money to her grandparents. Mei-Ling replied that all the Chinese people do that. 'My mum has always told me to take care of my grandparents and my little sister, if anything were to happen to them.' Mei-Ling told the researcher that she feels very responsible, because her parents have been working hard all their lives to bring them up and she is the eldest daughter in the family. 'There is no one else to help them, once they get old.'

Obedience

On one or two occasions, the researcher heard Yuen Yuee ask her father whether she could go on a school trip outing the next Saturday or Sunday with her class and teacher. Her father replied, 'No' without any explanation as to why she could not go, other than, 'You know Sunday school is on Sunday!' Yuen Yuee did not argue. She walked away from the situation.

Reading and Writing

The researcher's first impression of Mei-Ling's home was that she felt she had gone back to Hong Kong! There are two big Chinese-style paintings in the hall. In the lounge there is a pile of Chinese newspapers, magazines and equivalent of *TV Times*, all from Hong Kong. There is nothing in English. There are dozens of Chinese videos on the book shelf. Mei-Ling's mother told the researcher that Mei-Ling helps them to write letters to relatives in Hong Kong. 'That will keep Mei-Ling practising her Chinese writing. If we do not force her to write in Chinese, she will forget it all sooner or later. But Yuen Yuee cannot write a sentence in Chinese at all. What can we do? We keep asking her grandparents to post us some Hong Kong primary school text books and exercise books for her to practise her Chinese writing.'

On one occasion, the researcher was invited into Mei-Ling and Yuen Yuee's bedrooms. There were a few Hong Kong pop singers posters on the wall and half a dozen Chinese novels – love story novels and some magazines from Hong Kong. The researcher asked Mei-Ling what kinds of music she liked to listen to and she showed the researcher all her Hong Kong cassettes which she had bought from China Town on Sundays. Yuen Yuee's bedroom is full of primary school text books from Hong Kong. She had two English books from her present school. Yuen Yuee told the researcher that she hated writing in Chinese, as it is very hard and boring, 'My father makes me copy and copy my Chinese name more than 100 times until I get it correct.'

Family Time: Entertainment, Videos and Television

Mei-Ling's mother told the researcher that the family spends a lot of time together except when their two daughters go to school. 'Probably the *Gweilo* neighbour thinks that we use our two daughters as a sort of cheap labour because they often help us in the take-away shop after school. They should take the responsibility, let them know it is not easy to earn the pennies. If we work hard together, we can go back to Hong Kong every summer for a holiday and also we both do not like them to be hanging around in town with their *Gweilo* friends. Most of them are very naughty, because there is nothing to do in the evening. Their parents do not care about them and let them do what they want. But it would not happen in our family. My husband is very strict with his two daughters, especially Mei-Ling. He will not let Mei-Ling go to any of her friends' birthday parties or discos because he is concerned that she will have a boy friend and then get pregnant. You know here in England, 14 or 15 year-olds get pregnant.'

Mei-Ling and Yuen Yuee told the researcher that they hardly ever had time or the chance to sit down to watch programmes like *Neighbours* or *Blue Peter*. When we are in school, all our friends are talking about what happened to Sam and Annalise last night. We just feel fools because our parents always put Cantonese videos on the television. Yuen Yuee said that at the beginning that she did not like to watch the Chinese videos because it did not make sense to her. She did not know what they were talking about because it was all in Cantonese, it seemed to be as background music. Only on Monday evenings when our parents go to visit our uncle Wing, who is my father's brother, I do have a chance to see what I want to watch. My *Di Ga-Jay* (big sister) just stays in her bedroom listening to Cheung Kwok Wing tapes. He is a pop singer in Hong Kong or she revises for her GCSE examinations. She is boring.'

The sisters told the researcher, 'Saturday and Sunday are our favourite days. We can have a lie-in in the morning. Afterwards we watch Cantonese videos together because my mother records the Satellite Chinese Channel at night.' Most of the 'Chinese soaps' are all around family conflict or how people become successful, Mei-Ling said, 'You (the researcher) know! Last night you watched that programme with us, my mother kept saying that when we grow up, we would not treat our parents like that – would we?'

Family Activities

During the visit to the Mei-Ling's family ,the researcher was invited by Mei-

Ling's parents to stay over night so that the next morning the researcher could go to Mei-Ling's father's restaurant. They go to China Town in Manchester every Sunday. That is the only day they go out. It was 11:30 am by the time we arrived in China Town. Mei-Ling's father dropped Yuen Yuee off at Sunday school and Mei-Ling went to the Chinese Art shop to buy all Hong Kong cassettes and magazines or posters. Mei-Ling's mother told the researcher that they would meet us in the restaurant. Mei-ling's father treated the researcher as an honoured guest. He introduced her to all his friends and relatives in the restaurant.

Aspirations

Mei-Ling's father told the researcher that they encourage their two daughters to study as much as they want. 'It does not cost much to send them to school or university. The government pays for it. Education is most important for them. Not like us. It is a hard life and there are long working hours to earn our money. We do not expect our children to work in either the take-away or the restaurant, especially as they are both girls. When they grow up with a good education then they will marry a good man. We will sell our business and go back to our homeland, to Hong Kong, to retire.'

Case Study 3	**The Chan family**
Origin:	From Hong Kong's New Territories
Family members:	Grandfather (Mr Chan) Grandmother (Mrs Chan) Father Chan (Junior) Mother Five children: Wai Yee (14 yrs) daughter Wai Ling (11 yrs) daughter Wai Kit (8 yrs) daughter Wai Mei (5 yrs) daughter Wing Hing (two months old son)
General information:	Mr Chan's parents were immigrants to Britain from Hong Kong in 1958. Mr and Mrs Chan own a take-away shop in Manchester.

Family Background

Mr Chan's father is a first generation migrant to Hong Kong from China. He worked as an accountant in the International Textile Silk Company. His firm had different branches all over the world. His degree qualification was in Economics from Peking University. In addition to his hard-working attitude and his fluency in English, he was recommended by his manager to work in the head office in Britain. At that time, people like Mr Chan's father were in the minority. Working abroad was an honour to the family. He started to work in one of the branches in Liverpool. After working five years in Liverpool, he decided to return to Hong Kong to look for a wife. Eventually, he brought his wife as an immigrant into Britain from Hong Kong to start a family in Liverpool. They produced four sons, who were all born in England and were all educated in Liverpool.

The eldest son completed his secondary education in his local school and started working in a Chinese restaurant as a waiter which he has done for the last 10 years in Liverpool. His father then made an arrangement for him to marry a girl from China, because his father did not want his eldest son to marry an English girl. Now Mr and Mrs Chan (Junior) have four daughters and one son and live in Greater Manchester. They have their own take-away.

Their four daughters Wai Yee (14), Wai Ling (11), Wai Kit (8), Wai Mei (5) and the two months old son Wing Hing were all born in England. The Chan family live a 20 minutes walk from their take-away. The three elder girls go to the local school in Manchester. Wai Mei and Wing Hing stay at home with their grandparents who have now moved from Liverpool to Manchester and live with their eldest son.

Although Mr Chan (Junior) grew up and was educated in Britain, he feels more comfortable practising the Chinese traditional way of life. His wife, in particular, holds a strong belief in Chinese values. They teach their children to behave in particular ways so that they do not offend their grandparents who live with them. When all four daughters finish school the family intention is that they will go straight into the take-away to begin their working lives. Their newly-born son Wing Hing will go to University!

Language

Mr and Mrs Chan Junior's family spoke to the researcher in Cantonese all the time. Mr Chan Junior speaks fluent English, so he takes telephone orders and his wife does the cooking in the kitchen. All four daughters speak Cantonese with their parents and grandparents. Wai Yee (14), the eldest daughter, told the researcher that her mother cannot understand English, so they are better talking in Cantonese. 'Sometimes when I explain things to my father, I speak in English, because I do not know how to explain in Cantonese.' 'My grandfather always corrects our mistakes if we speak the wrong way round in Cantonese.'

Writing and Reading

Each Saturday, Wai Yee's grandfather teaches the children to write Chinese characters. Wai Ling told the researcher that grandfather is very strict and serious about it. 'If we do not sit straight or hold the pens properly, he will smack our hands, or he will hold our hand and move our hand with his hand, together with the pen, so we can follow his movement to copy the words. Normally, grandfather writes the word inside a square and asks us to copy exactly the same, until we can do it. We have repeated practice every single Saturday and we do it again in the Sunday school.'

In their middle room, is a pile of Chinese newspapers, magazines, Hong Kong primary school text books and exercise books for them to practise their Chinese writing. Wai Yee and Wai Ling told the researcher that they can only write their Chinese names and some simple words. The researcher heard the grandfather tell a story to the three younger granddaughters. The story began about the Chinese Confucian philosopher. When he was young, his mother insisted on moving three times to different neighbourhoods to find one that would be the most favourable for him to concentrate on studying. After the story finished, the grandfather told the children that they must be 'good girls' and love their parents, who do everything for them like the mother of Mencius.

A Sense of Respect

Whenever the researcher was with Mr and Mrs Chan's family, all their daughters addressed their sisters in terms of the position in the family. The younger children never call the elders by their first name. They say big sister number one, or sister number two or sister number three, etc. They always addressed the researcher as 'Miss S_____.'

The children regard Mr and Mrs Chan and grandfather as authority figures who are held in high regard. Grandfather, in particular, was very highly regarded. Some evidence indicated that the children always gave grandfather a cup of tea first or addressed him first rather than their parents.

Authority

On one occasion, when the researcher talked with Mr Chan about his teenage time in Britain, Mrs Chan was heard shouting at Wai Ling from the kitchen. 'Put the video back Wai Ling, I want to hear what happened to ...' because Wai Ling had switched on BBC1 to watch *Neighbours*. Wai Ling turned on the video for her mother without saying a word or displaying any angry expression. Mrs Chan came out and smacked her on the head.

Another instance, during the researcher's time with the Chan family, Wai Ling (number two) asked her mother if she could go out to her best friend's birthday party on Saturday afternoon. Her mother replied, 'No, you need to practise your Chinese writing.' Wai-Ling did not express her disappointment, she simply walked away from the situation. She did not argue at all.

Family Time: Entertainment, Television and Videos

Wai Yee's grandfather told the researcher that he spent a lot of time looking after the children for his son because they were busy at the take-away shop. 'We are a Chinese family living in a foreign land. We should look after and help each other to prevent Western people looking down on us.' Wai Yee's grandfather said that the elder granddaughter is very good at helping her parents during the evenings and that she understands that as a family we do need to help each other. She never asks to go out with her friends from the school, because she knows that if she goes out with her friends, her parents will have to work very hard without her help. We need to train them when they are still young, to make them realise the responsibility they are to themselves and to the family as a whole. They just do as they are told without negotiation, unlike many children in Britain. Most Sunday afternoons, their parents go to shopping in Manchester's China Town. Their daughters go to Sunday school to learn Chinese. On Mondays, which is their day off, they visit relatives or some friends come to their house to have dinner. The elder ones will do their homework or listen to their own music, the younger ones will watch Cantonese videos with their parents. The researcher never saw any toys or games around at their house, despite the presence of four young children.

Educational Expectations

Mr Chan attended all the parents' evenings when his elder daughter was in primary school to show that he cared about his daughters. But Mr Chan does not go any more as he believes that the education in England is of poor quality. His view is that the teachers do not care about their pupils' progress, there is no discipline and no homework. Mr and Mrs Chan (Junior) told the researcher that notwithstanding the faults of the state system, they will do everything to provide their children with a good education.

Case Study 4	**The Ho family**
Origin:	From Hong Kong's New Territories
Family members:	Father Mother Three children: Mei Fung (16 years old) daughter Tai Fai (14 years old) son Wai Fing (13 years old) daughter
General information	Mr and Mrs Ho's family have lived in Britain for 33 years. Mr and Mrs Ho own a take-away shop.

Family Background

Mr Ho came to Britain from Hong Kong's New Territories in 1963, and had previously lived in a small village. Mr Ho was about 10 years old when his parents died. He was brought up by his aunt, his father's sister. He did not have a chance to complete his primary school education. He cannot write or read Chinese.

He worked as a trainee chef in an open-street restaurant in Hong Kong from the age of 14 until he was 21. Many Hong Kong Chinese men who worked in the restaurant industry went abroad in the hope that it would provide a bright future, hoping to earn a lot of money so they would have a better life. Basically, he was sold to a Chinese restaurant owner in Scotland through an agency in Hong Kong. He started to work as a chef in a Chinese restaurant in Glasgow and lived with a group of Chinese workers in the restaurant's accommodation. He saved enough money to open a Chinese take-away shop in Manchester. He worked in England for 10 years before he went back to Hong Kong to get married through the matchmaking of his sister.

Mr Ho told the researcher that the reason he looked for a wife urgently was because he needed a person to help him to run the shop, without employing any workers. He also thought that he had reached the age to settle down and have a family (he was in his late 30s). Mrs Ho was almost 10 years younger than Mr Ho. Since then, they have had two daughters and one son. Mei-Fung the elder daughter (now 16) was born in Britain, and will soon take her GCSE examinations. She finds it extremely hard to study and at the same time help her parents in the take-away shop. She told the researcher that she feels she wants to sleep in many of the lessons and cannot concentrate on the lesson on many occasions. Tai Fai (now 14) was born in Britain. He has a quiet personality. His father frequently told the researcher that Tai Fai is a very clever boy who has good reports and good results in his examinations. He is very proud of his son and expects a lot of him.

The researcher has no evidence that during the visits to the Ho's family Tai Fai's father or mother ever mentioned their two daughters' school work at all. There was evidence of Mei-Fung's jealousy of her brother (Tai Fai). They do not 'get on'. Mei-Fung feels her brother is favoured by her parents because he is the only son in the family. He only helps in the shop for about two hours every day, during the rest of the evening he is allowed to do his homework, but not Mei Fung, who must work.

Wai Fung (now 13) was born in Britain. She is still in her local secondary school with her brother. They go to school together every morning. She gets on well with her brother. Wai Fung, like her elder sister, works in the shop after school. Mrs Ho seems to be very demanding of all her children, especially the two daughters. She expects them to work in the shop every evening for six days a week. She expects her son to do his homework and eventually go to university. She does expect him to do some work in the take-away but not as much as the girls.

Language

The Ho family speak Cantonese as their first language. Their three children were born and educated in Britain and they speak fluently in Cantonese and English. The researcher asked the children whether they find any difficulty in speaking Cantonese. The elder daughter said that she was forced to speak Cantonese as far back as she could remember. Her father would hit her hard with chopsticks if she spoke English to her parents at home. Tai Fai told the researcher that he could remember what his father said to them, 'Speak English at school, but speak Cantonese at home, no English!' Mr and Mrs Ho told the researcher that they stopped their children speaking English to them as soon as they started to go to school.

They believe that as they spend nearly eight hours in school every day, they will forget how to speak in Cantonese. Mr Ho told the researcher angrily that he does not allow his son and daughters to speak English. 'We just feel fools, we do not know what they are talking about, how can we tell them what is good or bad? We always tell them to be a "good boy" and "good girls" and the reason we work hard and long hours all our life is because we want to provide a better life for them in the future.' The youngest daughter told the researcher that while she watches videos with her mother, she keeps asking her mother 'What does this mean?' 'What is she talking about?' so that she picks up Cantonese language from all the videos.

A Sense of Respect

Although Mr and Mrs Ho only had a very limited education they still hold many traditional Chinese values. They do not allow their children to address their elder sister or brother by their first name. In one observed incident the youngest daughter called her brother by his first name. It was obviously just a joke between them, but Mrs Ho smacked Wai Fing (13) across her face without explanation. Wai Fing understood the message and why her mother was hitting her. Since then the researcher has heard the youngest daughter address her brother as '*Di Xiao*' which means big brother.

One evening, when the researcher had dinner with the Ho family, the youngest daughter was just sitting down and eating the meal without waiting for the rest of the family and the visitor (the researcher). Her father became very cross and smacked her head and told her not to do that, that it was bad manners and that Miss S____ would think that they had not taught her properly, no respect for seniors in the family, no table manners, no respect for guests.

A Sense of Loyalty

Mr Ho's son told the researcher that sometimes he feels very guilty doing his homework upstairs when he can hear how busy it is downstairs in the take-away. He finds it difficult to concentrate on doing his homework, so he goes downstairs to help the rest of the family.

Three months into the research period Mr Ho was told by his doctor that he had cancer in his nose which needed treatment. He and his wife did not believe the doctor. They went back to Hong Kong to look for the appropriate Chinese medicine. They left the shop for the elder daughter, Mei Fing (then 15), to look after. Because of her father's illness, she felt the burden of responsibility now. She looked after the youngest sister and brother while their parents were in Hong Kong, and managed the shop to maintain the income from the business. She told the researcher that if anything were to happen to her father, she feels she would have to be loyal to her brother and sister and give up her studies.

Reading and Writing

Mr and Mrs Ho cannot read and write Chinese so nobody in that family can teach the children to read or write Chinese. Mr Ho frequently asked the researcher to help them write letters to their Hong Kong relatives and to translate correspondence or assist with filling in forms. Mr Ho is too proud to ask his children to do things like that because he believes it is akin to begging. He does not want to 'lose face' as a father authority figure.

Family Time: Entertainment, Television and Video

The study of this family revealed no exceptions to the findings from the other studies. There are three televisions in the take-away shop. One on the counter shows BBC1 programmes in the evenings for the customers; the second television is in the middle room which is on for most of the day. The whole family watches video recordings of Hong Kong soaps, Chinese movies or satellite programmes. They receive special rates from the video shops in China Town. The third television is in the upstairs living room. This is used mostly on Mondays when they have their day off. The parents watch Hong Kong movies or videos recorded from the Satellite Chinese channel.

Mr Ho goes to the casino in China Town every Sunday night after business hours and stays until early morning, because he has a day off on Monday. Mrs Ho told the researcher that her husband stays in the casino until 3:00 am. She will stay at home trying to catch up on her sleep.

The elder daughter has a group of Chinese friends whom she meets in school. They will go shopping together in China Town. The second son and the youngest daughter will watch videos with their mother or catch up on their homework and revision on Monday evenings.

Expectation and Aspirations

Mr Ho told the researcher that he cannot read or write and this is the worst thing in his whole life. He and his wife do not want their three children to follow in their steps, especially their son who they believe has a bright future and will go to university to be a doctor. Their hopes for the two daughters when they reach a certain age are to find a good husband and have a family.Then they will have finished their responsibilities as parents. The Ho's son told the researcher that he wanted to take computer technology in his A-Level in order to take a degree in Computer Art. However his parents really want him to become a doctor. He said to the researcher, 'Most Chinese parents have expectations of their children, especially if you are the eldest son of the family. They just expect me to become an accountant or a doctor or a lawyer.'

Case Study 5	**The Chow family**
Origin:	From Hong Kong
Family members:	Father Mother Three children: Kowk Me (25 years old son) (lives in Hong Kong – works in bank) Kwok Sku (16 years old) son Kwok Fah (13 years old) son
General information:	Mr and Mrs Chow worked as police officers and came to England in 1992.

Family Background

In 1992, Mr and Mrs Chow and their two younger children migrated to England because of the impending uncertainty of the 1997 situation. Mr and Mrs Chow worked in the CID department of the Hong Kong Police for nearly 30 years, while Mrs Chow was a policewoman. They have three sons. The eldest, who is 25 years old, is still in Hong Kong and works in a bank. The second eldest son, Kwok Sku (now 16), goes to the local college and is studying a business course. The youngest son, Kwok Fah (now 13), goes to the local secondary school.

Four years ago when the Chow family arrived in Manchester, they bought a semidetached house. Mr and Mrs Chow planned to open a Chinese restaurant after they had decided to migrate to England. Some relatives of Mr Chow had already lived in Manchester for 30 years. They have a Chinese restaurant in a small village outside Manchester. Mrs Chow told the researcher that although they have good qualifications and can speak enough English to get by on a day to day basis, when, for example, she receives a form or letter from a housing agency, she finds it hard to follow and understand spoken English. Mr Chow also gets very frustrated and depressed. The reason they decided to become British citizens was because they both worked in a government department and had first priority to apply to emigrate. 'Really, it is not for us,' said Mrs Chow. 'We have reached 50 years of age, and it is not long to retirement age. It is hard to start again, especially in a Western country like Britain. Nevertheless, we need to think of our children's future first.'

The elder son, who is grown up (age 25), has his own way of life and decided to stay in Hong Kong. Their two younger sons are entitled to a free education in England. There are more universities than in Hong Kong, where there is too much competition. They are doing well in their school work after the first year; but as the Chows explained, it was a nightmare looking for suitable schools for their children when they first arrived. They were unable to find any help. They did not know where to start and who they could ask.

Mr Chow learnt how to cook in his relatives' restaurant. He came home late, tired out and slept all morning. Mrs Chow stayed at home all day long. There was nobody to talk to or see until the children return home from school. 'It was just like being in a prison. I was a career woman. I find it hard to live this kind of life, but I need to think of my children's future.'

After one and a half years, the family became more settled. They spent all their savings on the catering business and bought a restaurant. Mr and Mrs Chow now go to work in the evenings, while their two children stay at home after school. On Saturdays and Sundays their two children work in the restaurant helping in the family business so that Mr and Mrs Chow can keep their eyes on them.

Education

Kwok Sku (16) and Kwok Fah (13) told the researcher that when they were at school in Hong Kong they always stayed in the same class with the same pupils, but at school in England they had to move around from one lesson to another lesson. Each lesson has different pupils in the class. At the beginning of their school life in England it was confusing. 'It is always noisy in our class. You cannot hear what the teachers talk about in the lesson. The teachers spend most of the time telling pupils off and shouting at them. We do not have much homework to do, it is not like a Hong Kong school. The teachers always give us projects and tell us to work as a group in the lesson and give us a lot of freedom. The pupils in our class are usually messing about, they do not pay any attention to the teachers at all. Most days just go like that. We only have a few Chinese friends who look after us in school. If the rest of the pupils make fun of us, they will tell them off. We only play with our Chinese friends in school, we go to lunch and play in the school playground together.'

Mr and Mrs Chow talked about their expectations for their two sons' futures. They want them to go to university in Manchester, to gain a degree, to have a professional career rather than staying in their catering business, 'Catering is hard work, long hours, no life at all.'

Mrs Chow said she is not happy with her sons' education. 'Schools in England have no discipline, some of the pupils behave like animals in the zoo, fighting together in the class. They do not take any notice of the teachers and the teachers cannot do anything about it to control them. No homework! The teachers do not encourage pupils to work hard, there is no motivation.' She prefers the Hong Kong school system that pushed pupils to succeed. 'During the evening, when we go to work in the restaurant, we arrange for them to have private tutorials in Mathematics and English, so that they will not waste all evening watching videos or doing nothing. We get an indication by their school reports that their English is not very good.'

Reading and Writing

The boys said, 'At the beginning, we tried to read a local newspaper and watch BBC1 or ITV, but we found it hard to follow. Our mother tries very hard to encourage us to listen to and to speak English. She bought a lot of English speaking tapes for us to listen to and to practise our English, but we became bored.' Mrs Chow said, 'The children's school work and text books are not good enough for them to catch up in their English. We bought a lot of simple English story books and ordered English text books by post from Hong Kong for them. It is so difficult to make them develop their motivation to read and write in English.'

Family Time: Entertainment, Television and Videos

'We live away from our parents' restaurant. They go to work most evenings. We never see them, because they finish working at 2:00 am, when we are already in bed. In the morning, we go to school and they are still in bed. The only days we can see each other is Saturday and Sunday. We can go shopping with our father, go back to the restaurant and have lunch together and then we work together in the evening. We miss living in Hong Kong with our parents because they were always around in the house. We went out together most evenings or we had our meals together,' said the Chows' two sons. 'In this country the only chance we have to spend as a whole family is some Saturday or Sunday mornings and afternoons when we watch Hong Kong movies or videos together. We miss our Hong Kong TV programmes. After school we come home and there are only two of us, except that the private tutors come for two hours. We never have a chance to go out in the evening, because most of our Chinese friends need to be helping their parents in their take-away shops. We do not like hanging around with English boys, we have no common interests.'

Summary of Findings from the Five Case Studies

Each family followed a typical and familiar Hong Kong Chinese life style. They observed traditional customs, habits and cultural practices; eating their own Chinese food, using rice bowls, Chinese spoons and chopsticks, rather than using Western knives and forks; inculcating behavioural rules in all their children, particularly 'Respect superiors', 'Memorise lessons,' and 'Practise skills'.

Clearly, evidence from the five case studies showed that despite more than 30 years of migration, the adult British-Chinese have not yet fully adapted to the culture, language and behaviour of Britain. A survey by Yau (1983) in Lambeth showed that many Chinese people who were 25 years of age or over did not have a sufficient knowledge of English to participate confidently in daily life amongst British people. But Locke (1992) claimed that:

> While [in the short term] no people from outside cultures seem ever to have been fully absorbed by a host culture, the forms and techniques by which the Chinese have maintained their traditions are unique. Their cultural and social exclusivity within the cities of the host cultures is a phenomenon of worldwide historical significance (p. 83).

The case study research from Manchester confirms this idea.

Most of the British-Chinese live near or in larger cities, several of which have a Chinatown, for example, London, Liverpool and Greater Manchester. According to Owen (1993), 36 per cent of the Chinese population in Britain live in Greater London, 27 per cent in the South East and 10 per cent in the North West. They tend to read only Chinese newspapers, listen to Hong Kong music, eat Chinese food and only socialise with their Chinese relatives or friends (Locke, 1992, p. 84) Likewise, the families in the present study go to China Town every Sunday to do their grocery shopping, then go to the video shop to hire a number of Hong Kong films to watch for the week and go to Chinese Sunday school.

British-Chinese parents still hold on to their own culture value and norms in relation to child-rearing practices. According to a group of influential academic and professionals in this field such as Tseng and Hsu (1969–70), Tseng (1972), Ho (1979; 1981) and Bond (1992), they accept that there is a strong obligation which includes group loyalty and obedience, avoidance of embarrassing situations, modesty, humility, and respect in the presence of superiors, the absence of complaining in the face of hardship and the obligation of the individual to the family and to those of superior status which still exists in the traditional Chinese culture.

Kang (1984) observed that: 'Filial piety was perhaps the major goal that guided the socialization of children in the traditional Chinese family' (p. 1004). The case studies above confirm that Chinese children seem to be very well behaved, in the face of what to a European child would be unreasonable restraints. The conformity of Chinese children is based on the two strong principles of filial piety and respect for age. Chinese adults are still expected to be obedient and give complete devotion to their elderly parents, especially to their father rather than mother, and respect to their grandparents (as is illustrated in case study 3).

According to Roopnarine and Carter (1992), Chinese parents tend to discourage their children from becoming independent and do not encourage them to express their opinions. Chinese parents employ 'impulse control' throughout their children's life. Children tend to follow and obey their parents' wishes and guidance related to education, marriage, daily life and occupation. The parents and children the researcher interviewed fully confirmed and supported this observation. Sue (1981) reported that most Chinese parents tend to use two powerful psychological techniques to control their children, and to implement their cultural practices of filial piety. The first one is shame, frequently pointing out the bad behaviour of other children, so that the child will get the message that certain kinds of behaviour are not acceptable, as this would bring shame on the family. Shame is experienced not only by the individual but by the family as a whole. The second technique, is guilt. If the child tries to be independent or go against their parents' wishes, they are labelled selfish and not grateful for what their parents have done for them.

Traditional Chinese Family Structure

On the Marriage Law of China, Hinton (1986) observed that 'Parents have the duty to rear and to educate their children; the children have the duty to support and assist their parents' (p. 553). The Chinese people hold a strong kinship bondage throughout the whole life span. 'The general consensus which does not allow Chinese people to give up their responsibility to their aged parents when they grow up, get married and have their own children' (Ma, 1988, p. 207).

The detailed information from the five case studies entirely confirm the observations of these various studies carried out in China and Hong Kong: Chinese families in Britain are extremely traditional in their values and socialisation practices.

> The family, the oldest human institution, is the basic unit of a culture. The family is responsible for the production of children who will continue the culture, as well as for the socialization of those children. The manner in which the culture organizes itself in kinship patterns provides useful information on its structure. Factors such as who has authority in families and in what areas, the impact of marriage outside the cultural group, the nature of relationships among members of family, and how lineage is determined are useful in understanding the impact of family structure on the culture (Locke, 1992, p. 10).

Everybody plays a different role and acts out their behaviour differently according to their role in the society at a macro level. When we look at individual roles in a Chinese family from the micro level, the structure of the family itself is a model of social life. The Chinese philosopher Confucius had a great influence on the Chinese family system. His concept of the structure of the Chinese family depends heavily on the age, sex and generational status, and determines that individuals have a particular role and duty in the family.

In Britain in contrast, it seems that great emphasis is placed on the importance of the individual and on the development of an independent, self-motivated child. The situation is very different for British-Chinese families' children. The head of the household is the father in the traditional Chinese family system. He holds high authority, he is unquestioned. It is the male duty to be a good son, to be a good husband and a good father, especially the eldest son or the only son of the whole family. Sons play a very important role in the family lineage.

Boys have many duties to fulfil because they carry the family name and bear the burden of social and financial responsibilities. The family is constantly watching their every movement, achievement, or failure in their careers. We can see some evidence from case study 4, when Ho's son told the researcher, 'Most Chinese parents have expectations of their children, especially if you are the eldest son of the family. They just expect me to become an accountant or a doctor or a lawyer.' From case study 1, Ben and Ken's parents said, 'We keep telling Ken that once we reach retirement age, this business will belong to him. It is a profitable business. Ken is the eldest son in our family. He should take this responsibility.'

The traditional female duty is to be subservient to males (husband, son, brother) and look after all domestic work. This ancient principle is still at work, as evidenced by the sample's case studies. In case study 2, Mei-Ling's father told the researcher that they do not expect their daughters to become independent business people. When they grow up with a good education, they will marry a 'good' man, himself well-educated and prosperous. In case study 4, Mr and Mrs Ho's hopes for their two daughters were also that they would find good husbands.

The Chinese family pays a great deal of attention to the use of the correct forms of address in daily interaction. There is a different way to refer to or address your older or senior which shows respect. Often the Chinese parents refer to their children as 'the eldest' or 'the youngest'. Siblings in the family also address their brothers and sisters depending on individual positions in the family. The hierarchy of relationships in the family was confirmed by the case studies. Brothers and sisters were not allowed to call each other by their first name.

Language, Writing and Reading

Fewster (1989) shows that the Chinese language is extremely different in syntactical structure as compared to English, and lacks the complexities of verbs, tenses and conjugations which make English such a difficult language to learn for people whose first language is Chinese, Korean or Japanese. It has been estimated that the time needed for a native Chinese speaker to learn English is four times more than the time needed for a native English speaker to learn French or German.

However, the written forms of Chinese are not alphabetic or phonetic. The Chinese script is composed of ideograms, each word represented by a unique ideogram or 'picture', and these stylised pictures have been standardised as ideograms since 2212 BC (Han Dynasty). Chinese people are proud of the complex, aesthetic nature of the Chinese script which plays a very important part in Chinese culture. Around 3,000 characters are in use everyday, and the total includes over 200,000 characters. Each character must be learned by heart and practised endless times before an individual becomes literate. A university student will need to have learned at least 30,000 ideograms.

Typically, Chinese children learn reading and writing from the age of five to nine. The most important task is to learn to write one's own name. Written Chinese is produced in a vertical line from right to left. Most Chinese parents in Britain believe that their children should maintain their cultural identity through the learning of Chinese language (Wong, 1992). The case study evidence shows that the Chinese families have high expectations that their children will learn Chinese reading and writing. Practising individual words, especially their names and concentrating upon word accuracy is important.

According to the Haringey Chinese group's survey, 27 out of 52 Chinese parents only completed primary education (Wong 1992) and may have little knowledge of written Chinese. Most Chinese parents have little knowledge of English. They find it very difficult to be participants in their children's developing English vocabulary and conversation, even though they have 'close encounters' with their children.

Throughout the case study interviews, Cantonese was spoken on all occasions. As the researcher is Cantonese, this is perhaps not surprising. Occasionally, the researcher deliberately asked the children to speak in English when they were out of hearing of their parents. In most cases their command of English was good.

Lambeth reports that:

> Most children talk in Chinese at home with their parents but the majority of them do not read or write Chinese, and speak in English amongst themselves (Home Affairs, 1985, p. xii).

In case study 2, the parents were determined that their two daughters would speak Cantonese, although they preferred to communicate with each other in English. The girls were sent to China Town each Sunday to the Sunday school to learn to read, write and communicate in Cantonese. The daughters claimed, on occasions, that they did not understand some Cantonese words. The researcher sensed that a quiet generation battle may have been taking place. The behaviour rule of 'respect superiors' was being quietly challenged and there was evidence of their father's anger when he heard his daughters communicating in English. 'Speak to us in Cantonese,' he shouts to them in Cantonese. Both parents have lived in Britain for nearly 25 years.

These teenage girls were already becoming embarrassed by their parents' inability to pronounce English correctly and the traditional behavioural rule of 'respect superiors' was being challenged as they corrected their parents' pronunciation. In all five case studies this was the most clear evidence of the beginnings of a challenge to the authority, respect and dignity which should be afforded to the parents' generation. Interestingly, even though the father was demanding respect for his authority, he used a disrespectful term to tell his daughters that they were becoming more like *Gweilo/Gweilpor* – (slang for white people) in their disrespect for him.

In case study 3, one of the daughters preferred to speak English to her father who is a fluent English speaker because she has more English vocabulary than Chinese vocabulary.

In case study 4, English was spoken at school and Cantonese at home and this was strictly observed, with memories of being hit with chopsticks if English was used! More Cantonese is picked up from watching Chinese videos. In case study 5, no English was spoken in the household, although the parents were able to speak English. This professional family had recently settled from Hong Kong.

From the ethnic minority group parents' point of view, keeping their own mother tongue as a living language is the most important factor for several different reasons which includes cultural understanding and communication with relatives. Several of the parents faced a continuing dilemma about cultural and linguistic choice. Many parents understand that English oracy and literacy is the means of attaining a good education, an essential condition of living in Britain and the path to a successful future. On the other hand, many parents also wanted to avoid the loss of culture which accompanies their children's loss of language.

There was evidence to suggest that each of the five families feels it is very important to maintain and develop their mother tongue. It is important to speak, read and write in Chinese. All the children were brought up speaking Cantonese. The only evidence from the research which observed the children writing in English was in connection with their homework, although homework was rarely given. This in itself was an annoyance to the parents who believe that the children should as a behavioural rule 'practise the skill' of writing.

In the case of the engineering student however, there was ample evidence of written assignments in English, lecture notes and written notes from the text books which were in many cases copied carefully in order to assist memory. The behavioural rules 'memorise the lesson' and 'practise the skill' of writing were a result of early years of a Hong Kong education.

These stored behavioural rules, both general and specific, had been well internalised and affected Ken's behaviour in this regard. He knew that he would acquire the knowledge and remember it if he wrote it down. He knows how he learns best and is a diligent student. His younger brother Ben follows in his footsteps out of respect for his elder brother and his ways of working have been impressed upon him. The behavioural rule 'respect superiors' is well evidenced here.

In all cases, the parents wanted their children to learn to write in Chinese and most had sent or still sent children to a Chinese weekend school in China Town. Here they practised their writing. The most important aspect of this was the need to be able to write their name, which they wrote over and over again, in time-consuming practice, intended to develop their patience until the characters of their name were written perfectly.

The parents face a dilemma. They want their children to be able to write in both languages, Chinese and English, and yet the children seem to have little time to practise at home because they are working in the family business. The only writings which the researcher observed in addition to Ken's study notes were the notes for the food orders, in every case written in Chinese characters. There was a report of Chinese letter writing by the elder of two daughters and of weekend tuition by an authoritarian and punitive grandfather.

The evidence from the five case studies in relation to reading shows that there was generally very little indication of English reading materials, whether school books, novels, other books, newspapers, comics, magazines, puzzle books, and so on in the five households.

Obedience and a Sense of Respect for Elders

The behavioural rules by which children are reared stress the importance of obedience in all matters: 'respect superiors' is acquired during childhood. The authority of the parents must not be challenged and the children are frequently reminded of this. They seem to adopt a subservient attitude although the researcher observed on occasions that there was suppressed anger in front of their parents. Subservience and a lack of overt aggression characterised the relationship between children and parents even when the children wished to do something else, for example, an engineering assignment, or go to a disco, go to a best friend's birthday party, go on a school trip at the weekend or watch a different television channel.

The children in the case studies have never witnessed a home situation where children argue with their parents, express an alternative opinion or disobey their parents. These attitudes to authority figures transfer to their school life where they treat the teachers with respect and a degree of subservience to authority. They never question their parents and indeed find it difficult to ask questions; they find it difficult to have an independent opinion since opinions are formed and slavishly followed in a Chinese household from family authority figures.

The complexity of behavioural rules in this area of child-rearing affects the way children react to, and deal with adults (superiors) in everyday life. Children, through being obedient, are less original in their thinking and less creative and thus less fluent in their communication and ideas. Parents teach their children to be unassertive and to listen rather than talk. There seems to be little verbal interaction with their children although no studies have been done on Chinese families. A Japanese study by Caudill (1972) describes how the mother, in particular, controls the children, consistently teaching them what not to do. Likewise, obedience is an essential aspect of Chinese culture.

The behavioural rule 'respect superiors' has been taught to every child in the five case studies. In one case, the sons were frequently reminded to pass a cup of tea to the researcher with both hands in true respectful fashion and in a second case a teenage girl was reprimanded publicly for sitting down before she did. In all cases the children were instructed by their parents to call her 'Miss Sham'.

Every family member is kept in check by the duty to respect and obey in terms of strict hierarchical and gender control which each one owes to another. The sense of respect in relation to grandparents is also very closely held and is of the highest importance. One boy returned to Hong Kong for one week to visit all his relations and for one week to China to visit his grandmother. The whole holiday was spent with older relations and he enjoyed it immensely; all the more so, because he had done his duty and shown his respect for his older relatives, a duty he must do as is the eldest son in his family.

Family Time: Entertainment, Television and Videos

In all five case studies, family time together is demonstrably important to the parents and to the children. The parents in each case take parenting very seriously. They want to impress their family and cultural rules upon their children. They want to ensure that the children grow up to respect them and the elders in their family, that they learn the family values in connection with the importance of the family and the family business: thrift, team working, good manners, honesty, filial piety, hard work, and learning their responsibilities to care for their parents in their old age.

In each case, the family owned a take-away shop and in four cases the family lived on the premises which usually consisted of the living space above the shop of two bedrooms, one large and one small, a bathroom/toilet and a lounge. In every case, the researcher was invited to their private quarters on more than one occasion. In each case there were very few examples of English decor or furnishings. The furniture was usually English. Book shelves displayed videos not books. A very large television and video machine usually dominated the room.

School Achievement: Expectations and Aspirations

One wonders what effect the obvious overwork of the British-Chinese children who live in a take-away shop and their exclusive diet of Chinese language videos, will have upon their school achievement. The five case studies indicate that the parents were extremely ambitious for their children to succeed. The parents were not generally complimentary about British schools. One parent had himself experienced an English (Manchester) education but could also remember his days in a Hong Kong school and looked back on the Hong Kong discipline and rigour with affection and nostalgia. He described noisy classrooms in England, and teachers who do not care and provide no discipline. He now pays for extra evening tuition for his daughters in Maths and English.

Teaching methods are different in British schools. Teaching is child-centred. Children are encouraged to explore their environment and actively to seek knowledge. They are given a certain degree of freedom to move around the classroom. It seems less disciplined in Britain than in Hong Kong. Chinese parents believe that 'play' is a waste of time. They think their child should have a formal education. The Chinese education system encourages the 'learning by doing' approach rather than the British 'learning through play' approach (Sham, 1989).

One 16 year-old girl admitted to wanting to fall asleep in school lessons and being unable to concentrate in school as a direct result of working long hours in the take-away, and the lack of stimulation provided by the lessons. Lai (1975), Garvey and Jackson (1975) and Simpson (1987) have also identified British-Chinese families with take-away shops having children who were less successful in their education, due to spending much of their time helping along with the family business, with parents who were unable to help them with their school work, because most of the Chinese parents lack of a knowledge English and also work unsociably long hours. The conflict of roles for parents and children with respect to domestic work obligations, obedience within the family system, and adapting to the freedom of the British school system is clearly apparent in the present study.

Conclusions

Many questions remain to be answered or confirmed. Do British-Chinese pupils have a style of learning that is different from English pupils, particularly if their parents originate from Hong Kong? Are British-Chinese pupils really any different from English pupils in the way they learn? If such differences do exist, how have they developed? What are the effects upon their educational achievement and motivation in learning under British schools' teaching styles? What will be the obstacles they face? What can be done to improve the integration of Hong Kong pupils into English schools? These and many more questions underlie this research project.

These five case histories leave us with one word to describe the children in these families: heroic. They work loyally and with industry in their family catering businesses for long hours, still managing to do normal school work as well as learning spoken and sometimes written Chinese. They accept their parents with tolerant concern – particularly their anxious and sometimes autocratic fathers who demand standards of filial obedience which, for the western observer, are awesome. They suffer the external slights of racism with dignity and courage, but retain (like the young people whom David Parker interviewed) a keen interest in popular Cantonese culture. Many Chinese children, like those observed by the researcher, will become engineers, technicians, doctors, researchers and business people. What expectations will they have for their own children? This is an important question for future research.

11 Conclusions and Policy Recommendations

Introduction

In this chapter we return to the questions posed earlier, and using the data presented in the findings, attempt to provide some answers. For convenience we list the original questions here.

* How were the personal and cultural identities of Chinese adolescents affected by growing up in Britain and their attending British schools? Was there evidence of conflict arising from the differing cultures of home and school? If they were subject to conflicting expectations, how effectively were they coping? Was there evidence that racism and problems of cultural adaptation were adversely affecting their self esteem?

* What were their educational aspirations?

* How did they differ, if at all, from their European British peers as well as from young Chinese people growing up in Hong Kong?

* What appropriate measures should be adopted by schools, Local Education Authorities, community organisations and other agencies to meet the needs of British-Chinese adolescents?

* Were such measures also likely to be appropriate for those Hong Kong Chinese who have entered Britain before 1998? If not, what other kinds of responses might be appropriate?

What were the Personal and Cultural Identities of Chinese Adolescents Affected by Growing up in Britain?

In common with young people of other ethnic minority groups in Britain,

Chinese adolescents were faced with questions about their identities which their European British peers did not have to grapple with. As might be supposed, having regard to their youth, members of all three groups – European British, Hong Kong Chinese and British-Chinese – often found it difficult to say with confidence what it meant to them to be 'British' or 'Chinese'. The British-Chinese group, however were faced with the particular problem of defining themselves, knowing themselves to be ethnic Chinese but growing up in Britain with the recognition that it was here that their futures lay. Most of them (more than 50 per cent) thought of themselves as 'British-Chinese' but nearly 40 per cent still felt themselves to be 'Chinese' whilst a proportion, small but perhaps not trivial 3 per cent thought of themselves as 'British'. Each of those categories probably formed a continuum so that, for example, within the 'British-Chinese' there would be those who thought of themselves as nearly British but a little Chinese and others for whom being Chinese was at the centre of their identity with the British element very much at the periphery.

It seemed to be the case that in general, those who had lived longest in Britain were most likely to call themselves 'British' or 'British-Chinese' with the more recently arrived calling themselves 'Chinese'.

Interestingly, their dilemma was mirrored in the Hong Kong Chinese, who also struggled with the knowledge of being Chinese whilst at the same time having a sense of being different from those living on the mainland. For them, the awareness of difference sprang entirely from the sense of cultural difference.

As Verma with Ashworth (1986) argue, a culture is dynamic over time as its adherents make small adjustments which enable them to function in the environments in which they find themselves. Although such adjustments are necessary for the survival of both the individuals and the group of which they are members, there remain certain core areas which Smolicz (1984) attempted to define as follows:

> ... whenever people feel that there is a direct link between their identity as a group and what they regard as the most crucial and distinguishing element of their culture, the element concerned becomes a core value for the group.

Thus every culture has certain core elements which identify its members and with which they identify themselves. Compromise with these core elements is thus extremely difficult for them. Rejection of them implies rejection of the group of which they are members – a kind of self-imposed exile. For most cultures, these core elements include either one, or a combination of two or more, of the following: religion, family networks, clan, and *language*.

Our findings were very much in line with what might be expected from the above. We deal first with *language*.

> Language is not merely a medium of communication ... but a unifying factor of a particular culture and often a prerequisite for its survival (Giles and Saint-Jacques, 1979).

One of the clearest messages coming out of this study was the importance of the Chinese language and its maintenance to both the young people and their parents. There were, of course, practical reasons for this. Most parents lacked any real fluency in English so it was important to them that their children were able to communicate effectively in the mother tongue – usually Cantonese or Hakka. Only one out of 10 of the British-Chinese normally used English with their parents, even though seven out of 10 said that they were more fluent in English and that they normally used it when they were speaking to their brothers and sisters or friends. It was therefore not surprising to find that parents exerted a good deal of pressure on their children to send them to a local Chinese Community School, usually at weekends, where they could be taught Chinese and had opportunities to learn something of Chinese history and traditions.

However, it should be added that, although the youngsters often complained about parental pressures to attend these schools, the uninspiring teaching they were subjected to and the difficulty of learning the language, they nevertheless recognised its importance. This recognition was based not just on its practical value in terms of better communication within the family but for the significance it had for them in maintaining their cultural identity. But as they grew older and started to prepare for public examinations, many of them stopped attending these schools because this conflicted with demands of their formal education. It is worth noting that this was with the agreement of their parents who evidently accepted that success in examinations came first.

There was some evidence that, whilst fluent in spoken Chinese, many British-Chinese (especially those born in or long resident in the UK) had very little written expertise. The nature of written Chinese demands time and a level of commitment that were not available to them.

We turn next to *religion*. For many of the ethnic minority communities now living in Britain, religion is central to their personal and cultural identities. For the Chinese, this seemed at first sight not to be the case. During the Chou dynasty (1027–221 BCE) documents concerning gods of various origins and powers were created and still survive. They related to rivers, lakes, mountains and other natural manifestations. They had no particular images, but were represented by abstract symbols, and communication with them was through one's ancestors.

In Chinese thought, heaven and earth represent the primary forces in nature. The *I Ching* (Book of Changes) teaches that 'when heaven and earth exert their influences, all things are transformed and animated.' Everyone could observe the effects of these forces in the changes of the seasons and the growth of plants and animals so it was natural for them to be worshipped for their extraordinary powers. This gradually led to philosophical concepts like *tao* (the way) and the belief that happiness was made possible by living in harmony with nature. From this, it is not difficult to understand how various aspects of nature – the wind, the sun and moon, lightning, mountains and lakes – became objects of reverence.

The growth in the number of deities in China's early history made it particularly necessary to organise the practice of worship and the solution that was adopted was to use ancestors as the medium of communication with them. It was this which formed the justification for ancestor worship and it served two purposes. It retained a link with the past through former members of the family and personalised the process of seeking the intervention of remote deities.

As Kong (1989) puts it, 'It is a very flexible belief system, since any practice that might help to fulfil one's wishes is likely to be readily accepted.' He then goes on to observe that the Chinese were the only people to embrace three different belief systems – Taoism, Confucianism and Buddhism – believing that they were three different routes to one truth. This is followed by King's suggestion – and a significant one in the context of this study – that it was for this reason that 'Chinese culture remained intact when it came in contact with the major religions of other civilisations. Even Buddhism, the single foreign religion that gained a strong and lasting foothold in China, was significantly transformed by traditional modes of thought and belief.'

It is tempting to perceive strong similarities between China and India in the way that they coped with the influence of foreign thought. They both accepted new elements but did not reject their old beliefs and practices, rather the new was grafted on to the old and became part of it. Accommodations were made and just as Hinduism continued, powerfully but subtly, to inform the Indian civilisation over the millennia, despite all foreign influences, so with China: it accepted and transmuted external influences whilst its civilisation remained in its essence unchanged by them.

The information we collected on the religious beliefs of British-Chinese young people was, at first sight, contradictory, not to say confusing. To the direct question 'What, if any, is your religious belief?' more than six out of 10 said that they had no religious belief or were unsure. This might be compared with responses from the European British and Hong Kong Chinese samples of four and five out of 10 respectively. Elsewhere, however, they were asked for their response to the proposition that 'Worshipping ancestors during special festivals is important.' Only one out of 10 of British-Chinese disagreed with this. More than five out of 10 agreed with it with less than four out of 10 saying that they were uncertain. Responses from the Hong Kong Chinese were very similar.

What seems to be the case is that the Chinese community in Britain is retaining its religious practices in a form similar to and at about the same level as the Chinese in Hong Kong. What is confusing to the Western mind is the nature and practice of that religion. (Some might argue that these practices do not constitute a religion as normally understood. In response we can only say that they are a form of activity for which there seems no real alternative term.)

Perhaps three observations are possible. First, the tradition of a religious observance which is essentially domestic and can be conducted in the absence of priestly bureaucracies means that it can be continued and even flourish though its practitioners are widely dispersed and often isolated as is the case with the Chinese in Britain. Moreover, since it is not dependent on a priesthood and dedicated buildings but goes on in the home, it is invisible to the outside world. Second, the fact of its continued existence suggests that it forms a continuing link with the historic culture of the Chinese. Finally, it is possible that this link – invisible though it is to Western eyes – has a greater significance in the preservation of the sense of being Chinese than might be supposed. If this is so, the importance of our finding, that these religious practices are in as healthy a state among the British-Chinese as they are among the Hong Kong Chinese, is considerable. It suggests that they are seen as one of the core values of Chinese culture and are being successfully retained. That dimension of values in Chinese people described by Bond and Pang (1990) which combines a sense of inner spirituality with an outward practice of morality also seems to have survived the migration experience.

Finally in this section we consider the importance of the *family*. The family has, from earliest times, played the primary role in Chinese society. It was the model of the state. The father was the ruler of, and provider for, all the other family members. A similar relationship existed between the father and the government official who was the head of the town or region, and between him and the emperor who was the head of the country. Thus the whole of society was constructed on the hierarchical principle, with the father of the family, the smallest unit of the state, wielding imperial powers over his subjects whilst owing obedience to those in authority over him. Within the family, the same principle held good. Thus, for instance, children addressed their siblings not by their given names, which would have been impolite and lacking in respect, but by their position in the family. A younger son would call an older son *Di Xiao* (Number one) and, conversely, he would be called 'Little Brother'. To put it another way, the family, observed through a microscope, was indistinguishable from the state. In practice, this dominance over the family exerted by the father was tempered by other factors. Although the final decisions might be his to make, filial piety required him to respect the views of his parents and grandparents who were thus able to exert a significant influence on family affairs. In addition to his obvious responsibilities towards the family, a man's most important duty was to produce a male heir to continue the family lineage. The structure and importance of the family in Chinese culture is unique (Kong, 1989) There are, he suggests, two reasons for this. The first is that it is the family by which the ancestral cult is perpetuated – a person's life is extended by his children. Since there is no strong belief in an afterlife, devotion to the family and the extension of the family line is what gives meaning to life. The second important reason is that having children ensures that one is looked after in old age. Filial piety demands that, because parents brought you into the world and looked after you in infancy, you should look after them when they grow old.

At a more philosophical level, Confucius taught that harmony in society could be achieved through the observance of a set of principles called the *ng lun* or 'five relationships' which outlined the expectations and obligations of the persons involved. In Chinese society, these relationships could be identified as: (i) the governor and the governed; (ii) father and son; (iii) husband and wife; (iv) the elder brother and the younger brother; and (v) friends (Creel, 1954). The clear emphasis on relationships within the family carries with it the implication that the state should be rooted in the family. Confucius believed that the administration of the state should start from the family. A person who has been properly brought up to respect authority within the family would also respect authority outside the family and thus become a good and obedient member of the empire (Lang, 1946).

The importance of the family is not unknown in other cultures. In Pakistan, for instance, there is the *biraderi* (a complex of relationships both by blood and by marriage). Here, however, family relationships are strengthened by adopting endogamy as the normal practice in which quite closely related members of the family – frequently first cousins – are encouraged to marry. By comparison, China had established exogamy as the normal practice by about 500 BCE and this inevitably gave rise to the introduction of surnames in place of the former clan names. The surname had a number of important functions. First, it provided a means of ensuring that people who were related did not inadvertently marry each other. Another function was to unite people together. In early times, people often took their names from their village or district where they lived. Since the father's surname was passed on to his children, people who share the same name are, in theory, either descended from a common ancestor or from ancestors who lived in the same place. Thus, Chinese people have traditionally placed a good deal of importance on clan kinship as well as blood kinship.

During this century, China has been in a more or less continuous state of war or internal turmoil. There was the Revolution of 1911, the Second World War, 1939–45, the Communist Revolution in 1949 followed by the Cultural Revolution (1966–76) in which children were encouraged to spy on their parents and report them to the authorities for failing to adhere to party dogma. The significance of this last revolution to the people of mainland China cannot be exaggerated, since it sought effectively to destroy the traditional attitudes of respect and obedience owed by children to their parents and struck at the heart of the nature of the family and the culture which underpinned it, as it had existed for some 2,500 years. Because of its status as a Crown Colony until 1997, the Hong Kong Chinese were protected from these consequences of the Cultural Revolution, as, of course, were those who had migrated to Britain or elsewhere. Thus, as has been observed in other communities in diaspora, important elements of their culture – in this case the internal power structure of the family – have been preserved in them even though events, or indeed, the natural processes of cultural evolution, have substantially altered or removed them in the homeland.

It is difficult to overestimate the importance of the Chinese family in reproducing a range of core cultural values in the children and all the evidence suggests that it continues to do so in Britain. It serves to mould the characteristics of the children from the day of their birth. Traditional child-rearing practices often remain intact and whilst, to western eyes, the duties of respect and obedience might seem overpowering, leading to a passivity that approaches to subservience, there are countervailing benefits that include a sense of security within the family unit.

A family, structured and motivated in the way we have seen the Chinese family to be, might almost have been designed to survive intact in an alien culture. Its ordered, philosophically coherent structure consistently applied by its senior members provides great internal strength. Its cultural values are made concrete by its existence. Core cultural values are not dependent on external influences, they are what holds the family together and the survival of the family affirms the values which shape it. Even their religion serves to bind the family together, to preserve the link between the living and the dead thus emphasising its continuity through the generations.

Other investigations associated with this study have indicated the closed nature of the Chinese family. It is clear that many Chinese adolescents are the major link between parents and outside society. Many parents in our sample still do not speak English to any extent. The case studies dramatically underscore this point.

Thus, in the three core elements of family, religion and language, our findings strongly suggested that the British-Chinese adolescents were successfully preserving their cultural identities.

Was there Evidence of Conflict Arising from the Differing Cultures of Home and School?

One of the most interesting revelations of the study was the way that these young people were managing to deal with the daily transition from home (essentially Chinese) to school (profoundly western European). Although this seems, on the face of it, a fairly straightforward question, it requires answering in at least three ways.

i. What were the problems or challenges that they encountered?
ii. What strategies did they employ to deal with them?
iii. How successful were these strategies in dealing with the problems?

The nature of British schooling is the product of western European thought as interpreted by British educationists and modified by British history: it is a reflection of British culture. Leaving aside the economic functions of schooling – to provide pupils with knowledge and skills that will make them useful and productive members of the state – schools exist to reproduce in the next generation those modes of thought, skills, attitudes and behaviours believed to be fundamental to the nature of British society. A fundamental tenet of western thought is that knowledge is progressive – that is to say that previously held assumptions and beliefs are open to question and that progress can only be made by questioning them. Students in school are encouraged to bring a critical approach to bear on conventional wisdom because only by testing it can its value be established. If it cannot survive this critical test, then it has no value and must be replaced with a better alternative. The questioning of authority is seen to be at the heart of intellectual and moral progress.

The contrast between this and the assumptions which structure the traditional Chinese family is self-evident. On the one hand, the children attend schools which require as a condition of their academic success that they question authority and, on the other, they return to homes in which the father generally assumes autocratic power.

There is a parallel process which they were in a position to observe in the relationships between their European British peers and their parents which they are able to compare with their own experiences. Whilst their own families retain much of the Confucian principle of submission by the children to the authority of the father, British family structures are much more strongly influenced by Aristotelian concepts of man and society. This teaches that people in society are 'free men', capable of reasoning and behaving rationally. Knowledge emphasises logical explanations since free men are logical animals. As a result of adopting Aristotelian principles, governing power in Britain is subject to challenge from the people.

The rejection of authority leading to automatic respect and acceptance of the views, opinions and wishes of parents over a wide range of issues has resulted in a heavy reliance on negotiation between parents and children in British families. That is not to say that there are no non-negotiable issues but the recognition of even these have normally been arrived at, and preferably been recognised by both sides, as a result of the negotiation process. This led many of our British-Chinese interviewees to comment on what they saw as the greater levels of openness and understanding between parents and children leading to closer relationships in European British families than they experienced in their own.

Of course, the youngsters who formed our sample were unlikely to formulate the differences they perceived between their own and their European British peers' family lives in terms of the differences between Aristotelian and Confucian teaching. They were, however, certainly able to perceive that there were differences and recognise that they were fundamental and not merely cosmetic – that they were not merely superficial customs applied to the same underlying family structures.

It was possible to detect in our interviews with them a kind of wistfulness in their recognition of this difference, perhaps best exemplified by the comment of one youngster whom we cited earlier: 'The British family is more different from the Chinese. They are more open and their relationship is closer.' That having been said, there was little to suggest that the comparison between their own and their British peers' relationships with their parents resulted in dissatisfaction with or unhappiness in their own family lives. It certainly did not affect their recognition of their traditional duties and obligations to their parents. Observation in British-Chinese families again suggested the ability of these young people to maintain separate identities. Whilst recognising the quality of British parent/child relationships, and in the school context exhibiting some envy of that relationship, they were clearly comfortable and secure within the home, submitting willingly and without rancour to the hard discipline which obedience to the father demanded. It is also worth recalling that it was possible to detect similar feelings in the Hong Kong Chinese; 'We seldom talk; we have dinner while we watch television. We have little conversation at the dinner table. Usually our sisters would talk together.'

In reflecting on the way that the young British-Chinese manage the transition between school and home – effectively between western European and Chinese cultures – it may help to widen the focus of attention slightly to include the parents and the problems they face.

Among the most significant findings were those which showed that almost seven out of 10 of our sample of young Chinese people in Britain believed that the language they spoke best was English and that they normally used it when they were talking to their brothers and sisters and friends. As a mirror image of this, eight out of 10 normally used either Cantonese, Hakka or Mandarin when speaking to their parents. It could be that they did so out of a form of respect for their parents because it was their preferred language or because their parents insisted on it as part of a programme of reinforcing their cultural identity. A third possibility is that they did it because their parents were limited in their use of, and could not communicate effectively in, English. Of the three possibilities, the last seems most plausible and fits well with the estimate made by the Home Affairs Committee (1985) that between 65–75 per cent of first generation Chinese settlers were unable to use English effectively.

Behind these statistics, the domestic scene (as evidenced by the five case studies) is only too easily constructed. The children and their friends are busy talking to each other in English which the parents are unable properly to understand. They ask a question or give an instruction in Cantonese to which the children reply, also in Cantonese. They then revert to English as they resume their conversation and the parents are again distanced from whatever it is that their children are talking about. It is easy to see how this can lead to the parents feeling that they are being ignored, that their authority is diminished, that their control over them is waning, that their children are growing away from them. As Wong (1992) puts it, they begin to feel that their children are like 'bananas – with Chinese yellow skin on the outside but with European people's minds'. With this in mind, their enthusiasm for their children to attend Chinese Language Schools is readily understood.

Remaining within the family, what other important areas were found to be of interest? We explored attitudes towards sex equality and found that there was a tendency in both groups of Chinese female respondents to think that boys and girls should be treated differently when their replies were compared with their European British peers. The female British-Chinese respondents thought, for instance, that it was less important for them to go on to higher education than boys. Surprisingly, perhaps, significantly more girls than boys agreed with this proposition. In other respects, however, there was little difference: nine out of 10 boys and virtually 10 out of 10 girls said that they thought boys and girls should be treated the same.

These findings took on a particular interest when the interview evidence was reviewed, and revealed a good deal of indignation was voiced by the girls over what they perceived as the preferential treatment the boys received from their parents and the relative importance accorded to boys because they would perpetuate the family name.

What seems to be the case is that both boys and girls have rejected or are in the process of rejecting the traditional belief in the inferior status of women and that the girls, in particular, are resentful of parental attitudes of this kind. It seems reasonable to infer that these young people are adopting western European egalitarian beliefs and will put them into practice in their maturity. This might be seen as a 'culture free' adaptation – that is to say, one which does not threaten any of the core values of Chinese culture but one that happens because it makes sense for them in the social structures in which they are growing up.

It could be, however, that since they were interviewed in school, they adopted the views appropriate to that context. There is a clear problem in any inquiry that the distinction between the beliefs held in school and those held in the home could lead to simultaneously held conflicting beliefs. The ability and desire to conform to the society in which they find themselves is well known and is represented in the adoption of Western names by many Chinese settlers. When belief is determined by those in authority, it is not personalised in the way that Western individualised belief systems are.

To return, then, to the question: was there evidence of conflict arising from the differing cultures of home and school? On the basis of our study, it is possible to assert that the British-Chinese youngsters were well aware of differences but were avoiding conflict by successfully making accommodations to cope with them. Most importantly they were managing it without having to discard any of the core values by which they identified themselves.

What were their Educational Aspirations?

In seeking to answer this question, we first take the opportunity to reflect on schools and schooling as experienced by the British-Chinese. The evidence cited above suggests quite strongly that the British-Chinese youngsters were much closer in their experience of, and attitudes towards, school to their European British counterparts than they were to the Hong Kong Chinese. They seemed no less happy about going to school, they had at least as positive attitudes towards their academic achievement and general participation in school activities, their perceived relationships with their teachers were as good; and in terms of their post-school aspirations they scored highest of all three groups. In all these areas they were closely aligned to their European peers and generally scored better than their Hong Kong counterparts.

This is not to suggest that they did not experience some problems. As the interview material made clear, the chief amongst these was the demands placed on them by the English language. As almost nine out of 10 used their mother tongue in speaking with their parents, it is reasonable to conclude that a similar proportion first started their formal education with little or no English but with Chinese linguistic patterns already established. It is worth recollecting that the two languages have little in common. Chinese is monosyllabic, with no genders, plurals, tenses, cases or conjugations and exhibits a preference for short, simple sentences. The contrast between a language with these characteristics and the kind of English encouraged in schools needs little emphasis.

It was not part of this study to attempt an objective assessment of the youngsters' competence in English. They admitted it was a problem but believed that it was one that they were coping with. Our own perception was that they were certainly able to make themselves understood and could do so with some fluency but that there was a lack of accuracy in their usage. Reference to the interview data, which we were careful to present verbatim, provides support for this judgement. Additional support for our assessment is supplied by Wong (1992), using ILEA research material and studies undertaken by Kysel for the years 1981, 1983 and 1985 with pupils in Greater London, who gives figures of between 31–36 per cent of Chinese speakers who were 'fluent' in English. Unfortunately she does not define 'fluent' or indicate whether accurate usage formed part of the term.

Since there was no evidence from our own study, or from other sources, of special programmes designed to help them acquire fluency and accuracy in English language, it must be assumed that these are generally lacking. That does not of course, mean that individual teachers do not give such help as they are able to supply. Our work with other, South Asian, minority groups (Skinner, 1995) showed that they did. Unfortunately it also show, in the absence of properly constructed support programmes presented by teachers skilled in teaching English as a second language, their help was less effective than it might have been and needed to be.

On the basis of what little evidence exists, a plausible conclusion would be that too many Chinese youngsters now in school lack the language skills they need to function at the levels they are probably capable of across the curriculum and that this militates against their academic progress.

Another problem they have to contend with which their European peers largely escape is that of lack of parental support for their current educational experiences. As the case studies in chapter 10 show, parents have extremely positive attitudes to education, yet they are nevertheless often critical of the British school system. In this, as in other studies, it was clear that parents were very anxious for their children to succeed in the schools they attended.

The Chinese are at least equal to other ethnic minority groups in their tradition of respect for education. Confucius taught that knowledge was of supreme importance. It not only developed a person intellectually and morally but provided insights into the management of the family, the administration of a country, and illuminated the 'bright virtues' of the world. Among the hierarchies of the professions in ancient society, scholars were at the top of the social structure. Literacy training was seen by the common people as the high road to public service and consequently to wealth and prestige (Kiang, 1948). As Wah et al. (1996) remind us, the concept of competitive examinations were invented by the Chinese to select the finest minds to join the Emperor's Civil Service and become Mandarins. There is thus a tradition of some 2,000 years of seeing education as an escape from drudgery and hardship, a route to economic and social success for the scholar and his family.

The majority of the first generation settlers in Britain were well aware that in Hong Kong, executive positions in the civil service and other high prestige professions were filled by university graduates. Tradition and pragmatism thus combine in their minds to encourage their children to succeed in school. What they lack is the ability to give practical help. As we saw, fewer than one in 10 of parents had received university education. Many had stopped schooling at primary level and such education as they had received was very different both in form and content from the experience their children were having. Moreover, with more than 60 per cent of parents engaged in catering and allied industries with their notoriously long and antisocial hours, the time they had available to give to their children was very restricted. Add to that their inadequacy in English and it is clear that, however much they might want to help their children, they are unable to do so. This dilemma is brought out very clearly in the case studies.

Their only recourse is to exhortation and six out of 10 of our sample of British-Chinese adolescents said that their parents emphasised the importance of education 'very often' and a further three out of 10 did so 'often.'

The situation for both parties, children and parents, seems an unfortunate one. On the one hand, the children need help but cannot receive it and, on the other, the parents are anxious for their children's success but cannot do a great deal of a practical nature to promote it. It may be that a saving factor in this situation is the duty of obedience to parents, which is such a powerful force in the Chinese family.

Chinese youngsters are under great pressure from parents to succeed in their education with no recourse to help outside their schools. A solution adopted by some parts of the Afro-Caribbean community (Stone, 1981) – Saturday schools where youngsters can be given help in their school work – is beginning to be used by Chinese parents. In Canada, these Chinese Saturday schools are numerous.

A problem encountered both by pupils and schools arises from the geographical diffusion of Chinese families in the wider community. One result of this is that many schools have the children of only one or two families among their pupils. From this it follows that their opportunities to form friendships with other Chinese youngsters at school are limited. Interview evidence suggested that the longer they had lived in England the more likely they were to form friendships with British classmates but with the limited numbers involved it would be unwise to draw any firm conclusions about inter-ethnic friendships. It could be that such friendships will lead in the longer term to many inter-ethnic marriages, and certainly in Canada European-Chinese intermarriages are increasingly common (Bagley, De Klerk and Young, 1997). But as the case studies in Chapter 10 indicate, arranged marriages are still common amongst the Chinese community in Britain – in part a reflection of the isolation of many Chinese adolescents who do not have opportunities to meet a wide circle of Chinese friends.

Here we could perhaps point to the obvious fact that, with such small numbers of Chinese students in any one school, schools were faced with particular problems – resource utilisation, staffing and timetabling to name but three – if they were to arrange special provision for them in the way that they could, for example, be provided when perhaps more than half the students are of Afro-Caribbean or South Asian origin.

To return to more positive aspects of their school experience, the most notable fact is the way that the British-Chinese have adapted to the expectations, content and methods of working of schools which embody so many cultural assumptions differing from those of the home. Indeed, it would appear that they have been able to do more than come to terms with the transition from home to school: rather that they have learned how to embrace with pleasure the two worlds. All things considered, this was an unexpected finding but the conclusion seems inescapable when six out of 10 (similar to that of their counterparts in Hong Kong) were able to say that they 'always felt happy at school'. The surprise was perhaps the greater when compared with the response of their European British peers for whom the proportion was only four out of 10. It is tempting to suggest that what is happening here is that a core belief of respect for learning and the value it has for the individual and society has remained intact and has transcended the less significant issues of content and philosophical alignment.

Such a view would find some support from the fact that eight out of 10 of British-Chinese respondents said that they 'worked and tried very hard in school' and more than one in five said that they got very good marks in tests – a higher proportion than either the European British or Hong Kong Chinese groups. The success they claim is a self-assessment and it was no part of this study to obtain from schools their actual success in tests. However, some indirect support for their own assessment can be found in the results of the 1991 census, and the 1994 census of ethnic minorities. Using the results from London (since it provides the largest population), it is possible to identify by ethnic group the proportions of those with qualifications including all higher and first degrees, or their equivalent, nursing and teaching qualifications and their equivalent. This shows that over 30 per cent of the Chinese community held such qualifications as compared with 17 per cent of European British (London Research Centre, 1993; Modood et al., 1997).

These results align seductively with our findings, not least when nearly eight out of 10 (a higher proportion than in the European British and Hong Kong Chinese groups who were nearer to seven out of 10) of the British-

Chinese group in our sample said that they intended to continue their studies in college or at university after leaving school.

Also noteworthy is the relationship they felt they had with their teachers. Almost half felt that they were liked by their teachers and while a similar number were undecided, only one in 10 felt they were disliked. Whilst these figures might be held to be inconclusive, the significant fact is that their judgement of these relationships was more positive than those expressed by European British youngsters and much more positive than those of their Hong Kong peers. They were also more likely than the other two groups to be told that their work was good and they were doing well. The outcomes of questionnaires and interviews with the Hong Kong students require some caution however. The notion of teachers 'praising' students may well be more embedded in British schooling than in Hong Kong. This would make 'lack of praise' less significant in Hong Kong.

All these experiences are likely to improve their self esteem and as we noted earlier, some writers have argued that this, in itself, is likely to improve their actual performance. It also goes some way towards explaining the happiness they feel in school.

To conclude these reflections on schools and schooling and the educational aspirations of young British-Chinese, our findings seem to suggest the following. They were generally accommodating well to British school life which they were enjoying at least as well as, if not better than, their European British and Hong Kong counterparts. Their own assessment was that they were not only happy at school but were performing well in their studies. Finally, their aspirations, as measured by their intention to progress to some form of tertiary education, were somewhat higher than those of their Hong Kong or European British peers.

Was there Evidence that Racism was Adversely Affecting their Self Esteem?

As was seen in an earlier chapter, self esteem is a complex issue. In seeking to answer this question we reflect on the racism experienced by young British-Chinese whilst also taking into account the impact of home and school.

One of our most disturbing findings was the widespread experience of racism. Whilst analysis of racism is a commonplace in the literature devoted to Afro-Caribbean and South Asian communities, little attention has been given to the experience of the Chinese in Britain. As a consequence, it is easy to assume that it is not a problem for them. More than seven out of 10 of our British-Chinese sample had at one time or another experienced it themselves and over half of them had friends whom they knew had been subjected to it. For all practical purposes, the fear of it or the reality were universal. Interview evidence showed that it happened in school, on the streets and at home. At school and on the streets it took the form of name-calling and bullying with European children calling them 'Chink' or pushing them out of the way to get to the front of queues. Others spoke of more serious events in which their house or shop was attacked and doors and windows broken. A worrying refrain was their perception that teachers or the police did not seem to do anything about these events.

Such accounts told by children and adults have become commonplace in the literature dealing with ethnic minorities in Britain. Those engaged in this study have read of them and heard them at first hand for as long as they have been researchers. The saddening fact is that they seem to be as common now as they ever were. It is, of course, an inescapable part of life for them. What is extraordinary to anyone who has never had to face this is the courage and equanimity with which they spoke of it. That having been said, four out of 10 of our sample said that, at one time or another, they had wished they were not Chinese and it seems reasonable to suggest that this was one of the results of their experiences of racism. To be forced into a frame of mind so that one wishes to deny one's ethnic and cultural inheritance must be an unhappy experience. What is surprising is how these young people coped with it as our findings on their sense of self esteem suggest.

Coopersmith's adapted Self Esteem Inventory consists of three sub-scales, one of which seeks to measure school self esteem. Our results showed that in all four items on this scale, the British-Chinese group scored *higher* than their European British counterparts and significantly *higher* than the Hong Kong Chinese.

In the light of much of what we found about the school experience it was reasonable to expect that they would record reasonably good scores. What was surprising was that, as a group, they felt better about themselves than their European British peers. It seems that they feel that they are coping well with the demands school places on them and at the risk of being repetitious, we list the demands peculiar to them:

i. the medium of instruction is English;
ii. there is a gulf between the philosophical underpinnings of the home and the school;
iii. the ability of their parents to help them with English-language school work is very limited;

iv. their appearance marks them off as members of a minority community and therefore as targets for verbal and physical racist attacks.

In addition to these and in common with all young people at school, they have to cope with the normal stresses imposed by preparing for and taking public examinations.

One result in this sub-scale that did cause some surprise in the light of other findings related to racism was their rejection of the proposition that 'other kids pick on me very often'. It is difficult to reconcile the one with the other. Perhaps the result turned on their interpretation of the meaning of 'very often'. Another possibility is that they felt that racist name-calling and the like somehow did not count because it was not personal – that when it happened, it was an attack on them for being Chinese, not for being who they were. Whatever the reason, the findings are as they are, and are virtually identical to those obtained from a different sample over two years earlier.

A second sub-scale in the Self Esteem Inventory was concerned with home self esteem. In this, the British-Chinese group demonstrated a level of self esteem that fell between that of the European British (highest) and Hong Kong Chinese (lowest).

On the basis of interview evidence, it seems that a major problem for the British-Chinese was poor communication between parents and children – a complaint that was echoed by the Hong Kong Chinese. For both Chinese groups, the main cause of resentment was the autocratic nature of their parents, which, as we have seen, was a characteristic of Confucian family relationships. This emerges, with dramatic force, from the five case studies presented in chapter 10. The negotiation process normal in western European families (even though the final power of decision normally remains firmly with the parents) means that inter-generational communications have to remain open. Children and young people are thus given a sense of having some control over their lives and power to determine their actions. Even more important, they have some sense that they are part of the decision-making process affecting the family as a whole.

What is of particular interest here is that the British-Chinese group were aware of the difference between their experience and that of their European British peers so that they could, and did, make comparisons, from which they concluded that there was much to be said for the relative openness of European British family relationships.

The Hong Kong Chinese, on the other hand, had no such alternative family style at hand with which to compare their experiences and yet seemed *more* resentful of what they saw as the poor communications with and unreasonable exercise of power by their parents. This gives rise to a number of questions. Why, given this situation, did the British-Chinese have a better sense of home self esteem than their Hong Kong counterparts? Was it, perhaps, that they had looked at British family life and had come to the conclusion that, in spite of certain attractive features, it lacked some characteristics which they found in their own homes – characteristics which, consciously or not, they decided were of greater importance? Conversely, why did the Hong Kong Chinese group score lower when they had no alternative with which to compare themselves? Were their responses conditioned by what they had seen in Western films and TV programmes with their frequently idealised versions of family life?

Another reason which could be explored further is the interaction between the peer group and the home. The Hong Kong students are immersed in their own peer society and will be torn between an autocratic home culture and their peer pressures. The British-Chinese on the other hand will see the school/peer culture as quite different and may thus live more happily in their two separate worlds. There is evidence from family observation that, for the British-Chinese, the 'out of school society' of adolescents is largely an isolated family-based one rather than a peer society. For the Hong Kong students, the two are likely to interact much more strongly. Our study provides no answers to these questions but they seem central to a proper understanding of the psychological growth processes of these young people.

Finally we come to the Core Self Esteem scale. Here we find that the British-Chinese group generally perceive themselves as capable, successful and worthy. In fact of the three groups in our sample, they emerge as the best adjusted. The effects of racism on their self esteem are unquantifiable but are certainly not substantial.

The Hong Kong Chinese

Thus far, we have directed our attention primarily to the Chinese in Britain and used the Hong Kong Chinese for comparative purposes. It remains, therefore to consider the insights we were able to gain on them, having regard to the British Nationality Act (Hong Kong) 1990.

As our interviews illustrated, there was a widespread problem of identity in which they knew themselves to be ethnic Chinese but felt that there were cultural differences between themselves and those who were citizens of the

People's Republic of China. These they identified in economic and political terms and many clearly felt that the absorption of Hong Kong within the PRC would be disadvantageous to the territory in general, and to them in particular. They were worried about the consequences to their education and future chances of a career. Some worried because they knew that their families were planning on moving, but they did not know where, others worried because they knew that their family could not afford to move and were fearful of the consequences of remaining. Those who were moving were distressed at the thought of losing their friends, those who were staying were concerned at the anticipated loss of freedom when China took control. Indeed, it had been our assumption when planning this study that the Hong Kong Chinese would emerge, as a group, secure in their cultural and ethnic identities and a high level of personal esteem, befitting a community at ease with itself. It was the British-Chinese, living as a minority amid a society holding many values very different from their own, which we expected to show signs of stress.

What we found was almost the reverse. The British-Chinese youngsters seemed largely to have come to terms with their situation, seemed to have adopted strategies to preserve what they felt was central to their cultural identities and made what adaptations were necessary at the periphery to enable them to form a positive social identity. It was the Hong Kong Chinese, on the verge of unknown but certain changes to their lives, who were the more insecure. For the British-Chinese, there was some security in belonging to relatively isolated but secure family units in terms of knowing where and who you are. This could well lead to the British-Chinese community being very slow to form a closer relationship with British society. Certainly the experience of the older members of the Chinese community would confirm this.

It is clear, writing in 1998, that many of the fears of those who stayed in Hong Kong were, in economic terms, justified. This was not due to any particular political pressures or policy, but a reflection of the general economic malaise of South East Asia, which has seen for the first time in 30 years, substantial unemployment and wage decline in Hong Kong.

The Case Studies

The case studies show very clearly that families in the catering trade are locked in drudgery, marginalised in an occupational system that although allowing the acquisition of capital nevertheless isolates Chinese families, and forces them to employ their children as units of labour. These children cope with their multiple roles – as student of English and Chinese, as obedient child, as willing preparer of food for several hours each day, as supporter and translator for their isolated parent – with such cheerfulness, goodwill and success that as researchers we are stunned in admiration at the success of these children.

It will be the next generation of Chinese people who will break out of the ghetto of the take-aways, who will often be university and college educated, and who will choose their own marital partners. Yet, we expect, they will still hold to values of filial piety, supporting their parents with respect and affection.

These case studies, together with the material from questionnaires and more formal interviews give an encouraging picture, despite the multiple stresses which face Chinese youth in Britain today. In terms of identity models, there is no evidence of 'foreclosure' or reliance on rigid models of identity, despite the fact that many of the youth are still immersed in the symbols of popular Cantonese culture. These youth have 'roots' in traditional family forms, but they also have 'routes' into British culture, and into upward mobility. In Ghuman's (1991) term, despite multiple pressures they are often getting 'the best of both worlds'. Their identities illustrate the phenomenon described by Weinreich et al. (1986) of 'situated identities', which are part of an adaptational process.

Policy Recommendations

One of the major problems encountered by our sample of British-Chinese adolescents was that of mastering the English language in a sophisticated form. It is self-evident that their success in education is contingent on this and that insufficient resources are being made available to the day schools for them to meet this challenge. It is also our belief from other studies we have undertaken that such resources as are made available are not being used as effectively as they might be.

Recommendations for improving the teaching of English as a second language to Chinese students date back to 1985 when the Home Affairs Committee suggested that Local Education Authorities should supply bilingual teachers to schools with Chinese pupils for this purpose and that the Department of Education and Science (now the Department for Education and Employment) should monitor their availability and take steps to increase the supply if necessary. The Home Office's reply was to emphasise the problems of monitoring and to remain silent on the subject of increasing the supply. In fact, nothing was done.

We recommend that Chinese community organisations, Local Education Authorities and schools should join together and bring their influence to bear on the DfEE to review present provision and to take action along the lines suggested by the Home Affairs Committee.

It was also clear that few Chinese parents were in a position to help their children with the general, day-to-day, educational problems which they might encounter. Two strategies might be adopted here which give rise to two recommendations.

I We recommend that they consider setting up Saturday Schools (or their equivalent) where students could be given personalised help with their school work by professionally qualified teachers.

Alternatively or additionally,

II We recommend that groups of Chinese adult workers be deployed to discuss the education of their children with parents and to act 'in loco parentis' where necessary or desirable with schools.

As we have seen, the maintenance of the mother tongue is recognised by both parents and children as central to preserving their cultural identity. The United Nations Convention on the Rights of the Child, 1989, to which Britain is a signatory, laid down certain principles among which is the right of minority communities to enjoy their own cultures, religions and languages and that the state has an obligation to protect them.

Most Chinese parents in Britain are ill-equipped to teach their children themselves. Many are ill-educated and most are engaged in occupations which allow them little free time with their children at home. If Chinese youngsters are to learn their mother tongue, particularly in its written form, provision has to be made outside the home. Such provision as currently exists is supplied by the Chinese community out of its own limited resources.

Unfortunately, the problem faced by the Chinese community is identical to the one faced by all ethnic minorities living in Britain. The DfEE, the Home Office and Local Authorities have resolutely refused to accept any responsibility for the education of the children of minority groups in their mother tongues in spite of their obligations which Britain freely entered into.

We therefore recommend that the Chinese community explore, perhaps through the CRE, the possibility of recourse through European legislation to put pressure on the Home Office or the DfEE to meet its moral obligation under the UN Convention on the Rights of the Child.

The British Nationality Act (Hong Kong) 1990 made provision for up to 50,000 heads of household in Hong Kong to be permitted entry with their families to the United Kingdom as a result of the ceding of Hong Kong to the People's Republic of China in 1997. Applications were to be considered on a case by case basis but it was clear that a major factor in the decisions would be the economic situation of the applicants. In short, only those applicants who were educationally well-qualified and with adequate financial resources so that they would not be a 'burden' on the British economy, would be admitted. The effect of this is that those who settled in Britain under the Act were a very different kind from most of the existing members of the Chinese community in Britain. They are members of the professional middle-class and will not meet many of the problems faced by their fellow countrymen who arrived in the 1950s and 1960s.

Their children, however, are likely to have similar problems with respect to the English language will require the same help. It may be that, with their better connections, their parents will be able to apply pressure for the kind of improved provision, both in respect of English language and mother tongue teaching that we recommended earlier.

Although our respondents seemed to be coping with racism it remains an evil. Whilst one of the strengths of the Chinese community lies in its determination to deal with its own problems, it is also one of its weaknesses. Racism is not something within its power to stop. It is all the more important, therefore, that the host community, and especially teachers and those professionally concerned with young people, are brought to recognise that Chinese children and young people are its victims, just as much as those who are from the South Asian and Afro-Caribbean communities.

We recommend that the DfEE and CRE jointly circulate schools to raise the awareness of headteachers and teachers to the problems faced by Chinese youngsters arising from racism in school and elsewhere.

References

Bagley, C. (1975), 'Sequels of Alienation: A Social Psychological View of the Adaptation of West Indian Immigrants in Britain', in K. Glaser (ed.), *Case Studies on Human Rights and Fundamental Freedoms* (pp. 252–85), The Hague: Nijhof.

Bagley, C. (1983), 'Alienation and Identity in Young West Indians in Britain and the Netherlands', in C. Bagley and G.K. Verma (eds), *Multicultural Childhood: Education, Ethnicity and Cognitive Styles* (pp. 180–93), Aldershot: Gower Press.

Bagley, C. (1989a), 'Development of A Short Self-Esteem Measure for Use with Adults in Community Mental Health Surveys', *Psychological Reports*, 65, pp. 13–14.

Bagley, C. (1989b), 'Self-concept and Achievement in British and Anglo-Canadian High School Students', *Canadian and International Education*, 18, pp. 77–8.

Bagley, C. (1993a), 'Social and Psychological Adjustment of Migrant and Non Migrant Elderly in Canada and Hong Kong', *Asia Pacific Journal of Social Work*, 3, pp. 67–76.

Bagley, C. (1993b), 'Psychological and Social Adjustment in Racially-mixed Marriages', *International Journal of Marriage and the Family*, 1, pp. 53–9.

Bagley, C. (1994), 'Mental Health and Social Adjustment of Elderly Chinese Immigrants to Canada', *Canada's Mental Health*, 41, pp. 6–10.

Bagley, C. (1997), 'Mental Health and Migration in West Indians: British and Canadian Comparisons', in I. Al-Issa and M. Tousignant (eds), *Ethnicity, Immigration and Psychopathology* (pp. 300–15), New York: Plenum.

Bagley, C., Bolitho, F. and Bertrand, L. (1997), 'Norms and Construct Validity of the Rosenberg Self-Esteem Scale in Canadian High School Populations: Implications for Counselling', *Canadian Journal of Counselling*, 31, pp. 82–92.

Bagley, C. and Evan-Wong, L. (1975), 'Neuroticism and Extraversion in Response to Coopersmith's Self Esteem Inventory'. *Psychological Reports*, 36, pp. 253–4.

Bagley, C., Ko, G. P.-C. and O'Brian, C. (1997), 'The Development of Foster Care in Hong Kong', in M. Colton and M. Williams (eds), *The World of Foster Care: An International Sourcebook on Foster Family Care Systems* (pp. 99–106), Aldershot: Arena.

Bagley, C. and Mallick, K. (1978), 'Development of A Short Form of the Piers Harris Self-Concept Scale', *Educational Review*, 30, pp. 265–8.

Bagley, C. And Mallick, K. (1995), 'Negative Self-Perception and Components of Stress in Canadian, British and Hong Kong Adolescents', *Perceptual and Motor Skills*, 81, pp. 123–7.

Bagley, C. and Mallick, K. (1998), 'Adjustment, Stress and Family Life in Adolescents in Canada, Britain, Hong Kong, India, Pakistan and The Philippines', paper given to *First International Conference on Child and Adolescent Mental Health*, Hong Kong, June.

Bagley, C. and Mallick, K. (1999), 'Field Independence, Cultural Context and Academic Achievement', *British Journal of Educational Psychology*, 65, pp. 58–8.

Bagley, C., Mallick, K., Verma, G.K., Madrid, S., Bertrand, L., Bolitho, F. and Tse, J. (1998), 'Adjustment, Stress and Family Life in 16–18 Year Olds in Canada, Britain, Pakistan, India, Hong Kong and the Philippines', paper given to *First International Conference on Child and Adolescent Mental Health*, Hong Kong, June.

Bagley, C., Van Huizen, A. and Young, L. (1997), 'Multi-Ethnic Marriages and Intercultural Relations in Britain and The Netherlands', in D. Woodrow et al. (eds), *Intercultural Education: Theories, Policies and Practice* (pp 317–28), Aldershot: Ashgate.

Bagley, C. and Verma, G.K. (1978), 'Development, Norms and Factorial Validity of Scales for Measuring Racial Attitudes in Adolescents in Multi-Ethnic Settings', *Educational Studies*, 4.

Bagley, C. and Verma, G.K. (1979), *Racial Prejudice, the Individual and Society*, Farnborough: Saxon House.

Bagley, C. and Verma, G.K. (1980), 'The Structure and Validity of Self-concept Measures in Multi-Ethnic Populations', *British Journal of Educational Psychology*, 50, p. 77.

Bagley, C., Verma, G.K. and Mallick, K. (1979), 'Pupil Self-Esteem: A Study of Black and White Teenagers in British Schools', in G.K. Verma (ed.), *Race, Education and Identity* (pp. 176–91), London: Macmillan.

Bagley, C., Verma, G.K., Mallick, K. and Young, L. (1979), *Personality, Self Esteem and Prejudice*, Farnborough: Saxon House.

Bagley, C., Verma, G.K. and Mallick, K. (1982), 'The Comparative Structure of Self-Esteem in British and Indian Adolescents', in C. Bagley and G.K. Verma (eds), *Self-Concept, Achievement and Multicultural Education* (pp. 212–26), London: Macmillan Press.

Bagley, C. and Young, L. (1988), 'Identity, Self-esteem and the Personal Evaluation of Colour in Young Children in Canada, Jamaica, England and Ghana', *International Journal of Intercultural Relations*, 12, pp. 45–60.

Bagley, C. And Young, L. (1990), 'Depression, Self-Esteem and Suicidal Behaviour As Sequels of Sexual Abuse in Childhood: Research and Therapy', in M. Rothery and G. Cameron (eds), *Child Maltreatment: Expanding Our Concepts of Helping* (pp. 183–219), Hillsdale, NJ: Lawrence Erlbaum 1990.

Bagley, C. and Young, L. (1994), 'Immigration and Social Policy', *Policy Options*, 8, pp. 20–4.

Bagley, C. and Young, L. (1999), 'Evaluation of Group Counselling for Women Survivors of Child Sexual Abuse', *Social Work with Groups*, in press.

Barker, H. (1968), *A Chinese Lineage Village: Sheung Shui*, London: Frank Cass & Co. Ltd.

Barth, F. (1969), *Ethnic Groups and Boundaries: the Social Organization of Culture Difference*, Boston: Little Brown.

Bell, J. (1989), *Doing Your Research Project: A Guide for First-time Researchers in Education and Social Science*, Buckingham: Open University Press.

Bhavnani, K. (1991) *Talking Politics: A Psychological Framing of Views from Youth in Britain*, Cambridge: Cambridge University Press.

Bond, M. (1991), *Beyond the Chinese Face. Insights from Psychology*, Oxford University: Oxford University Press. Hong Kong.

Bond, M. (1992), *The Psychology of the Chinese People*, New York: Oxford University Press.

Bond, M. and Pang, M.-K. (1990), 'Trusting the Tao: Chinese Values and the Re-centring of Psychology', in U. Gielen (ed.) *Chinese Morality: Values, Reasonings, and Education*, New York: Academic Press.

Bond, M. and Smith, B. (1993), *Social Psychology Across Cultures. Analysis and Perspective*, London: Harvester Wheatsheaf.

Boudon, R. and Bourricaud, F. (1982), *A Critical Dictionary of Sociology*, London: Routledge.

Bray, T. (1991), 'Hong Kong Education in an International Content. The Impact of External Forces', in L. Postinglione (ed.), *Education and Society in Hong Kong, Toward One Country Two Systems*, London: East Gate Books.

Breakwell, G. (ed.) (1983), *Threatened Identity*, Chichester: Wiley.

Breakwell, G. (1986), *Coping with Threatened Identities*, London: Methuen.

Brookover, W. (1965), *Self-Concept of Ability and School Achievement*, Michigan: Michigan State University Press.

Brookover, W.B. (1967), 'Self Concept, Ability and School Achievement', *Sociology of Education*, 37, pp. 1–14.

Bullivant, B.M. (1981), *The Pluralist Dilemma in Education: Six Case Studies*, Sydney: Allen and Unwin.

Burgess, R.G. (1984), *Field Methods in the Study of Education*, Brighton: Falmer Press.

Burkitt, I. (1991), *Social Selves: Theories of the Social Formation of Personality*, London: Sage.

Burns, R.B. (1979), *The Self Concept: Theory, Measurement, Development and Behaviour*, London: Longman.

Burns, R.B. (1982), *Self Concept, Development and Education*, Eastbourne: Holt, Rinehart and Winston.

Carter, B., Harris, C. and Joshi, S. (1987), *The 1951–55 Conservative Government and the Racialisation of Black Immigration*, Warwick: Policy Papers in Ethnic Relations No. 11, Centre for Research in Ethnic Relations, University of Warwick.

Caudill, W. (1972), 'Tiny Dramas: Vocal Communication Between Mother and Infant in Japanese and American Families', in W.P. Lebra (ed.), *Transcultural Research in Mental Health* (pp. 25–48), Honolulu, Hawaii: University Press Hawaii.

Census (1991), *Labour Force Survey*, London: HMSO.

Chan, D. And Lee, H.-C. (1993), 'Dimensions of Self-Esteem and Psychological Symptoms Among Chinese Adolescents in Hong Kong', *Journal of Youth and Adolescence*, 22, pp. 425–40.

Chan, Y.M. (1994), *The Educational Needs of Chinese Children*, University of Manchester: PhD thesis.

Chann, F. (1976), *Conference on Chinese in Scotland, May 1976*, London: Hong Kong Government Office.

Chen, C. and Uttal, D. (1988), 'Cultural Values, Parents' Beliefs and Children's Achievements in the United States and China', *Human Development*, 31, pp. 351–8.

Cheung, S.-K. and Bagley, C. (1998), 'Validating An American Scale in Hong Kong: The Center for Epidemiological Studies Depression Scale (CES-D)', *Journal of Psychology*, 132, pp. 169–86.

Cheung, W. (1975), *The Chinese Way: A Social Study of Hong Kong Chinese Community in a Yorkshire City*, University of York: MPhil thesis.

Cheung, C.-K., Lee, J.-J. and Chan, C.-M. (1994), 'Explicating Filial Piety in Relation to Family Cohesion', *Journal of Social Behavior and Personality*, 9, pp. 565–80.

Cheung, P.C. and Lau, S. (1985), 'Self-Esteem: Its Relationship to the Family and School Social Environments Among Chinese Adolescents', *Youth and Society*, 16, pp. 438–56.

Chiam, H.-K. (1987), 'Change in Self-Concept During Adolescence', *Adolescence*, 12, pp. 70–8.

Choy, W. (1987), 'I'm a Banana and Proud of It', *Toronto Globe and Mail*, 18 July, p. 20.

Clegg, J. (1988), *History of the Chinese Community in Britain*, Manchester: Chinese Information Centre.

Cohen, L. and Mannion, L. (1985), *Research Methods in Education*, London: Croom Helm.

Cook, T.D. and Reichardt, C.S. (1979), *Qualitative and Quantitative Methods in Evaluative Research*, London: Sage.

Cooley, C.H. (1902), *Human Nature and the Social Order*, New York: Scribener.

Coopersmith, S. (1967), *The Antecedents of Self Esteem*, San Francisco: Freeman.

Coopersmith, S. (1975), 'Self-Concept, Race and Education', in G.K. Verma and C. Bagley (eds), *Race and Education Across Cultures* (pp. 145–67), London: Heinemann.

CRE (1988), *Learning in Terror*, London. Commission for Racial Equality.

Creel, H.G. (1954), *Chinese Thoughts From Confucius to Mao Tse-Tung*, London: Eyre and Spottiswode.

Crittenden, K. and Bae, H. (1994), 'Self Effacement and Social Responsibility: Attribution As Impression Management in Asian Cultures', *American Behavioral Scientist*, 37, pp. 653–71.

Department of Education and Science (DES) (1985), *The Education of Immigrants (Circular 7/65)*, London: HMSO.

DES (1985), *Education for All: Report of the Committee of Inquiry Into the Education of Children From Ethnic Minority Groups* (The Swann Report, Cmnd 9453), London: HMSO.

Edgar, P. (1974), *An Analysis of the Coopersmith Self Concept Theory*, California: Goodyear.

Erikson, E.H. (1965), *Childhood and Society*, New York: Norton.

Erikson, E.H. (1968), *Identity, Youth and Crisis*, London: Faber.

Feldman, S. and Rosenthal, D. (1990), 'The Acculturation of Autonomy Expectations in Chinese High Schoolers Residing in Two Western Nations', *International Journal of Psychology*, 25, pp. 259–81.

Fewster, C. (1989), 'Chinese Revolution', *Nursing Times*, 19 July, pp. 48–9.

Fitchett, N. (1986), *Chinese Children in Derby*, Oxford: Oxford University Press.

Fong, Y. (1981), *Teachers' and Pupils' Perceptions of Effective Geography Teaching in Hong Kong Schools*, University of Hong Kong: MEd thesis.

Fox, D.J. (1969), *The Research Process in Education*, New York: Holt, Rinehart and Winston.

Francis, L. and Wilcox, C. (1995), 'Self-Esteem: Coopersmith and Rosenberg Compared', *Psychological Reports*, 76, p. 1050.

Garvey, A. and Jackson, B. (1975), *Chinese Children – Research and Action Project into the Needs of Chinese Children*, London: National Children's Bureau.

Geertz, C. (1963), *Old Societies and New States: the Quest for Modernity in Asia and Africa*, New York: Free Press.

Ghuman, P. (1991), 'Best Or Worst of Two Worlds? A Study of Asian Adolescents', *Educational Research*, 33, pp. 121–32.

Gibbons, J. (1982), 'The Issues of the Language of Instruction in the Lower Forms of Hong Kong Secondary Schools', *Journal of Multilingual and Multicultural Development*, 3 (2), pp. 117–28.

Giles, H. and St-Jacques, B. (1979) (eds), *Language and Ethnic Relations*, London: Pergamon Press.

Gransow, B. (1995), 'Chinese Modernization and Cultural Self-Conception', *Zeitscrift Fur Soziologie*, 3, pp. 183–95.

Grotevant, H.D. (1987), 'Towards A Process Model of Identity Formation', *Journal of Adolescent Research*, 2, pp. 5–21.

Hammersley, M. and Atkinson, P. (1983), *Ethnography: Principles in Practice*, London: Tavistock.

Hauser, S. (1971), *Black and White Identity Formation*, London: Wiley.

Hinton, H.C. (ed.) (1986), *The People's Republic of China, 1979–1984: A Document Survey*, Vol. II, Wellington, DE: Scholarly Resources Inc.

Ho, D.Y.F. (1979), 'Parental Education Is Not Correlated With Verbal Intelligence or Academic Performance in Hong Kong Pupils', *Genetic Psychology Monographs*, 100, pp. 3–19.

Ho, D.Y.F. (1981), 'Traditional Patterns of Socialization in China Society', *Acta Psychologica*, 23, pp. 81–95.

Hogg, M.A., Abrams, D. and Patel, Y. (1986), 'Ethnic Identity, Self Esteem and Occupational Aspirations of Indian and Anglo-Saxon British Adolescents', *Genetic, Social and General Psychology Monographs*, 113, p. 4.

Home Affairs Committee (1985), *The Chinese Community in Britain: Second Report*, London: HMSO.

Howard, J.A. and Callero, P.L. (1991), *The Self-Society Dynamic: Cognition, Emotion and Action*, Cambridge: Cambridge University Press.

Jones, D. (1979), 'The Chinese in Britain: Origins and Development of a Community', *New Community*, 11, p. 3.

Jowett, A., Li, F., Findlay, A. and Sheldon, R. (1995), 'Discourse on Migration and Ethnic Identity: Interviews With Professionals in Hong Kong', *Transactions of the Institute of British Geographers*, 20, pp. 342–56.

Kahn, R.L. and Cannell, C.F. (1967), *The Dynamics of Interviewing: Theory, Technique and Cases*, New York: John Wiley.

Kaplan, H. (1975), *Self-Attitudes and Deviant Behavior*, California: Goodyear.

Kaplan, H. and Pokorney, A. (1976), 'Self-Derogation and Suicide', *Social Science and Medicine*, 10, pp. 113–18.

Kelly, G. (1955), *The Theory of Personal Constructs*, New York: Norton.

Kemp, S. and Watkins, D. (1996), 'Anonymity of Responses to Self-Evaluations: Are We Misinterpreting Self-Concept Research?', *Psychological Reports*, 79, pp. 1187–94.

Kerlinger, F.N. (1970), *Foundations of Behavioural Research*, New York: Holt, Rinehart and Winston.

Kiang, W.H. (1948), *The Chinese Student Movement*, New York: King's Crown Press.

Knight, G., Kagan, S., Nelson, W. and Gumbiner, J. (1978), 'Acculturation of Second and Third Generation Mexican-American Children', *Journal of Cross-Cultural Psychology*, 9, pp 87–97.

Kong, S.L. (1989), *Chinese Culture and Lore*, Ontario: Kensington Educational.

Ladlow, D.E. (1980), *Suggestions and Background Information for Teachers of Chinese Children*, Hong Kong: University of Hong Kong.

Lai, K.C. (1975), *Problems Facing Chinese Immigrants from Liverpool*, University of Hull: Dip. Applied Social Studies thesis.

Lai, L. (1975), *Chinese Families in London: A Study into their Social Needs*, Brunel University: MA thesis.

Lai, M. (1976), 'Why Did the Chinese Migrate? Excerpt from Blood and Sweat in the Golden Mountains', *East/West*, January, p. 1.

Lang, O. (1946), *Chinese Family and Society*, New Haven: Yale University Press.

Lange, A and Westin, C. (1985), *The Generative Mode of Explanation in Social Psychological Theories of Race and Ethnic Relations*, Research Group on Ethnic Relations, Social Cognition and Cross-Cultural Psychology, Dept. of Education and Centre for Research in International Migration and Ethnicity, Report No. 6, University of Stockholm.

Lau, S. and Cheung, P.C. (1987), 'Relations Between Chinese Adolescents Perception of Parental Control and Organization and Their Perceptions of Parental Warmth', *Developmental Psychology*, 23, pp. 726–9.

Lawrence, D. (1996), *Enhancing Self-Esteem in the Classroom*, London: Chapman.

Lee, L. (1985), 'Social Stress and Coping Behaviour in Hong Kong', in W.S. Tseng and D. Wu (eds), *Chinese Culture and Mental Health* (pp. 193–214), New York: Academic Press.

Leung, K. and Lau, S. (1989), 'Effects of Self-Concept and Perceived Siapproval of Delinquent Behavior in School Children', *Journal of Youth and Adolescence*, 18, pp. 345–59.

Leung, W., Zhao, J. and Wu, Y. (1992), 'A Survey of Mental Health Level of 1,088 Middle School Students', *Chinese Mental Health Journal*, 6, pp. 100–2.

Llewellyn, Sir John (Chairman) (1982), *A Perspective on Education in Hong Kong Report by a Visiting Panel*, Hong Kong: Government Secretariat.

Locke, D. (1992), *Increasing Multicultural Understanding– A Comprehensive Model Multicultural Aspects of Counselling*, Series 1, London: Sage.

London Research Centre (1993), *London's Ethnic Minorities: One City Many Communities. An Analysis of 1991 Census Results*, London: London Research Centre.

Luk, C.-L. and Bond, M. (1992), 'Explaining Chinese Self-Esteem in Terms of the Self-concept', *Psychologia*, 35, pp. 147–54.

Lynn, I. (1982), *The Chinese Community in Liverpool: Their Unmet Needs with Respect to Education, Social Welfare and Housing*, Liverpool: Merseyside Area Profile Group.

Ma, H.K. (1988), 'The Chinese Perspectives on Moral Judgment Development', *International Journal of Psychology*, 23, pp. 201–27.

Marcia, J.E. (1966), 'Development and Validation of Ego Identity Status', *Journal of Personality and Social Psychology*, 3, pp. 551–58.

Maslow, A. (1954), *Motivation and Personality*, New York: Harper and Row.

Mason, E.J. and Bramble, W.J. (1978), *Understanding and Conducting Research: Application in Education and Behavioral Science*, New York: McGraw-Hill.

McFee, G. (1992), 'Triangulation in Research: Two Confusions', *Educational Research*, 34, pp. 3–14.

Mead, G.H. (1934), *Mind, Self and Society*, Chicago: University of Chicago Press.

Measor, L. (1984), 'Interviewing: A Strategy in Qualitative Research', in R. Burgess (ed.), *In the Field: An Introduction to Field Research*, London: Allen and Unwin.

Milner, D. (1997), 'Racism and Childhood Identity', *The Psychologist*, March, pp. 123–5.

Mishler, E.G. (1979), 'Meaning in Context: Is There Any Other Kind?', *Harvard Educational Review*, 49, pp. 1–19.
Mitchell, G.D. (1968), *A New Dictionary of Social Science*, New York: Aldine.
Modood, T., Berthoud, R., Lakey, J., Nazroo, J., Smith, P., Virdee, S. and Beishon, S. (1997), *Ethnic Minorities in Britain*, London: The Policy Studies Institute.
Morris, P. (1981), ''Reports: The Adoption of the Formal Doctrine of an Imported Curriculum Innovation, *Journal of Curriculum Studies*, 3, pp. 257–9.
Murphy, D. (1987), 'Offshore Education: A Hong Kong Perspective', *Australian Universities Review*, 30, 2, pp. 43–4.
Murray, M. and Dunn, R. (1979), 'Matching Preferred Cognitive Mode with Teaching Methodology in Learning a Novel Motor Skill', *Research Quarterly*, 50, pp. 80–7.
Newble, D. and Entwistle, N. (1986), 'Learning Styles and Approaches: Implications for Medical', *Education Medical Education*, 20, pp. 162–75.
Ng, K.C. (1968), *The Chinese in London*, London: Oxford University Press.
Oakley, A. (1981), 'Interviewing Women: A Contradiction in Terms?', in H. Roberts (ed.), *Doing Feminist Research*, London: Routledge.
Oatey, H. (1984), 'Teaching Training in the People's Republic of China', *A Case Report Language Learning and Communication*, 3, pp. 353–63.
Olafson, G.A. (1991), T'riangulation in Comparative Research: Mixing Qualitative and Quantitative Methods', in K. Hardman and J. Standevan (eds), *Sport for All: Into the 90s: Comparative Physical Education and Sport*, Vol. 7, Aachen: Meyor and Meyor.
O'Neill, J. (1972), *The Role of Family and Community in the Social Adjustment of the Chinese in Liverpool*, University of Liverpool: MA thesis.
OPCS (1990), *Total Period Fertility Rate Tables*, London: Office of Population, Censuses and Surveys.
Owen, D. (1993), *Ethnic Minorities in Great Britain: Age and Gender Structure*, National Ethnic Minority Data Archive 1991 Census, Statistical Paper No. 2, University of Warwick: Centre for Research in Ethnic Relations.
Oxford, R., Hollaway, E. and Horton-Murillo, D. (1992), 'Language Learning Styles: Research and Practical Considerations for Teaching in the Multicultural Tertiary ESL/EFL Classroom', *System*, 20, pp. 439–56.
Pan, P. and Goldberg, D. (1990), 'A Companion of the Validity of GHQ-12 and CHQ-12 in Chinese Primary Care Parents in Manchester', *Psychological Medicine*, Vol. 20, pp. 931–40.
Parker, D. (1994), *The Chinese in Britain: Annotated Bibliography and Research Resources*, Warwick: Centre for Research in Ethnic Relations, University of Warwick.
Parker, D. (1995), *Through Different Eyes: The Cultural Identities of Young Chinese People in Britain*, Aldershot: Avebury, for the Centre for Research in Ethnic Relations, University of Warwick and the Economic and Social Research Council.

Phillpotts, G. (1990), *The Chinese Community in Thameside*, London: Report of the Race Relations Adviser to the Equal Opportunities Sub-Committee, Thameside Council.

Reid, I. (1986), *The Sociology of School and Education*, London: Fontana.

Rex, J. (1991), *Ethnic Identity and Mobilisation in Britain*, Warwick: Monograph in Ethnic Relations No. 5, University of Warwick, Centre for Research in Ethnic Relations.

Robson, C. (1993), *Real World Research – A Resource for Social Scientists and Practitioner-Researchers*, London: Blackwell.

Roopnarine, J. and Carter, B. (1992), 'Parent-Child Socialization in Diverse Cultures', *Annual Advances in Applied Developmental Psychology*, Vol. 5, New Jersey: Ablex Corporation.

Rose, J. and Deakin, N. (1969), *Colour and Citizenship*, London: Oxford University Press.

Rosenberg, M.J. (1965), *Society and the Adolescent Self Image*, Princeton: Princeton University Press.

Rosenthal, D. and Feldman, S. (1992), 'The Nature and Stability of Ethnic Identity in Chinese Youth', *Journal of Cross Cultural Psychology*, 23, pp. 214–27.

Rushton, P. (1995), *Race, Evolution and Behavior*, New Brunswick: Transaction Press.

Sabin, T. and Scheibe, K.E. (1983) (eds), *Studies in Social Identity*, New York: Praeger.

Scovel, J. (1983), 'English Teaching in China: A Historical Perspective in Language', *Learning and Communication*, 2, pp. 1105–09.

Seabrook, J. (1987), 'Anger in Chinatown', *New Society*, 82.

Sham, Y.M. (1989), 'Different Altogether', *Nursing World*, July, pp. 20–1.

Sham, Y.M. (1991), *Reaching Chinese Families – A Study of Services for Chinese Families in Greater Manchester with a Member with Learning Difficulties*, unpublished BA dissertation.

Shek, D. (1991), 'What Does the Chinese Version of the Beck Depression Inventory Measure in Chinese Students – General Psychopathology or Depression?', *Journal of Clinical Psychology*, 47, pp. 381–90.

Simpson, M. (1987), *Children of the Dragon*, Bradford and Ilkley Community College.

Simsova, S. and Chin, W. (1982), *Library Needs of Chinese in London*, London: School of Librarianship and Information Studies, Polytechnic of North London

Skinner, G.D. (1995), *Primary Schools with All Pupils From South Asian Backgrounds*, Manchester: Report for the Leverhulme Trust, University of Manchester.

Smith, D.J. and Thomlinson, S. (1989), *The School Effect: A Study of Multi-Racial Comprehensives*, London: Policy Studies Institute.

Smolicz, J. (1984), 'Multiculturalism and An Overarching Framework of Values: Some Educational Responses for Ethnically Plural Societies', *European Journal of Education*, 19, pp. 20–9.

Song, M. (1997), 'You're Becoming More and More English: Investigating Chinese Siblings Cultural Identities', *New Community*, 23, pp. 343–62.

Spradley, J.P. (1979), *The Ethnographic Interview*, New York: Holt, Rinehart and Winston.

Stenhouse, L. (1975), *An Introduction to Curriculum Research and Development*, London: Heinemann.

Stevenson, H. and Stigler, J. (1984), 'Reading Disabilities: The Case of Chinese Japanese and English', *Child Development*, 53, pp. 1164–81.

Stone, M. (1981), *The Education of Black Children in Britain*, Glasgow: Fontana.

Sue, D.W. (1981), *Counselling the Culturally Different: Theory and Practice*, New York: John Wiley.

Suzuky, H. (1980), 'The Asian-American Family', in M.D. Fautini and R. Cardenas (eds), *Parenting in a Multi-Cultural Society* (pp. 74–102), New York: Wiley.

Tajfel, H. (1987), *The Social Psychology of Minorities*, London: Minority Rights Group.

Tam, S.-F. (1995), 'Relationship of Self-Concept and Social Desirability Tendency of Hong Kong Chinese Adults with Physical Disabilities', *Perceptual and Motor Skills*, 81, pp. 731–8.

Taylor, M.J. (1987), *Chinese Pupils in Britain*, London: NFER/Nelson.

Tse, J., Bagley, C. and Mak H.-W. (1994), 'Prevention of Teenage Suicidal Behaviour in Hong Kong: Development of the Health Intervention Training-Mutual Aid Network', *School Psychology International*, 15, pp. 99–114.

Tse, J., Bagley, C. and Yau, A. (1998), 'Suicidal Risk Scale for Hong Kong Students', *Core: Collected Original Resources in Education*, in press.

Tseng, W.S. (1972), 'On Chinese National Character from the Viewpoint of Personality Development', in Y.Y. Li and K.S. Yang (eds) *The Character of the Chinese: An Interdisciplinary Approach* (Monograph Series, B, No. 4, pp. 227–50), Taipei Institute of Ethnology Academic Sinican (in Chinese),

Tseng, W.S. and Hsu, J. (1969–70), 'Chinese Culture, Personality Formation and Mental Illness', *International Journal of Social Psychiatry*, Vol. 16, pp. 5–14.

Tsow, R. (1984), *Mother-Tongue Maintenance: A Survey of Part-Time Chinese Language Classes*, London: CRE.

Tu, W.-M. (1985), *Confucian Thought: Selfhood as a Creative Transformation*, New York: Albany State University of New York.

Tuckman, B.W. (1972), *Conducting Educational Research*, New York: Harcourt, Brace Jovanovich.

Ullah, P. (1990), 'Rhetoric and Ideology in Social Identification: The Case of Second Generation Irish Youths', *Discourse and Society*, 1, pp. 167–88.

Verma, G.K. with Ashworth, B. (1986), *Ethnicity and Educational Achievement in British Schools*, Basingstoke: Macmillan.

Verma, G.K. and Darby, D.S. (1994), *Winners and Losers: Sport and Leisure with Reference to Ethnic Minorities*, Brighton: Falmer Press.

Verma, G.K. and Mallick, K. (1998), *Researching Education: Perspectives and Techniques*, London: Falmer Press.

Verma, G.K., Zec, D. and Skinner, G.D. (1994), *The Ethnic Crucible*, Brighton: Falmer Press.

Wah, Y.-Y., Avari, B. and Buckley, S. (1996), *British Soil, Chinese Roots: Chinese Life in Britain*, Liverpool: Countrywise.

Walker, R. (1985), *Doing Research*, London: Methuen.

Wallman, S. (1983), 'Identity Options', in C. Fried (ed.), *Minorities: Community and Identity*, Berlin: Springer-Verlag.

Wang, Y. (1982), 'English Teaching and English Studies in China', *Language Learning and Communication*, 1, pp. 5–20.

Watkins, D., Akande, E, Cheng, C. and Regmi, M. (1996), 'Culture and Gender Differences in the Self-Esteem of College Students: A 4 Country Comparison', *Social Behavior and Personality*, 24, pp. 321–7.

Watkins, D. and Kemp, S. (1996), 'Self-Esteem and Academic Streaming in Hong Kong', *Journal of Social Psychology*, 136, pp. 651–3.

Watkins, D. and Qi, D. (1994), 'Assessing Self-Esteem in Chinese School Children', *Educational Psychology*, 14, pp. 129–37.

Watson, J.L. (1977), 'The Chinese: Hong Kong Villagers in the British Catering Trade', in J.L. Watson (ed.), *Between Two Cultures: Migrants and Minorities in Britain*, Oxford: Blackwell.

Weinreich, P. (1979), 'Cross-Ethnic Identification and Self-Rejection in a Black Adolescent', in G.K. Verma and C. Bagley (eds), *Race, Education and Identity*, London: Macmillan.

Weinreich, P. (1989), 'Conflicted Identifications: A Commentary on Identity Structure Analysis Concepts', in K. Leibkind (ed.), *New Identities in Europe*, Aldershot: Gower.

Weinreich, P., Kelly, A.J.D. and Maja, C. (1986), *Situated Identities, Conflicts in Identification and Own Group Preference in Racial and Ethnic Identifications: Rural and Urban Black Youth in South Africa*, International Association for Cross Cultural Psychology, 8th International Congress, Istanbul.

Wells, L.E. and Marwell, G. (1976), *Self-Esteem: Its Conceptualisation and Measurement*, Beverly Hills: Sage.

Werbner, (1991), *The Migration Process: Capital, Gifts and Offerings Among British Pakistanis*, New York: Free Press.

Westcott, K. (1979), *Survey of the Use of English in Hong Kong*, Hong: mimeo.

Wilpert, C. (1989), 'Ethnic and Cultural Identity: Ethnicity and the Second Generation in the Context of European Migration', in K. Liebkind (ed.), *New Identities in Europe*, Aldershot: Gower.

Wong, L.F. (1992), *Education of Chinese Children in Britain: A Comparative Study with the United States of America*, Clevedon: Multilingual Matters.

Wong, T. (1996), 'The Ethnic and National Identities of the Hong Kong People - A Liberal Explanation', *Issues and Studies*, 32, pp. 105–30.

Woo, J. (1985), *The Chinese Speaking Student: A Composite Profile*, New York: New York Bilingual Education Multi-functional Support Centre.

Wood, F. and Johnson, A. (1972), 'Coopersmith SEI Scores of Boys with Severe Behaviour Problems', *Exceptional Children*, 38, pp. 46–8.

Worsley, P. (1984), *The Three Worlds: Culture and World Development*, London: Weidenfeld.

Yang, K.-S. and Bond, M. (1980), 'Ethnic Affirmation by Chinese Bilinguals', *Journal of Cross Cultural Psychology*, 11, pp. 411–25.

Yang, K.-S. and Bond, M. (1990), 'Exploring Implicit Personality Theories with Indigenous or Imported Constructs: the Chinese Case', *Journal of Personality and Social Psychology*, 58, 6, pp. 1087–95.

Yau, L. (1983), *Report on the Chinese Community in Lambeth* (unpublished), London: Community Relations Council for Lambeth.

Yik, M. and Bond, M. (1993), 'Exploring the Dimensions of Chinese Person Perception with Indigenous and Imported Constructs: Creating A Culturally Balanced Scale', *International Journal of Psychology*, 28, pp. 71–95.

Young, L. and Bagley, C. (1982), 'Identity, Self-Esteem, Self-Concept and the Development of Black Identity: A Theoretical Overview', in G.K. Verma and C. Bagley (eds), *Self-Concept, Achievement and Multicultural Education* (pp. 41–59), London: Macmillan.

Zhou, Z. (1988), 'Historical Contexts of Educational Reforms in Present Day China', *Interchange*, Vol. 19, No. 3/4, pp. 8–18.

Zimmerman, M., Copeland, L., Shope, J. and Dielman, T. (1997), 'A Longitudinal Study of Self-esteem: Implications for Adolescent Development', *Journal of Youth and Adolescence*, 26, pp. 117–41.